Output, Employment, Capital, and Growth

Output, Employment, Capital, and Growth

A QUANTITATIVE ANALYSIS

By
HANS BREMS
University of Illinois

HARPER & BROTHERS, Publishers, New York

OUTPUT, EMPLOYMENT, CAPITAL, AND GROWTH: A Quantitative Analysis

Library of Congress catalog card number : 58-59884

TO ULLA

Contents

Preface

In the present volume the author attempts to restate and occasionally to refine and extend modern and neoclassical models of output, employment, capital, and growth. The construction of one all-embracing model, capable of simultaneously illuminating all aspects of output, employment, capital, and growth was beyond the powers of the writer—and its development might have overtaxed some readers. Instead, several chapter-length models have been produced, each designed specifically to aid in the study of one particular aspect of output, employment, capital, or growth. This method, aptly called "case theorizing" by an early reader of the present volume, illustrates the inherent flexibility of our general theoretical apparatus. In treating alternative approaches such as statics versus dynamics or linear programming versus infinitesimal calculus as supplements rather than substitutes, the method also guards against throwing too many babies out with the water.

The writer believes that economic models should be operationally significant. In other words, a model should permit of the drawing of specific conclusions about economic relationships. From any but the most trivial models the extraction of specific conclusions is greatly facilitated by the use of mathematics; hence elementary mathematics has been used freely. The book proceeds from familiar and simple models to the less familiar and more powerful ones. The kind of mathematics used describes a similar crescendo. Parts I, II, and III use no mathematics beyond elementary algebra and elementary calculus. Indeed the first and only integral sign of this book appears in the last chapter of Part III. Until then, the reader will need no more calculus than the definition of a derivative and mastery of the simplest cases of the technique of derivation. In Part IV, no more is required for the perusal of Chapters 20, 21, and 25 either. But Chapters 22 and 23 use linear difference equations in one variable, so admirably taught by Baumol in his *Economic Dynamics* (New York: Macmillan, 1951). Chapter 24 uses a system of two linear difference equations in two variables, implying a bit of matrix algebra. Finally, Chapter 26 uses linear as well as nonlinear difference equations in one variable.

The teacher considering the use of the present volume in his graduate economic theory course would probably wish to skip Chapters 24 and 26 and perhaps also Chapters 22 and 23.

During the preparation of this book, the writer received invaluable help from many sources. For unlimited access provided to modern computing equipment he is grateful to the Digital Computer Laboratory of the University of Illinois. For tutoring in what must have seemed to them very trivial subjects he is indebted to Professors David E. Muller and Abraham H. Taub of the Laboratory. For a grant to complete a programming project beyond his own powers he is grateful to the Research Board of the University of Illinois, and for executing the project to Mr. Gene H. Leichner of the Digital Computer Laboratory. For a grant to have all mathematics examined and all operations checked he is grateful to the Research Board, and for the actual checking to Charles W. Gear of the Digital Computer Laboratory and John Shih-yao Chiu of the Department of Economics.

Manuscripts of individual chapters have been read, criticized, and in some cases considerably improved by colleagues at home and overseas. The writer is particularly grateful to William J. Baumol, Edward H. Chamberlin, Sven Danö, Robert Dorfman, James Duesenberry, Marianne Ferber, Marvin Frankel, Walter Galenson, Robert A. Gordon, Alvin H. Hansen, Harry Johnson, Wassily W. Leontief, P. Nörregaard Rasmussen, Paul A. Samuelson, Robert M. Solow, G. Stuvel, Earl R. Swanson, Frederick Williams, Frederik Zeuthen, and Johan Åkerman.

For ever-ready coöperation and clerical assistance the writer is indebted to the College of Commerce and its Department of Economics of the University of Illinois.

Roughly one-third of the material presented in the present volume has appeared previously; such material was published as articles in *The American Economic Review, Econometrica, The Economic Journal, Kyklos, The Quarterly Journal of Economics, The Review of Economics and Statistics,* and *The Review of Economic Studies.* For the care with which the manuscripts have been criticized and improved, the writer is deeply grateful to the editors and referees of these journals.

H. B.

December, 1958

Acknowledgments

To the publishers of the following journals the writer expresses his appreciation for permission to reproduce partly or fully:

TO Kyklos-Verlag for "A Generalization of the Foreign Trade Multiplier," *Kyklos*, Vol. IX, Fasc. 4 (1956), used in Chapter 4.

TO the Harvard University Press for "A Solution of the Keynes-Hicks-Hansen Non-linear Employment Model," *The Quarterly Journal of Economics*, Vol. LXX, No. 2 (May, 1956), used in Chapter 5; for "Employment, Prices, and Monopolistic Competition," *The Review of Economics and Statistics*, Vol. XXIV, No. 4 (November, 1952), used in Chapters 7 and 9; and for "Growth Rates of Output, Labor Force, Hours, and Productivity," *The Review of Economics and Statistics*, Vol. XXXIX, No. 4 (November, 1957), used in Chapter 21.

TO The Econometric Society for "Employment and Money Wages under Balanced Foreign Trade," *Econometrica*, Vol. 25, No. 2 (April, 1957), used in Chapter 11; and for "The Foreign Trade Accelerator and the International Transmission of Growth," *Econometrica*, Vol. 24, No. 3 (July, 1956), used in Chapter 24.

TO The American Economic Association for "Input-output Coefficients as Measures of Product Quality," *The American Economic Review*, Vol. XLVII, No. 1 (March, 1957), used in Chapter 17.

TO The Royal Economic Society for "Stability and Growth," *The Economic Journal*, Vol. LXV, No. 260 (December, 1955), used in Chapters 20 and 25.

TO *The Review of Economic Studies* for "Constancy of the Proportionate Equilibrium Rate of Growth: Result or Assumption?" *The Review of Economic Studies*, Vol. XXIV, No. 2 (February, 1957), used in Chapter 22.

TO The University of Chicago and to Professor Simon Kuznets for the latter's Table 1 in "Quantitative Aspects of the Economic Growth of Nations," *Economic Development and Cultural Change*, Vol. V, No. 1 (October, 1956), p. 10, used in Chapter 22.

Output, Employment, Capital, and Growth

1

Substance, Operational Significance, Generality, Validity, and Mathematics in Economic Theory

Uebers Verallgemeinern :
Niemals richtig
Immer wichtig

Erich Kästner

1. SUBSTANCE AND OPERATIONAL SIGNIFICANCE

By the *substance* of an economic theory is meant the specificity of its premises. Closely related to the substance of a theory is its *operational significance*, by which is meant the specificity of the conclusions that can be drawn from the theory. Usually, the more specific the premises, the more specific the conclusions. For example in order to gain operational significance in the cobweb theorem and reveal whether price will display damped or explosive oscillations, one must specify the slopes of the demand and supply curves used. Merely specifying the sign of each slope is not enough. The task of extracting the conclusions from premises at a high degree of specificity may well be a formidable one. In some cases only the use of high-speed electronic computers can

1

bring such conclusions within reach.   For this reason the recent use of computers has greatly increased the operational significance of certain economic models.

2. GENERALITY AND VALIDITY

The *generality* of an economic theory refers to the extent to which its premises cover real-world facts in time and space. Closely related to the generality of a theory is its *validity*, by which is meant the extent to which conclusions drawn cover real-world facts in time and space.   Thus generality and validity are both measures of realism, but it is important to distinguish between the realism of the premises and that of the conclusions.   The importance of making this distinction becomes evident as soon as we realize that no theory can ever hope to achieve full generality by covering all real-world facts.   If it did, it would indeed have ceased to be theory.   Yet by being selective in our choice of premises, we may hope to formulate a theory that can achieve a quite high degree of validity.   Success lies in including only relevant and typical facts among the premises.   Nonrelevant facts would clutter up the argument, and nontypical positive and negative deviations might well cancel.   Needless to say, in selecting the relevant and typical facts to be included among our premises we frequently have "bad luck," which normally appears as lack of validity of our theory.   But not always.   For example, we do not know whether orthodox profit-maximization or the full-cost principle is the more realistic premise.   But we do know that if the elasticity of the demand curve faced by the firm is a constant, and marginal cost is a constant, then the two premises will lead us to exactly the same conclusion about price behavior.   Thus even though we may have picked the less realistic premise we may arrive at the more realistic conclusion.   Our theory, then, is valid without being general.   In Milton Friedman's "positive economics," validity is all that matters.

3. THE COMPROMISE BETWEEN SUBSTANCE AND GENERALITY

Substance and generality are frequently alternatives. The only truly general statement about the behavior of economic subjects is the proposition that households, firms, labor unions, etc., act as they do. But such propositions are empty of substance. They permit no predictions and have no operational significance. By making a premise more specific we add substance, but at the same time we reduce the number of real-world facts of which the premise is a good description. For instance, we can specify firm behavior as the attempt of a firm to maximize dollar profits within the calendar year with no regard to customer relations, public relations, or labor relations. While this specification will give our model great operational significance, it may be a poor description of the behavior of the large majority of firms in the real world. This kind of dilemma has been with us for a very long time. Either we have been quite unspecific, not indicating any exact relationships between our variables—with the result that we have achieved generality while exposing ourselves to the criticism that not much is said—or, alternatively, we have committed ourselves to specific hypotheses, rigorously expressed, with the result that we have achieved operationally significant models with sufficient substance while this time exposing ourselves to the criticism that we have dealt with only a very special case.

Must substance be bought at the expense of generality? Clearly, the answer is in the negative. One example supporting a negative answer is the design of the Leontief dynamic input-output model. The use of the very large number of specific interindustry input-output and capital-output coefficients in the Leontief model does not reduce its generality but merely keeps separate those categories that behave differently, thus maintaining generality by avoiding premises which are poor descriptions of real life. This involves heavy disaggregation and the consequent swelling of the number of variables in the model.   There is a price to be paid for simultaneous advance on the road towards generality and the road towards substance, or the advance would have been made long ago.   That price is advance in the mathematical education of economists as well as advance in the technology of the electronic high-speed digital computer and the electro-analog computer.[1]

4. MERITS OF MATHEMATICS

Quite apart from the fact that mathematics is unrivaled in offering a means of solution of really complicated problems in economics, it may contribute to the clarification of any economic model.   It is impossible to set out one's ideas in a rigorous fashion without disclosing one's premises.   In this process the model builder himself may become more aware of his own assumptions. Furthermore, once formulated rigorously, they are exposed for all to see and criticize.   But this is not all; few of us can set out things in a rigorous fashion without gaining better understanding of such terms as "determination," "cause," and "effect."   The use of mathematics will drive home the lesson that usually in a multi-variable system the values of all variables are simultaneously determined by the values of all the parameters.

A third merit of mathematics is that it is international.   As such it is likely to facilitate international exchange of ideas, a good thing which has greatly enriched our science in the past.

5. LIMITATIONS OF MATHEMATICS

First and foremost of the obvious limitations of mathematics is that of measurability being a prerequisite for the application of

---

[1] A vivid impression of the advance during less than 20 years in mathematical economics (as distinct from econometrics) is gained from a comparison of the size and content of R. G. D. Allen's *Mathematical Analysis for Economists* (London: Macmillan, 1938) with those of his new *Mathematical Economics* (London: Macmillan, 1956).   On the role of the digital computer, see for example, Oskar Morgenstern, "Experiment and Large Scale Computation in Economics," *Economic Activity Analysis*, Morgenstern, ed. (New York: Wiley, 1954), pp. 484–549.

most branches of mathematics. In economics three different degrees of this limitation are found.

A. The first and strongest degree is that some of the categories we wish to analyze *are not measurable*. Utility does not seem measurable, not even at the individual level. This problem, however, has been solved or by-passed long ago by a number of writers.[2] In the theory of nonprice competition certain aspects, both of the quality of the product and of the selling effort accompanying it, are usually thought of as nonmeasurable. But given certain assumptions, the theory of nonprice competition can be made fully quantitative.[3] A hard core of nonmeasurable categories includes such realities as the politics of union leadership and union strategy, still waiting to be incorporated into the economics of labor.

B. The second degree of difficulty of measurement is found when certain categories, although measurable, *are not actually being measured*. This group is of ever-decreasing size. The last few decades have seen tremendous improvements in the quantity and quality of statistical data published periodically by the governments of such countries as the United States, Great Britain, Canada, the Netherlands, and the Scandinavian countries, to mention the best. Even expectations are being measured now! The real handicap, not likely to be overcome soon, is the lack of data on underdeveloped economies and, for the economic historians, the lack of data about the relatively distant past.

C. The third and weakest degree of difficulty of measurement

[2] Eugen E. Slutsky, "Sulla teoria del bilancio del consumatore," *Giornale degli Economisti*, Vol. LI, No. 7 (July, 1915), translated as "On the Theory of the Budget of the Consumer," in *Readings in Price Theory*, K. E. Boulding and G. J. Stigler, eds. (Homewood, Ill.: Irwin, 1952), pp. 27–56; J. R. Hicks, *Value and Capital* (Oxford: Clarendon Press, 1939); John von Neumann and Oskar Morgenstern, *Theory of Games and Economic Behavior* (Princeton: Princeton University Press, 1944), pp. 15–31; and Milton Friedman and L. J. Savage, "The Utility Analysis of Choices Involving Risk," *The Journal of Political Economy*, Vol. LVI, No. 4 (Aug., 1948), pp. 279–304, reprinted in *Readings in Price Theory, op. cit.,* pp. 57–96.

[3] In chap. 17 the author has made an attempt in this direction.

is the case of certain categories that, although actually being measured, *are not being measured with enough precision.* A Swedish treatment [4] of the terms of trade, defined as the ratio between the indices of export and import prices, is preceded by the motto: "Only economists can believe that by dividing one fiction of the mind by another one comes out with a reality." Only too frequently do we lump nonhomogeneous things together into aggregates, and the index-number problem rears its ugly head. But while the difficulties associated with the index-number problem are very real ones, they are only remotely related to the use of mathematics. Certainly, neither literary nor geometrical economic theory has eschewed such concepts as "land," "labor," "capital," "the wage rate," and "the interest rate," etc. Too, the practical forecaster speaks bluntly about "manufacturing output" and "the wholesale price level." The real remedy, then, is not the abandonment of mathematical economics, but rather the disaggregation of the aggregates. However, disaggregation, which results in an increase in the number of variables, will cause the model to rapidly grow beyond the capacity of literary treatment as well as of two-dimensional geometry. Accordingly, the model becomes more, not less, amenable to mathematical treatment.

6. A PROBLEM OF COMMUNICATION

A final limitation, not inherent but serious enough for the time being, is the lack of communication between mathematical and nonmathematical economists. This lack of communication is very harmful indeed: an increasing amount of scholarly work in their own discipline is incomprehensible to the nonmathematicians and consequently not subject to their criticism. Moreover, powerful intellects are barred from working on important and promising problems, because the appropriate tools have not been mastered.

[4] Kurt M. Savosnick, "Några anmärkningar om autonoma och inducerade förändringar i terms of trade för ett litet land," *Ekonomisk Tidskrift*, Vol. LVII, No. 2 (July, 1955), p. 106.

Add to this misfortune what Paul Samuelson calls "the psychological problem presented by mathematics." Mathematics and its increasing use by economists generates in the innocent either inferiority complexes or hostility, which is equally unproductive and uncomfortable.

Realizing that the difficulty of communication between mathematical and nonmathematical economists exists, what can we do about it? In our discipline this is not the first time we have faced a language barrier. Fortunately for the Anglo-Saxon economist, most of what was really good in our field came from the Anglo-Saxon countries. Consequently, most Anglo-Saxon economists felt it safe not to read foreign languages. But there were, of course, names like Walras, Böhm-Bawerk, Wicksell, and Slutsky, to mention only the dead. These Continentals did read foreign languages; above all, they read English. Thus the language barrier was a one-way barrier. The mathematical language barrier is also a one-way barrier: While most economists are innocent of mathematics, the mathematical economists are fully literate. This suggests that the remedy is not simply a demand that the mathematical economists must themselves translate their contributions into literary form. It does not seem fair to shift the burden altogether to one side.

PART I

The Keynesian Model

City and State, North, South, item and aggregate . . .
                                        WALT WHITMAN

A major problem of economic theory is the determination of aggregate output. Because of its simplicity the Keynesian theory of aggregate output serves as an excellent introduction to modern economic theory. Indeed, most of what is offered in the present volume is presented as qualification of the Keynesian model.

Chapter 2 locates the Keynesian theory in its historical perspective, and the three subsequent chapters develop the theory itself. Development proceeds best, perhaps, in three successive stages. First, Chapter 3 develops the crude theory of aggregate static equilibrium output in a closed economy, excluding money and the rate of interest. Second, Chapter 4 extends the crude theory to two countries and develops the theory of foreign-trade multipliers. Third, Chapter 5 by adding money and the rate of interest to the theory, gives us the complete Keynesian model. A critique in Chapter 6 completes the presentation of Keynesian analysis.

The content of Part I is thoroughly conventional, but the emphasis in treatment is on formal precision. Presented in rigorous form, the Keynesian model very readily yields important conclusions about the effects upon output of changes in autonomous consumption, autonomous investment, money supply, liquidity preference, and the propensities to import and consume. Such conclusions are obtained from application of elementary calculus wherever possible or, alternatively, from numerical solutions of the model (illustrated graphically).

2

The Beginnings of Aggregation

1. THE FORERUNNERS

An analysis of aggregates is an analysis of large categories of things. For example, the analysis of aggregate output is the analysis of the sum total of all things produced in an economy, with little or no regard to the individual things. The analysis of aggregate employment is the analysis of all employment in an economy, with no regard to the employment in any individual trade.

Aggregation is a very old procedure in economics. Indeed, one of the oldest of all economic theories, the quantity theory of money, was an aggregative one. It can be derived as follows. Take the Fisher equation of exchange $MV = PT$, where M is money supply, V the velocity of money, P the price of the average good to be transacted, and T the amount of goods to be transacted. Assume M to be the independent variable, P the dependent variable, and V and T parameters. Writing the equation as

$$P = \frac{V}{T} M$$

we have the proposition that price is in direct proportion to the money supply, the factor of proportionality being the parameter V/T.

The ingenious refinement of economic theory achieved in the nineteenth century, culminating in Walras' *Elements* (1874) and

11

Marshall's *Principles* (1890), carried disaggregation down to the smallest units of the economy, the firm and the household. Within a short time, aggregate output could no longer be seen for all its component parts. In the Anglo-Saxon countries Marshall's authority overshadowed that of the new analysis of aggregates emerging on the continent shortly before the turn of the century. In 1888 Böhm-Bawerk[1] presented his aggregative model of the mutual interdependence of wages, profits, capital, and output. In 1898 Böhm-Bawerk's exact contemporary and pupil, Wicksell[2] developed his cumulative process of expansion, in which aggregate demand was determined by the volume of investment in conjunction with a marginal propensity to consume equaling one in labor households. In turn, the volume of investment was determined by the internal rate of return in conjunction with the money rate of interest.

The collision of the "Old" with the "New" was illuminated with singular clarity in the famous discussion between Keynes and Ohlin in the 1929 *Economic Journal*[3] analyzing the mechanism of Germany's payment of reparations, imposed upon her by the Treaty of Versailles. Curiously enough, in this discussion Keynes was still heavily influenced by Marshallian tradition; in his opinion Germany could pay only if the relative price of her exports could be reduced enough to secure for them a substantially larger market abroad, a condition necessitating a reduction of the German money wage rate. While Keynes did not think of the international demand curve for German exports as being entirely

---

[1] Eugen von Böhm-Bawerk, *Positive Theorie des Kapitales* (Innsbruck: Wagner, 1888), translated by William Smart as *Positive Theory of Capital* (New York: Stechert, 1891), book VII, "The Rate in Market Transactions," and "The Market for Capital in its Full Development," pp. 381–424.

[2] Knut Wicksell, *Geldzins und Güterpreise* (Jena: Gustav Fischer, 1898), translated by R. F. Kahn as *Interest and Prices* (London: Macmillan, 1936).

[3] J. M. Keynes, "The German Transfer Problem," *The Economic Journal*, Vol. XXXIX, No. 153 (March, 1929), pp. 1–7; and Bertil Ohlin, "Transfer Difficulties, Real and Imagined," *ibid.*, Vol. XXXIX, No. 154 (June, 1929), pp. 172–178, both reprinted in *Readings in the Theory of International Trade*, Howard S. Ellis and Lloyd A. Metzler, eds. (Philadelphia: Blakiston, 1949), pp. 161–178.

immovable under the impact of reparations, he certainly did expect a "substantial" reduction in the German money wage rate to be necessary. Against this, Ohlin advocated the views of a later Keynes: The amount the reparations-receiving country would absorb at a given German price would depend on its "buying power," and reparations were nothing but huge international transfers of "buying power." Indeed, according to Ohlin, the reparations-paying country "need not offer its goods on cheaper terms of exchange to induce [the other] to take a greater quantity of them." But Ohlin assumed full employment in both countries. An over-all variation of employment and output was not yet in sight; the foreign-trade multiplier was not yet operating; these were to come much later.[4]

2. EARLY AGGREGATIVE DYNAMICS

By 1930 the "New Economics" was gaining momentum in Sweden. In Erik Lindahl's *Penningpolitikens medel* (Malmö, Sweden, 1930, partially translated as *Studies in the Theory of Money and Capital*, London: Allen & Unwin, 1939), he refined the Wicksellian analysis of a cumulative process of expansion and added to it a government sector that furthered or hampered the process by governmental purchase of goods and services and collection of taxes. Although the cumulative process is primarily one of expansion of the price level in a full-employment economy, Lindahl sprinkled his text with passages on the special case of unemployed resources. In such a case, output but not prices would expand cumulatively as the money rate of interest was lowered relative to the internal rate of return. Lindahl also had an aggregate consumption function in his analysis : consumption

[4] Lloyd A. Metzler, "Underemployment Equilibrium in International Trade," *Econometrica*, Vol. 10, No. 2 (April, 1942), pp. 97–112, or his "The Transfer Problem Reconsidered," *The Journal of Political Economy*, Vol. L, No. 3 (June, 1942), pp. 397–414, reprinted in *Readings in the Theory of International Trade*, Howard S. Ellis and Lloyd A. Metzler, eds. (Philadelphia: Blakiston, 1949), pp. 179–197.

was made a function not only of income but also of income distribution. A Wicksellian cumulative expansion, whether of the price level or of the level of aggregate output, is initiated by a lowering of the money rate of interest relative to the internal rate of return. The expansion itself will cause a redistribution of income such that those with a relatively strong disposition to save (the entrepreneurs) will gain at the expense of those whose disposition is weak (the capitalists and the workers).

In the theory of interest and money, Ohlin[5] anticipated the Keynesian liquidity-preference schedule and made the observation that its high elasticity at low money rates of interest, rather than the scarcity of saving, constitutes the real floor under the rate of interest. With the publication of Lundberg's *Studies*[6] the flourishing Stockholm School reached its climax. Using the multiplier and the accelerator, Lundberg offered a large number of numerical sequence models of aggregate output, aggregate investment, and aggregate consumption. Lundberg, however, failed to find the roots of the difference equations he implicitly employed.[7] But here Frisch had already made substantial progress. In his celebrated contribution to the Cassel volume,[8] Frisch set out his dynamic macroeconomic system in terms of differential and difference equations with all their paraphernalia of complex roots in polar form, familiar to all of us since the publication of Samuelson's "Interactions"[9] and Baumol's *Economic Dynamics*.[10] But let us return to Keynes who had completely liberated himself in 1936 from the Marshallian tradition.

[5] Bertil Ohlin, *Penningpolitik, offentliga arbeten, subventioner och tullar som medel mot arbetslöshet* (Stockholm: Statens offentliga utredningar, 1934).

[6] Erik Lundberg, *Studies in the Theory of Economic Expansion* (London: P. S. King, 1937).

[7] Lloyd A. Metzler, "The Nature and Stability of Inventory Cycles," *The Review of Economic Statistics*, Vol. XXIII, No. 3 (Aug., 1941), pp. 113–129.

[8] Ragnar Frisch, "Propagation and Impulse Problems in Dynamic Economics," *Economic Essays in Honour of Gustav Cassel* (London: Allen & Unwin, 1933).

[9] P. A. Samuelson, "Interactions between the Multiplier Analysis and the Principle of Acceleration," *The Review of Economics and Statistics*, Vol. XXI, No. 2 (May, 1939), pp. 75–78, reprinted in *Readings in Business Cycle Theory*, Gottfried Haberler, ed. (Philadelphia: Blakiston, 1944), pp. 261–269.

[10] (New York: Macmillan, 1951).

3

A Keynesian Determination of Aggregate Static Equilibrium Output

1. AN AGGREGATIVE LAW OF OUTPUT AND DEMAND

The Keynesian model, reduced to the barest essentials, determines aggregate output as follows. Aggregate demand is the sum of consumption demand and investment demand. Consumption demand is a function of aggregate output; investment demand is a parameter. Aggregate demand must equal aggregate output.

The Keynes model has three important properties. In the first place, it is *aggregative*; no attempt is made to examine the composition of aggregate output, except for the rough distinction between consumption and investment. In the second place, the model is *static*; what is determined is a level of output, not the time path of output. In the third place, the model is an *equilibrium* model, for only in equilibrium will aggregate demand and aggregate output have to be equal. Should the former exceed the latter, inventory depletion would take place, but at constant demand inventory depletion will sooner or later induce increased output. On the other hand, should aggregate demand fall short of aggregate output, inventory would accumulate. Again at constant demand, inventory accumulation would induce reductions in output. Consequently, the only level of output that does not have an inherent tendency to change itself is the level at which aggregate demand equals aggregate output. In this sense the model is nothing but an aggregative version of the law of supply and demand. However, as an introduction to vastly more complicated models it is useful and worth setting out rigorously.

2. THE VARIABLES

This torso of the Keynesian model has merely three variables.

1. C = Aggregate desired consumption outlays by households, in billions of constant-value dollars per year
2. I = Aggregate desired net investment by business, in billions of constant-value dollars per year
3. Y = Actual net national product, in billions of constant-value dollars per year

In order to determine the equilibrium value of each of the three variables, three linear equations are set up.

3. THE EQUATIONS

The first equation is a behavior equation, specifying the way in which consumption demand depends upon output:

(1) $$C = a + bY$$

where a and b are parameters. The former is called autonomous consumption, the latter the marginal propensity to consume.

The second equation, also a behavior equation, states that investment is a parameter:

(2) $$I = \text{a parameter}$$

The third equation states the equilibrium condition: the sum of consumption and investment must equal national output; if such were not the case, inventory would either accumulate or be depleted, either circumstance inducing changes in output.

(3) $$C + I = Y$$

4. THE SOLUTION

Now solving for output, insert (1) and (2) in (3), rearrange, and get

(I) $$Y = \frac{I + a}{1 - b}$$

This solution indicates that the equilibrium value of the net national product is equal to a ratio whose numerator is the sum of autonomous investment and autonomous consumption, and whose denominator is equal to unity minus the marginal propensity to consume. The denominator, of course, may also be called the marginal propensity to save. A more intimate understanding of the properties of this solution, if cast in graphical form is possible for many readers.

In a diagram, measure Y on the horizontal axis, $C + I$ on the vertical axis. Equation (3) will then appear as a straight line running through zero and forming a 45° angle with each axis. In our diagrams the line representing equation (3) will be broken. Equations (1) and (2) may now be used to form a second relationship between $(C + I)$ and Y. One gets $C + I = a + I + bY$. Such a relationship in a diagram of the type we are studying must be a straight line. In our diagrams the line representing this relationship will be solid. Equilibrium net national output must satisfy both relationships; consequently, it must be equal to the abscissa to the point of intersection between the two straight lines, if any.

Figures 1 through 6 show some hypothetical cases. In Figure 1, where $I + a$ is positive but $b = 1$, the solid and broken lines are parallel; no finite value of equilibrium net national product is

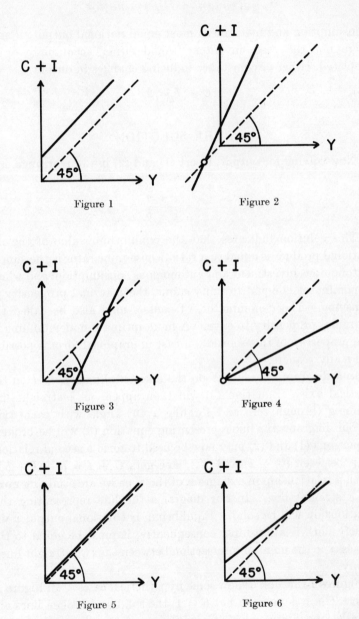

Figure 1

Figure 2

Figure 3

Figure 4

Figure 5

Figure 6

possible. In Figure 2, where $I + a$ is still positive but b is now in excess of unity, an intersection of the solid and broken lines is now possible but, alas, not for a positive value of net national output. When b is in excess of unity, Y can be positive only if $I + a$ is negative, as illustrated in Figure 3. Next, let us examine the special case where $I + a = 0$. If b differs from unity, the solid and broken lines will intersect at the point of origin, showing the equilibrium value of net national output to be zero, as illustrated in Figure 4. When $I + a$ still equals zero but b equals unity, the solid and broken lines will coincide, as shown in Figure 5, and any value of Y will satisfy our equations. Equilibrium net national output is then indeterminate.

Fortunately, in the real world the sum of autonomous investment and autonomous consumption $(I + a)$ is positive, and the marginal propensity to consume (b) is less than unity. Under such circumstances, as shown in Figure 6, the equilibrium value of net national output is positive and finite. For example the following set of values of our parameters might not seem entirely implausible:

$$a = 30$$
$$b = 0.75$$
$$I = 21$$

For these three values, equation (I) will give us the value $Y = 204$. To get an impression of the significance of the specific value attached to each of the three parameters, let us vary each of them in turn and watch the effect upon Y according to equation (I). To facilitate interpretation, the results, shown in Table 1, are also shown in graphical form, in Figures 7 through 9 on double-logarithmic scales. Such scales cause the elasticity of national output with respect to any of the parameters I, a, or b to appear visibly as the steepness of the curve. It appears that the elasticity of equilibrium net national output with respect to I is moderate, with respect to a somewhat higher, and with respect to b very high indeed. An alternative measure of these effects is found in the multipliers, treated in the following sections.

TABLE 1. Effects of Changing Three Parameters upon National Output

I	Y	a	Y	b	Y
1	124	10	124	0.65	145.7
11	164	20	164	0.70	170.0
21	204	30	204	0.75	204.0
31	244	40	244	0.80	255.0

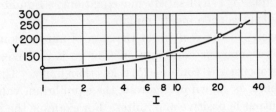

Figure 7

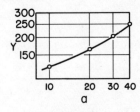

Figure 8

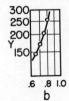

Figure 9

5. THE AUTONOMOUS-INVESTMENT MULTIPLIER

It is very easy to find, mathematically, the effect of a change in a parameter, say I, upon a variable, say Y. Equation (I) expresses the relationship between the variable Y on the one hand and any one parameter, including I, on the other. We have only to take the derivative[1] of Y with respect to I

[1] On the technique of differentiation, see for example, section 4 of chap. 9 of D. W. Bushaw and R. W. Clower, *Introduction to Mathematical Economics* (Homewood, Ill.: Irwin, 1957).

(II) $$\frac{\partial Y}{\partial I} = \frac{1}{1-b}$$

Equation (II), the famous Keynesian multiplier (Keynes did not mention any others), indicates that the derivative of equilibrium net national output with respect to autonomous investment equals the quotient of one divided by the marginal propensity to save. Tabulations for (II) are shown in Table 2. When, for

TABLE 2. The Keynesian Multiplier

b	$\dfrac{\partial Y}{\partial I}$
0.6	2.5
0.7	3.3
0.8	5.0
0.9	10.0

instance, the marginal propensity to consume equals 0.8, every additional dollar's worth of autonomous investment will raise the equilibrium value of net national output by five dollars. However, when the economy is thriftier, with the marginal propensity to consume perhaps being only 0.6, one additional dollar's worth of autonomous investment is not quite so potent, raising output merely by $2.50.

6. THE AUTONOMOUS-CONSUMPTION MULTIPLIER

Although we have three parameters in the model, multipliers, strangely enough, are never calculated with respect to the last two. Since it is easy enough to generalize the multiplier concept, let us now find the effect of a small change in the parameter a, autonomous consumption, upon Y, output. Using (I), we find the derivative of Y with respect to a to be

(III) $$\frac{\partial Y}{\partial a} = \frac{1}{1-b}$$

By analogy, we might call this the autonomous-consumption multiplier; it happens to have the same value as the autonomous-investment multiplier (II). Thus the injection of one additional dollar's worth of autonomous consumption or the injection of one additional dollar's worth of autonomous investment is equally beneficial, for either will raise the equilibrium value of net national output by a like amount, that is, one dollar divided by the marginal propensity to save.

7. THE INDUCED-CONSUMPTION MULTIPLIER

Finally, let us find the effect of a small change in the parameter b, the marginal propensity to consume, upon Y, output. Again using (I), we find that the derivative of Y with respect to b is

(IV)
$$\frac{\partial Y}{\partial b} = \frac{I + a}{(1 - b)^2}$$

which we shall call the induced-consumption multiplier. Unlike the values of the two other multipliers, the value of this multiplier depends upon the initial value of the parameter we are varying (b). But we can at least say that for positive values of $I + a$, the induced-consumption multiplier is positive.

8. CONCLUSION

We have found that for positive values of $I + a$, and for values of b less than unity, the equilibrium value of net national output is positive and finite and that it will rise with a rise in the value of (1) autonomous investment I, (2) autonomous consumption a, or (3) the marginal propensity to consume b.

9. TESTING THE STABILITY OF EQUILIBRIUM

By stability of equilibrium is meant the property of the equilibrium that results in deviations from the equilibrium to be self-correcting. In order to test the stability of our equilibrium solution (I) we merely assume that in a certain period, net national output deviates from the value defined by equation (I). The consequences of such deviation will become readily apparent from Figure 6, in which all investment was assumed to be autonomous and in which a constant volume of investment expenditure, irrespective of the level of national output, was added vertically to the consumption function; hence aggregate demand appeared as a curve whose slope was the marginal propensity to consume. Since the latter was less than one, the aggregate demand curve would run above a 45° line for outputs less than equilibrium output, but below the 45° line for outputs greater than equilibrium output. When output is less than equilibrium output, aggregate demand will *exceed* output, and inventory must fall. Falling inventory will induce firms to expand output, with the eventual result that the economy will be driven back to equilibrium. Conversely, when output is greater than equilibrium output, aggregate demand will *fall short of* output, and inventory must rise. Rising inventory will induce firms to reduce output, and in this situation, also, the economy will be driven back to equilibrium. We can only conclude that as long as the slope of the aggregate demand function is less than one, our net national output equilibrium will be stable.

Further aspects of the stability of static equilibrium will be studied in Section 12 of Chapter 7. The stability of dynamic equilibrium will be studied in Chapters 25 and 26.

4

The Foreign-Trade Multiplier

1. TWO COUNTRIES

We shall now expand the simple Keynesian model to the case of two countries. To compensate for the added complication we shall assume all import and consumption functions to be homogeneous, resulting in only one parameter per equation. In our two-country static Keynesian equilibrium model, the variables are:

C = a country's aggregate consumption of its own products

I = a country's aggregate net investment of its own products

M = a country's aggregate import

X = a country's aggregate export and

Y = a country's net national product

All variables are measured in billions of constant-value dollars per year, and relative price changes are ignored. All variables referring to country 1 will carry the subscript "1," and all variables referring to country 2 will carry the subscript "2." Having five variables for each of two countries, we have a total of ten variables.

NOTE: The present chapter is a slightly revised reproduction of the author's "A Generalization of the Foreign-Trade Multiplier," *Kyklos*, Vol. IX, Fasc. 4 (1956).

In order to determine the equilibrium values of the ten variables, the following ten linear equations are set up. First, in each country the aggregate consumption of own products is in proportion to net national product:

$$(1) \qquad C_1 = c_1 Y_1 \qquad\qquad (2) \qquad C_2 = c_2 Y_2$$

where c_1 and c_2 are the national propensities to consume own products.

Second, in each country aggregate net investment of own products is a parameter:

$$(3) \qquad I_1 = \text{a parameter} \qquad (4) \qquad I_2 = \text{a parameter}$$

Third, in each country import is for consumption purposes only, and aggregate import is in proportion to net national product:

$$(5) \qquad M_1 = m_1 Y_1 \qquad\qquad (6) \qquad M_2 = m_2 Y_2$$

where m_1 and m_2 are the national propensities to import. Fourth, one country's import is the other country's export, of course:

$$(7) \qquad M_1 = X_2 \qquad\qquad (8) \qquad M_2 = X_1$$

Finally, in equilibrium the net national product must be equal to the aggregate demand for it. This must be true in both countries:

$$(9) \qquad Y_1 = C_1 + I_1 + X_1 \qquad (10) \qquad Y_2 = C_2 + I_2 + X_2$$

2. SOLUTION

Our system of ten equations and ten unknowns can be solved with respect to the two equilibrium national products; the solutions are:

$$(I) \qquad\qquad Y_1 = \frac{(1 - c_2)I_1 + m_2 I_2}{(1 - c_1)(1 - c_2) - m_1 m_2}$$

$$(II) \qquad\qquad Y_2 = \frac{(1 - c_1)I_2 + m_1 I_1}{(1 - c_1)(1 - c_2) - m_1 m_2}$$

Now assume for both countries that the propensity to save is positive. In each country this propensity is equal to one minus the sum of the propensities to consume own products and to import. Consequently,

$$1 - (c_i + m_i) > 0 \qquad i = 1 \text{ or } 2$$
$$1 - c_i > m_i$$

For country 1:

$$1 - c_1 > m_1$$

(11) $$(1 - c_1)m_2 > m_1 m_2$$

And since for country 2

$$1 - c_2 > m_2$$

in inequality (11) when the m_2 on the left-hand side is replaced by $(1 - c_2)$, the result is

$$(1 - c_1)(1 - c_2) > m_1 m_2$$

Consequently, the common denominator of (I) and (II) is positive. Since both terms of the two numerators are also positive, the values of equilibrium national output in both countries are positive.

3. THE TWELVE NATIONAL-OUTPUT MULTIPLIERS AND THEIR SIGNS

In each of our solutions (I) and (II), all six parameters: c_1, I_1, m_1, c_2, I_2, and m_2, appear. For each country, then, there are six national-output multipliers. For country 1 they are:

(III) $$\frac{\partial Y_1}{\partial c_1} = \frac{(1 - c_2)Y_1}{(1 - c_1)(1 - c_2) - m_1 m_2}$$

(IV) $$\frac{\partial Y_1}{\partial I_1} = \frac{1 - c_2}{(1 - c_1)(1 - c_2) - m_1 m_2}$$

(V) $$\frac{\partial Y_1}{\partial m_1} = \frac{m_2 Y_1}{(1 - c_1)(1 - c_2) - m_1 m_2}$$

(VI) $$\frac{\partial Y_1}{\partial c_2} = \frac{m_2 Y_2}{(1 - c_1)(1 - c_2) - m_1 m_2}$$

(VII) $$\frac{\partial Y_1}{\partial I_2} = \frac{m_2}{(1 - c_1)(1 - c_2) - m_1 m_2}$$

(VIII) $$\frac{\partial Y_1}{\partial m_2} = \frac{(1 - c_2) Y_2}{(1 - c_1)(1 - c_2) - m_1 m_2}$$

According to our assumption that in both countries the propensity to save is positive, all six derivatives are obviously positive. In words they may be stated as: A country's equilibrium net national product will rise if (a) that country's own propensity to consume own products rises, (b) that country's own autonomous investment rises, (c) that country's own propensity to import rises, (d) the other country's propensity to consume own products rises, (e) the other country's autonomous investment rises, or (f) the other country's propensity to import rises.

All six multipliers (III) through (VIII) refer to the national output of country 1. Since solutions (I) and (II) are symmetrical in the sense that (II) can be derived from (I) merely by an interchange of the subscripts "1" and "2," the six remaining multipliers for country 2 can be easily derived from (III) through (VIII) by such interchange and need not be written.

4. GRAPHICAL ILLUSTRATION

The Keynesian multiplier, being a ratio between incremental output and incremental investment, both of which are measured in dollars per unit of time, is a pure number. The same is true of multipliers (IV) and (VII), but the remaining multipliers are ratios between incremental output (measured in dollars per unit of time) and incremental propensities (expressed in pure numbers). The numerical value of such multipliers obviously depends upon the unit of measurement adopted for output, and it might be desirable to look into the dimensionless elasticity instead. The easiest approach is to plot on double-logarithmic paper output as a function of the parameter in question. The elasticity of output with respect to that parameter will then appear visibly as the steepness of the curve.

Figures 10 through 15 show in double-logarithmic scale the equilibrium national output of country 1 as a function of each of the six parameters in turn. These six graphs were constructed as follows. To illustrate the interaction between two countries of substantially different sizes, we assigned the following values to the six parameters:

$$c_1 = 0.6 \qquad c_2 = 0.8$$
$$I_1 = 5 \qquad I_2 = 30$$
$$m_1 = 0.3 \qquad m_2 = 0.1$$

According to (I) and (II), the values shown will give $Y_1 = 80$ and $Y_2 = 270$. Except for the obvious requirements that the propensity to save should in each country be positive, and that the larger economy should be much less dependent upon import than the smaller economy, the values shown have been chosen arbitrarily. Each of the six parameters has, one by one, been varied, the values of the remaining five remaining constant, and the corresponding value of national output of country 1 has been found and shown successively in the six figures.

The general impression is that, within the ranges studied, equilibrium national output is more elastic with respect to the propensity to consume in each of the two countries, c_1 and c_2, than with respect to any other parameter. After all, consumption of own products in either country is the largest single component of national demand. If the two elasticities with respect to c_1 and c_2 are compared, we find the latter to be larger. This fact is hardly surprising since country 2 has a much larger equilibrium national output than has country 1. The four elasticities with respect to autonomous investment and the propensities to import are distinctly lower, but they do not seem to differ significantly from one another, at least within the range examined.

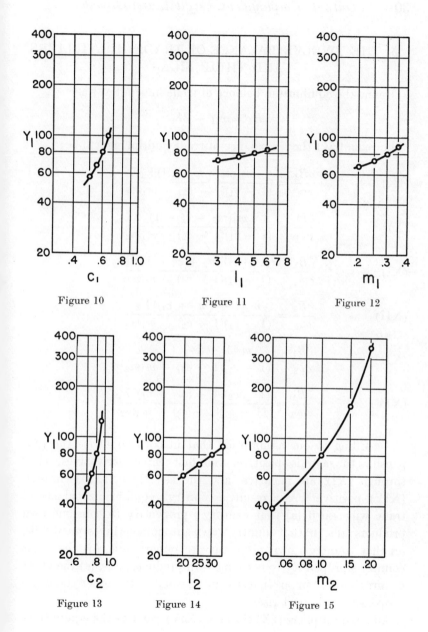

Figure 10

Figure 11

Figure 12

Figure 13

Figure 14

Figure 15

5. THE TWELVE BALANCE-OF-TRADE MULTIPLIERS AND THEIR SIGNS

Define the equilibrium balance of trade in country 1 as:

$$B_1 = X_1 - M_1$$

For country 1 the six balance-of-trade multipliers will be:

(IX)
$$\frac{\partial B_1}{\partial c_1} = \frac{m_1(m_2 + c_2 - 1)Y_1}{(1 - c_1)(1 - c_2) - m_1 m_2}$$

(X)
$$\frac{\partial B_1}{\partial I_1} = \frac{m_1(m_2 + c_2 - 1)}{(1 - c_1)(1 - c_2) - m_1 m_2}$$

(XI)
$$\frac{\partial B_1}{\partial m_1} = \frac{(1 - c_1)(m_2 + c_2 - 1)Y_1}{(1 - c_1)(1 - c_2) - m_1 m_2}$$

(XII)
$$\frac{\partial B_1}{\partial c_2} = \frac{m_2[1 - (m_1 + c_1)]Y_2}{(1 - c_1)(1 - c_2) - m_1 m_2}$$

(XIII)
$$\frac{\partial B_1}{\partial I_2} = \frac{m_2[1 - (m_1 + c_1)]}{(1 - c_1)(1 - c_2) - m_1 m_2}$$

(XIV)
$$\frac{\partial B_1}{\partial m_2} = \frac{(1 - c_2)[1 - (m_1 + c_1)]Y_2}{(1 - c_1)(1 - c_2) - m_1 m_2}$$

According to our assumption that in both countries the propensity to save is positive, the first three derivatives, (IX) through (XI), are negative, and the last three, (XII) through (XIV), positive. As a result, a country's equilibrium balance of trade will rise if (a) that country's propensity to consume own products falls, (b) that country's own autonomous investment falls, (c) that country's own propensity to import falls, (d) the other country's propensity to consume own products rises, (e) the other country's autonomous investment rises, or (f) the other country's propensity to import rises.

All six multipliers (IX) through (XIV), refer to the equilibrium balance of trade of country 1.   The equilibrium balance of trade of country 2 is

$$B_2 = X_2 - M_2$$

By using equations (7) and (8) we obtain

$$B_2 = M_1 - X_1$$

As a result $B_2 = -B_1$, and $dB_2 = -dB_1$.   Consequently the remaining six balance-of-trade multipliers for country 2 can easily be derived from the derivatives (IX) through (XIV), merely by a replacement of B_1 with B_2 on the left-hand side and by the addition of a minus sign on the right-hand side of each equation.

6. GRAPHICAL ILLUSTRATION

In order to determine the elasticity measure we plot our results in double-logarithmic graphs.   Figures 16 through 21 show the equilibrium balance of trade of country 1 as a function of each of the 6 parameters in turn.   The numerical values of the 6 parameters used as a point of departure are the same as before. Accordingly, country 1 has an equilibrium national product of 80, an equilibrium import of 24, an equilibrium export of 27, saves 8, invests 5, and lends 3 abroad.   Country 2 has an equilibrium national product of 270, an equilibrium import of 27, an equilibrium export of 24, saves 27, invests 30, and borrows 3 abroad. The variations of the 6 parameters, one by one, are the same as those in Figures 10 through 15.

The general impression is that the elasticities with respect to the two propensities to consume c_1 and c_2 are far greater numerically than any other elasticities shown.   In fact, with respect to these two propensities, the equilibrium balance of trade seems to be numerically even more elastic than was the equilibrium national output.   One difference, of course, is that while the elasticities of national output with respect to c_1 and c_2 were both positive, the elasticity of the balance of trade with respect to c_1 is negative but with respect to c_2 positive.

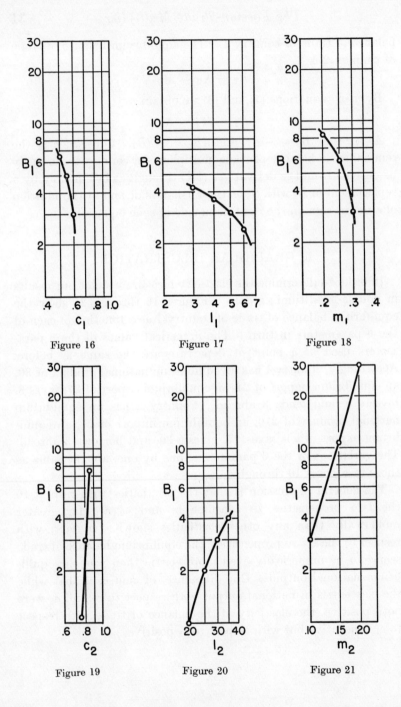

Figure 16

Figure 17

Figure 18

Figure 19

Figure 20

Figure 21

All four elasticities of the equilibrium balance of trade with respect to autonomous investments and the propensities to import are numerically somewhat lower than the propensity-to-consume elasticities. At the same time, however, they are numerically somewhat higher than the four corresponding elasticities of equilibrium national output, at least within the range studied.

7. LIMITS OF THE ANALYSIS

Only at the beginning of a course in the theory of international trade would material such as that presented here be at all useful. The rest of the course would devote itself to the mending of some of the gaping holes of our structure. First, there is the assumption of linear and homogeneous import and consumption functions. The homogeneity assumption is not our worst, however, for our autonomous investments could, in fact, take care of anything which happens to be autonomous. Second, there is the complete neglect of prices and exchange rates.[1] Such neglect is far more serious; but alas, necessary if one wishes to use for parameters the propensities to consume own products and to import. Third, there is the ease with which a country runs into international debt.[2] Fourth, there is the assumption of a two-country world. This is a heroic aggregation, only surpassed by the assumption of a closed economy, not infrequently made in economics. Fifth, there is the static character of our analysis: no accelerators, no growth.[3]

[1] On prices and wages, see chap. 11.
[2] On balanced foreign trade, see chap. 10.
[3] On international transmission of growth, see chap. 24.

5

The Complete Keynesian Model

1. GOODS AND MONEY

The beauty of the Keynesian system, refined by Hicks,[1] Hansen,[2] and others, was its successful integration of the theory of goods with the theory of money. In fact, there was a three-fold symmetry between the two spheres. First, in both there was the equilibrium condition that demand and supply must be equal. Equality between the demand for, and the supply of, goods would define the equilibrium level of output, and equality between the demand for, and supply of, money would define the equilibrium level of the rate of interest. Second, in both spheres demand was composed of two elements, one depending upon the level of output (the consumption function and the active-money function, respectively), and one depending upon the rate of interest (the investment function and the idle-money function, respectively). Third,

---

[1] J. R. Hicks, "Mr. Keynes and the 'Classics,' a Suggested Interpretation," *Econometrica*, Vol. 5, No. 2 (April, 1937), pp. 147–159, reprinted in *Readings in the Theory of Income Distribution*, William Fellner and Bernard F. Haley, eds. (Philadelphia: Blakiston, 1946), pp. 461–476.

[2] Alvin H. Hansen, *Monetary Theory and Fiscal Policy* (New York: McGraw-Hill, 1949); *Business Cycles and National Income* (New York: Norton, 1951); *A Guide to Keynes* (McGraw-Hill, 1953).

NOTE: The present chapter is a slightly revised and expanded reproduction of the author's "A Solution of the Keynes-Hicks-Hansen Nonlinear Employment Model," *The Quarterly Journal of Economics*, Vol. LXX, No. 2 (May, 1956).

the symmetry between the two spheres was complete to the extent that the two functions whose independent variable was the level of output were both usually assumed to be linear, whereas the two functions whose independent variable was the rate of interest were both nonlinear.

With few exceptions,[3] elementary texts have confined themselves to a Keynesian model from which the money sphere has been entirely eliminated. With the nonlinear functions thus eliminated the model becomes very easy to handle. However, with the post-1950 revival of interest in monetary policy in leading countries, it has become desirable to put the monetary sphere back into the model. Hicks, Hansen, and Baumol, in the works cited, did this by successive reduction of the system into two functions, the "IS" function and the "LL" function, both of which could be handled in a two-dimensional graph. The present chapter suggests a straightforward algebraic solution. If the nonlinear investment and idle-money functions can be represented by quadratic equations, the entire system can be reduced to a fourth-degree equation for output. On electronic computers this equation can be solved in less than one-half minute, and thus the effect upon output of manipulation of any of its parameters can be studied very easily. The present chapter will show such effects for a system containing eight parameters, not only for the sake of the model studied but also of providing an example of the usefulness of the electronic digital computer.

2. THE VARIABLES OF THE MODEL

The simplest possible full-sized Keynes-Hicks-Hansen model has seven variables in it:

C = Aggregate desired consumption outlays by households, in billions of constant-value dollars per year

---

[3] For example, William J. Baumol and Lester V. Chandler, *Economic Processes and Policies* (New York: Harper, 1954), chaps. 10 and 11.

I = Aggregate desired net investment by business, in billions of constant-value dollars per year

i = Actual market rate of interest, in a pure number per year

L_L = Aggregate desired volume of "asset" cash balances, in billions of constant-value dollars

L_T = Aggregate desired volume of "transactions" cash balances, in billions of constant-value dollars

M = Actual quantity of money supplied by the monetary authorities, in billions of constant-value dollars

Y = Actual net national product, in billions of constant-value dollars per year

In order to determine the equilibrium value of the seven variables, a system of equations must be set out. The first four equations are behavior equations, each relating a pair of variables to one another. The next two are equilibrium conditions, and the last will be a policy parameter.

3. THE REAL-SPHERE BEHAVIOR EQUATIONS

First of the four behavior equations is the consumption function. This is not the place to enumerate empirical contributions whose number has been *legio*. Without attempting to give reasons we shall adopt the simple and customary linear equation

(1) $$C = a + bY$$

where a and b are parameters.

Much less has been found about the investment function. Net investment is a function of the rate of interest: the lower the rate of interest, the larger the volume of net investment. Most specifically, Hansen has added the observation that the investment curve "is fairly elastic with respect to the rate of interest at *high* interest rate levels, and is fairly inelastic within a rather wide range of interest rates at the *lower* levels."[4]

---

[4] Alvin H. Hansen, *Business Cycles and National Income, op. cit.*, p. 133.

The latter half of Hansen's statement is well borne out by empirical findings. In a statistical study of the business cycle from 1919 through 1932 in the United States Tinbergen[5] found that the influence of discount rates and of other short-term rates upon investment was "very small." The influence of long-term interest rates on investment activity in durable goods was "moderate." The findings of the two Oxford surveys were similar to Tinbergen's. The first Oxford survey[6] included a great many questions asked of a small number of firms (37). The gist of the answers was that short-term rates had no influence upon investment. A majority of firms answered that the long-term rates had no direct effect, also. The second Oxford survey[7] included a small number of questions asked of a large number of firms (1308). The gist of the questions was whether the rate of interest, in any of its forms, had ever affected the decisions of the firm to invest in plant extension, maintenance, repairs, or inventory. The majority of the firms did not answer, but of the one-quarter that did, three-quarters answered no. Rather than asking borrowers, Jørgen Pedersen and C. E. Sørensen[8] asked lenders. All Danish banks were asked whether, within the interval from 4 to 8 percent per annum, variations in the rate of interest would affect the desire to borrow. The majority of the banks did not think so.

The first half of Hansen's statement, stating that investment is elastic with respect to interest at high rates of interest, has not been empirically tested—for the simple reason that in mature

---

[5] J. Tinbergen, *Business Cycles in the United States of America* (Geneva: League of Nations, 1939), p. 184 *et passim*.

[6] J. E. Meade and P. W. S. Andrews, "Summary of Replies to Questions on Effects of Interest Rates," *Oxford Economic Papers*, No. 1 (October, 1938), pp. 14–31, reprinted in *Oxford Studies in the Price Mechanism*, T. Wilson and P. W. S. Andrews, eds. (Oxford: Clarendon Press, 1951), pp. 27–30.

[7] P. W. S. Andrews, "A Further Inquiry into the Effects of Rates of Interest," *Oxford Economic Papers*, No. 3 (March, 1940), pp. 32–73, reprinted in *Oxford Studies in the Price Mechanism, op. cit.*, pp. 51–67.

[8] Jørgen Pedersen and Carl Erik Sørensen, "Hvorledes reagerer bankerne?" *Nationaløkonomisk Tidsskrift*, Vol. 88, No. 3–4 (1950), pp. 93–124.

capitalist economies, in which the data and tools for testing are available, the rate of interest has never been very high.   But on a priori grounds Hansen's statement sounds plausible enough. H. D. Henderson[9] and others have pointed to uncertainty of demand and cost conditions in the distant future as a factor that will swamp the rate of interest in the entrepreneurial mind.   But surely there would exist a rate of interest which would be high enough to swamp uncertainty.   Whether rates would have to go as high as 10 or 20 or more percent per annum is hard to say, but after everything has been taken into account, it seems at least safe to use an ellipse-shaped investment function like

$$(2) \qquad\qquad I = \sqrt{c - ei^2}$$

where c and e are parameters.   Both are positive, and e indicates the extent to which the ellipse is stretched.[10]   We are ignoring the parts of the ellipse lying outside the first quadrant.

4. THE MONEY-SPHERE BEHAVIOR EQUATIONS

Little needs to be said about the active-money function. Neither firms nor households can synchronize income and outlay, hence their need for active or transactions money.   Ignoring both autonomous consumption and transactions of intermediate and second-hand goods, we shall follow common usage and make active money L_T a linear and homogeneous function of output:

$$(3) \qquad\qquad L_T = fY$$

where f is a parameter.

Next the idle-money function L_L.   As Hansen says,[11] "this matter—the interest-elasticity of the L_L function—is stressed very

---

[9] H. D. Henderson, "The Significance of the Rate of Interest," *Oxford Economic Papers*, No. 1 (Oct., 1938), pp. 1–13, reprinted in *Oxford Studies in the Price Mechanism, op. cit.*, pp. 16–27.

[10] If $e = 1$ the ellipse becomes a circle.

[11] *A Guide to Keynes, op. cit.*, p. 130.

much by Keynes." Using linear relationships, A. J. Brown[12] found a very close relationship between idle money on the one hand and the rate of interest and the change of wholesale prices on the other, concluding: "If it is a criterion of the importance of a relation that it should emerge clearly in practice, this form of the liquidity-preference schedule would appear to be of very considerable importance." Using a Keynesian liquidity function, Tobin[13] found a clearly hyperbolic shape. Latané[14] and Polak-White[15] added income as an independent variable to the Keynesian liquidity function and at the same time replaced idle cash by *all* cash balances. Latané used M/Y as his independent variable and found a clearly hyperbolic shape. Polak-White used M in terms of the 1953 income level and on a semilogarithmic scale found a straight-line postwar liquidity function. Scandinavian writers have found hyperbolic liquidity-preference functions, too: Philip[16] found a Keynesian liquidity-preference function for Danish banks during World War II when the German-sponsored inflation made it possible to catch glimpses of the far end of the curve, normally hidden. Schlebaum Larsen[17] refined Philip's analysis by separating actual from expected future rates of interest. Börje Kragh[18] devoted an entire book to a partial

[12] A. J. Brown, "Interest, Prices, and the Demand Schedule for Idle Money," *Oxford Economic Papers*, No. 2 (May, 1939), pp. 46–69, reprinted in *Oxford Studies in the Price Mechanism, op. cit.*, pp. 31–51.

[13] James Tobin, "Liquidity Preference and Monetary Policy," *The Review of Economic Statistics*, Vol. XXIX, No. 2 (May, 1947), pp. 124–131.

[14] Henry Allen Latané, "Cash Balances and the Interest Rate—A Pragmatic Approach," *The Review of Economics and Statistics*, Vol. XXXVI, No. 4 (Nov., 1954), pp. 456–60.

[15] J. J. Polak and William H. White, "The Effect of Income Expansion on the Quantity of Money," *International Monetary Fund Staff Papers*, Vol. IV, No. 3 (Aug., 1955), pp. 398–433.

[16] Kjeld Philip, "A Statistical Measurement of the Liquidity Preference of Private Banks," *The Review of Economic Studies*, No. 40 (1949–1950), pp. 71–77.

[17] Heinrich Schlebaum Larsen, "Bankernes likviditetspraeference," *Ekonomisk Tidskrift*, Vol. LI, No. 1 (March, 1949), pp. 39–46, and "Om rentedannelsen for kreditforeningsobligationer," *Nationaløkonomisk Tidsskrift*, Vol. 87, No. 5 (1949), pp. 336–346.

[18] Börje Kragh, *Prisbildningen på kreditmarknaden* (Uppsala, Sweden: Appelbergs, 1951).

analysis of the Keynesian liquidity function, including a statistical study for Sweden 1931–1939. In a later paper Schlebaum Larsen [19] studied, for the period 1948–1953 in Denmark, the liquidity-preference schedules for banks as well as for private individuals. All three investigators found a hyperbolic shape.

As a first approximation, we shall adopt a hyperbola-shaped liquidity-preference function like

$$(4) \qquad L_L = \frac{g}{i - h}$$

where g and h are parameters. The parameter g is a measure of the total mass of assets; the parameter h indicates the minimum rate of interest at which L_L approaches infinity.[20] Thus the asymptotes of the hyperbola are the i-axis and the line parallel to the L_L-axis at the distance h from the latter.

5. TWO EQUILIBRIUM CONDITIONS

In both the goods and money spheres, demand must equal supply. First, in the goods sphere the sum of consumption and investment must equal national output, for if that were not the case inventory would either accumulate or be depleted, and either circumstance would induce changes in output. Thus

$$(5) \qquad C + I = Y$$

Second, in the money sphere the sum of demand for active and idle money must equal the available money supply, for if that were not the case individuals, in their attempt either to hold more money or to get rid of money, would either sell or buy bonds, and again, either circumstance would change the interest rate. Thus

$$(6) \qquad L_T + L_L = M$$

[19] Heinrich Schlebaum Larsen, "Udviklingen på det danske penge- og kapital-marked i årene 1948–1953," *Nationaløkonomisk Tidsskrift*, Vol. 92, No. 3–4 (1954), pp. 117–134.

[20] The notion of a minimum rate of interest at which L_L approaches infinity has been criticized by Don Patinkin in his *Money, Interest, and Prices* (Evanston, Ill.: Row, Peterson and Co., 1956), pp. 245–249.

6. A POLITICALLY GIVEN PARAMETER

The seventh and last equation is provided by the assumption that the monetary authorities will fix the money supply at some particular value:

(7) $$M = \text{a parameter}$$

7. SOLUTION

We have seven variables, and we have seven equations containing the eight parameters $a, b, c, e, f, g, h,$ and M. Since we are primarily interested in national output, let us solve for Y. Equations (2) and (4) being quadratic and the rest of the equations being linear, we obtain a rather complicated fourth-degree equation in Y:

(I) $$m_1 Y^4 + m_2 Y^3 + m_3 Y^2 + m_4 Y + m_5 = 0$$

where the m's are the following agglomerations of our parameters $a, b, c, e, f, g, h,$ and M

$$m_1 = + (1 - b)^2 f^2$$
$$m_2 = -2(1 - b)f[af + (1 - b)M]$$
$$m_3 = + (1 - b)M[4af + (1 - b)M] + f^2(a^2 - c + eh^2)$$
$$m_4 = - 2\{M[a(1 - b)M + (a^2 - c)f] + efh(g + hM)\}$$
$$m_5 = + (a^2 - c)M^2 + e(g + hM)^2$$

As a first step of our solution let us select a set of values for our parameters:

$$
\begin{array}{llll}
a = & 30 & f = & 0.50 \\
b = & 0.75 & g = & 1.16 \\
c = & 457 & h = & 0.02 \\
e = & 10{,}000 & M = & 160
\end{array}
$$

For these values, our crucial behavior equations will appear as

shown in Figures 22 through 25.   If these values are substituted
into the m's, equation (I) will be

(I) $0.015625Y^4 - 13.75Y^3 + 4111.75Y^2 - 455,752Y$
$$+ 11,530,900 = 0$$

Of the four roots in this polynomial (I), only one lies within the
interval considered in the present chapter (the interval in which

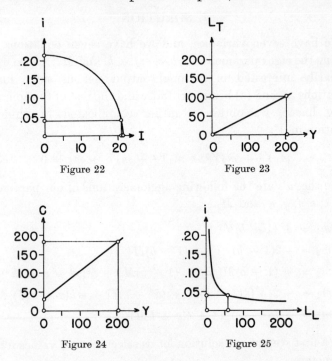

Figure 22

Figure 23

Figure 24

Figure 25

$h < i < \sqrt{c/e}$ and all variables assume real and nonnegative
values).   That root is $Y = 204.00$.   When Y assumes that value,
real and nonnegative values of consumption, investment, and
demand for active as well as idle balances result and are shown in
Figures 22 through 25.

8. THE SENSITIVITY OF NATIONAL OUTPUT TO CHANGES IN THE PARAMETERS

Finding the root $Y = 204.00$ itself, not easily obtained in any other way, would hardly justify the use of the digital computer. But the ease with which the computer handles a fourth-degree equation like (I) makes possible the important second step, varying each of the parameters a, b, c, f, g, h, M in turn, and watching the corresponding effect upon Y. To each parameter we have attached three values different from the value used first, but the values of all other parameters have been set equal to the corresponding value used first. Consequently, we obtain four different observations for each parameter, or 22 different versions of (I), all of which were solved in nine minutes by the computer, the resulting solutions are reproduced in Table 3, and in the interest

TABLE 3. Effects upon National Output of Changing Seven Parameters

a	Y	b	Y	c	Y
10	124.55	0.65	146.05	257	182.41
20	164.36	0.70	170.27	357	194.00
30	204.00	0.75	204.00	457	204.00
40	243.12	0.80	253.32	557	212.92

f	Y	g	Y	h	Y
0.30	204.56	0.66	204.58	0.01	204.66
0.40	204.37	1.16	204.00	0.02	204.00
0.50	204.00	1.66	203.29	0.03	203.15
0.60	203.10	2.16	202.44	0.04	202.11

M	Y
80	147.29
110	193.72
160	204.00
210	204.62

of easy interpretation, are shown in graphical form on double-logarithmic scale in Figures 26 through 32. The use of such scales makes the elasticity of national output with respect to any of the parameters a, b, c, f, g, h, and M appear as the steepness of the curve.

9. CONCLUSION

Conclusions may now be drawn directly from Figures 26 through 32. It appears that the value of national output is far more sensitive to changes in some parameters than in others. Within the fairly wide ranges studied, the parameter to whose changes national output is most sensitive is undoubtedly b, the marginal propensity to consume, vide the steepness of the Y-b relationship in Figure 27. Next, results in the case of the two parameters referring to autonomous consumption and autonomous investment, a and c, would seem to justify the usual emphasis upon the goods sphere, and particularly the Keynesian emphasis upon the multiplier as derived from the marginal propensity to consume. In the money sphere, national output seems to be sensitive only to changes in the parameter M, the money supply, and even here the sensitivity occurs only within that one interval involved when the economy is relatively starved of money. Within the rather wide intervals examined, national output seems to be singularly insensitive to changes in any of the parameters f, g, and h. It is negatively correlated with each of these parameters, as we would expect: Raising the transaction need for money per unit of output, f; raising the total mass of assets to be held possibly in money form, g; or raising the minimum rate of interest that people are willing to expect for any length of future time, h, will in each case lead to lower national output, but the elasticity of such output is numerically very small indeed.

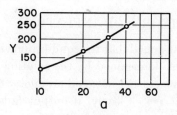

Figure 26

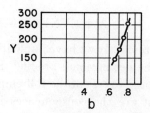

Figure 27

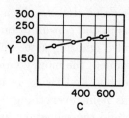

Figure 28

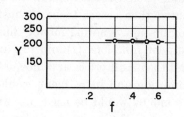

Figure 29

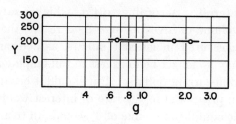

Figure 30

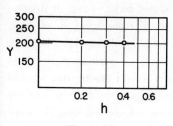

Figure 31

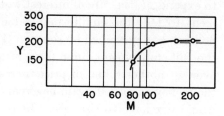

Figure 32

10. A KEYNESIAN THEORY OF INFLATION

Previously we have implicitly assumed that the equilibrium value of the net national product Y, as determined by the solution (I), is not in excess of the full-employment net national product. But what are the consequences if it is? Clearly, if output fails to catch up with demand, there will be, first, depletion of inventory and, second, an upward pressure upon prices.

Under such circumstances, the dollar in which everything is measured then ceases to be a constant-value dollar. As a first approximation, ignoring money illusions in the consumption and investment functions (1) and (2), and also ignoring asset effects, we find that if all prices and incomes doubled, the money value of consumption and investment would double, and twice as much active money would be needed. At this point everything would depend upon the monetary policy. Should the monetary authorities refuse to expand M, the money supply, more active money would mean less idle money which in turn, according to (4), raises the rate of interest. According to (2), a higher rate of interest reduces the volume of investment. As a result, the equilibrium value of Y, measured in current dollars, as determined by the solution (I) may no longer be in excess of full-employment output, also measured in current dollars. But should it be, another round of increases in prices and in the rate of interest would ensue, and eventually the equilibrium value of Y would fall to a point within the full-employment limit. When that happens, inflation stops.

On the other hand, should the monetary authorities be willing to expand M, the rate of interest would not have to rise or investment to fall; the equilibrium value of Y (measured in current dollars), as determined by solution (I) would still be as far beyond the full-employment limit (also measured in current dollars) as ever. Another round of price increases would ensue, but should the money supply M again be expanded, again the rate of interest would not have to rise, etc. In this case inflation would never stop.

The conclusion is, then, that by restricting M, the money supply, the monetary authorities can eventually stop inflation, whereas by continuing to increase M, they may keep it going. Is this the same thing as the time-honored quantity theory of money (sketched in Chapter 2)? If so, it is a far more refined and realistic version of the theory, for it includes the consumption function, the investment function, the liquidity-preference function, and the rate of interest, all four of which are not taken into account in the quantity theory. Above all, the monetary authorities, according to the Keynesian model, may check an inflation, but they by themselves cannot always generate one. Their expansion of M is a necessary but not a sufficient condition for inflation, cf. Figure 32.[21]

---

[21] Other aspects of inflation are to be studied in chaps. 7 and 8.

6

A Critique of Keynesian Analysis

1. THE OPERATIONAL SIGNIFICANCE OF THE KEYNESIAN MODEL

Like all widely accepted economic theories, that of Keynes is simple. Heavy aggregation had reduced the number of variables so drastically that very simple algebra or geometry or indeed, even verbal reasoning, could handle them. The ease of handling the Keynesian model is one important reason for the swiftness of its acceptance. Another is the practical importance of the questions to which it offered an answer, including mass unemployment, wartime inflation, the limits of monetary policy, and the threat of long-run stagnation. In the specificity of such answers is found the great operational significance of the Keynesian system.

2. A QUANTITY MARKET AND A PRICE MARKET

The price to be paid for the almost dramatic operational significance of the Keynesian model is lack of generality in several important respects, one of which Hicks [1] has described in a recent paper on methodology, as follows. Within a given period, one

---

[1] J. R. Hicks, "Methods of Dynamic Analysis," *25 Economic Essays in Honour of Erik Lindahl, 21 November 1956* (Stockholm: Ekonomisk Tidskrift, 1956), pp. 139–151.

can choose price for a parameter and let quantity transacted be a variable to be explained, as Keynes did in his determination of the flow of aggregate output. In this situation the flow of output would have to be such as to generate exactly a flow of income which in turn would generate exactly a flow of aggregate demand that would equal the flow of aggregate output. This flow equilibrium would ensure absence of inventory accumulation or depletion, but it would ignore stock equilibrium: the actual inventory coefficient might well differ continuously from that desired.

But one could instead choose quantity transacted for a parameter, letting price be the variable to be explained, as Keynes did in his determination of the rate of interest. In these circumstances the stock of bonds would at any moment of time be a constant, and the price of bonds would be determined by the willingness of the asset-owners to hold bonds rather than money. Such a stock equilibrium would ignore additions to or subtractions from the stock of bonds. The Keynesian theory of interest ignored such flows by use of a period of time so short that it approximated a moment of time.

Thus, according to Hicks, Keynes "boiled down" the whole economy into two markets: one quantity market ignoring stocks and one price market ignoring flows, the two linked by a single price chain, conceived of as the effect of the rate of interest upon investment. Keynes achieved his simplicity by choosing a short enough period in the price market and by suppressing the price mechanism in the quantity market. (To the choice and use of an ultrashort period we shall return shortly.) Such suppression of the price mechanism actually occurred during the 'thirties because of the depression and during the 'forties because of controls. But in Hicks' words, "the world of the 'fifties is not Keynesian in either of these ways; it may be Keynesian in its policies, but it is not Keynesian in its working." [2]

[2] Chaps. 7 and 11 of the present volume are devoted to a study of the role of the prices in the Keynesian model.

3. THE KEYNESIAN CHOICE OF AN ULTRASHORT PERIOD

The net flow of water into a reservoir can be assumed to leave the level of water in the reservoir unaffected only if an ultrashort period of time is considered. The Keynesian model did exactly this. In it, the level of water in the reservoir is represented by capital stock and the net flow of water into the reservoir by net investment. Hence the paradox that the Keynesian model treats net investment as positive, yet evidently considers capital stock a constant. Had longer periods been considered, a positive net investment would have expanded capital stock and with it output, thus incessantly forcing output to move from one level to the next. Modern growth models of the Cassel-Harrod-Domar [3] type retrieve proper perspective: We are interested not only in the *level* of output but also in the *growth path* of output. The new emphasis is more than a minor revision of Keynesian thinking: technically it substitutes difference or differential equations for equations whose variables carry no reference to time. Economically it restores thriftiness to its former place of honor, showing that the proportionate equilibrium rate of growth is in direct proportion to the propensity to save. While in Keynesian short-run analysis, an increase in the propensity to save would reduce the equilibrium level of output, in the Cassel-Harrod-Domar models, such an increase would accelerate equilibrium growth. [4] The striking contrast between the two effects vividly illuminates the lack of generality and validity in the Keynesian model.

[3] In Section 7 of Gustav Cassel, *Theoretische Sozialökonomie* (Leipzig: A. Deichertsche Verlagsbuchhandlung, Fifth Ed., 1932), translated by S. L. Barron as *The Theory of Social Economy* (New York: Harcourt, Brace, 1932), p. 61, we find a growth equation which, except for notation, is identical with Harrod's equation $GC = s$. See R. F. Harrod, *Towards A Dynamic Economics* (London: Macmillan, 1948), pp. 63–100; Evsey D. Domar, "Capital Expansion, Rate of Growth, and Employment," *Econometrica*, Vol. 14, No. 2 (April, 1946), pp. 137–147, and "Expansion and Employment," *The American Economic Review*, Vol. XXXVII, No. 1 (March, 1947), pp. 34–55.

[4] Part IV of the present volume is devoted to a study of such models.

4. DISEQUILIBRIUM IGNORED

Comfort is sometimes found in the belief that equilibrium solutions, although not holding in an ultrashort run, may hold in a longer run. A Keynesian paradox is the insistence both on an ultrashort period and on the exclusion of disequilibrium. By contrast, the Scandinavians had offered an analysis of successive disequilibria. Disequilibrium, manifesting itself as a discrepancy between the ex ante and the ex post values of a variable, might well persist. Particularly the nonmathematical early Swedish contributions left the impression that anything could happen and thus were long on generality and validity but had little substance. The mathematical models of the Lundberg[5] and Frisch[6] variety, although still disequilibrium models, had more substance and operational significance. But even more substance and operational significance were found in the Keynesian model according to which expectations, if not compatible with equilibrium, would be brought into line so quickly that disequilibrium could safely be ignored. One might submit that the *General Theory* can be operated so sure-footedly and can yield such magnificently clear answers precisely because it is *less* general than any other model enjoying widespread acceptance!

5. THE NEED FOR DISAGGREGATION

For all its lack of generality, the Keynesian model when modified is still an aid well suited to the study of certain problems of public policy. But frequently it is desirable to distinguish between output and income, output and employment, goods prices and factor prices, and the private and public sectors. If some disaggregation is acceptable, these distinctions can be made. In such disaggregation the summary Keynesian notation with its C, I, and Y is best replaced by a modified Leontief[7] notation.

[5] Erik Lundberg, *Studies in the Theory of Economic Expansion* (London: P. S. King, 1937).

[6] Ragnar Frisch, "Propagation and Impulse Problems in Dynamic Economics," *Economic Essays in Honour of Gustav Cassel* (London: Allen & Unwin, 1933).

[7] Wassily Leontief, "Static and Dynamic Theory," *Studies in the Structure of the American Economy* (New York: Oxford, 1953), pp. 53–90.

CONCLUSIONS

Part I was devoted to setting out the Keynesian system, one of the most significant systems, operationally, of which we know. Economic models must be operationally significant if policy conclusions are to be drawn from them. The preliminary policy conclusions drawn from Part I are: The level of national output would rise, if a rise occurred in national autonomous investment, national autonomous consumption, or the national marginal propensity to consume. In an open model, national output also would rise if a rise occurred in the corresponding parameters abroad or in the domestic or foreign propensity to import. Any increase in the country's own investment, consumption, or import demand, however, would be followed by a deterioration of the balance of trade.

Taking money and interest into account, we may conclude that increases in the demand for money would reduce, but only slightly, the national output. Reducing the money supply would also reduce national output, but more powerfully.

PART II

Disaggregation of the Keynesian Model

The machinist rolls up his sleeves,
the policeman travels his beat,
the gate-keeper marks who pass.
WALT WHITMAN

Part II is devoted to the modification of the Keynesian model in the one particular direction of disaggregation. In Chapter 7 the first step in that direction is the differentiation of the firm, household, and government sectors of a closed economy. In this chapter the prices of goods and factors are explicitly introduced. The resulting conclusions about effects upon output of changes in price policy, productivity, tax rates, and government expenditure on goods and services are drawn. Equilibrium employment is assumed to fall short of full employment in Chapter 7, but in excess of full employment in Chapter 8. In the latter the author submits that the model developed in Chapter 7 may be useful in the study of inflation, whether of the repressed or the open type. The effect of price policy upon output is examined in Chapter 7; by contrast, the effect of nonprice competition upon aggregate output, a most neglected subject, is treated in Chapter 9.

In Chapters 10 and 11 more steps in the direction of disaggregation are made possible by a relaxation of the assumption of a closed economy. Analogous to the balanced-budget multiplier developed in Chapter 7 is the balanced foreign-trade multiplier of Chapter 10. In Chapter 11 another aspect of balanced foreign trade, that of the effects of wage and price policy upon employment in an open economy fully exposed to foreign competition, is investigated.

In Chapters 12 and 13 the ultimate step in the direction of disaggregation, the presentation of the Leontief interindustry model, is taken. Chapter 12 develops the static open Leontief model, and Chapter 13 closes it.

7

Price Policy and Fiscal Policy at Less than Full Employment

1. THE NEED FOR SOME DISAGGREGATION

A priceless virtue of the Keynesian model of employment, interest, and money is its inherent simplicity. The price to be paid for simplicity, heavy aggregation, is well worth paying, at least in the introductory stage of exposition. Sooner or later, however, the need for some disaggregation will arise. For example, the description of the consumption function necessitates the distinction between national output and disposable personal income. Or, the examination of the role of prices in the model demands that distinction be made between factor prices and goods prices. Most importantly, the private and public sectors of the economy must be differentiated. Finally, a distinction between output and employment must be made.

2. A NEW MODEL

As the very first step toward disaggregation a simple three-sector model meeting the needs mentioned is presented.

NOTE: Chaps. 7 and 9 represent a completely rewritten and substantially expanded version of the author's "Employment, Prices, and Monopolistic Competition," *The Review of Economics and Statistics*, Vol. XXIV, No. 4 (Nov., 1952).

The notation[1] is:

Variables

X_j = output of goods produced by sector j, in physical number of goods per unit of time

x_{ij} = purchase of the product or the factor of sector i by sector j in physical number of goods, or factors, per unit of time, except $*x_{ff}$, $*x_{fg}$, and $*x_{hg}$ which are parameters

σ_{ij} = sale of the product or the factor of sector i to sector j. Dimension: same as x_{ij}

Parameters

A_{fh} = autonomous consumption, in physical number of consumers' goods per unit of time

a_{fh} = marginal propensity to consume expected real disposable income, a pure number

A_{gh} = autonomous income tax payment, in billions of dollars per year

a_{gh} = marginal income tax rate, a pure number

A_{hf} = autonomous factor purchase by firms, in physical number of units of input per unit of time

a_{hf} = marginal factor purchase by firms, in physical number of units of input per additional physical unit of output

λ = the mark-up coefficient by which the money value $\pi_h a_{hf}$ of the input of factors per marginal unit of output should be multiplied

π_f = price of output, charged by firms

π_h = price of input, charged by households

$*x_{ff}$ = gross private investment, in physical number of goods per unit of time

$*x_{fg}$ = government purchases of goods from firms, in physical number of goods per unit of time

$*x_{hg}$ = government purchases of services from households, in physical number of factors per unit of time

---

[1] For the understanding of any economic model, the distinction between variables and parameters is absolutely essential. Therefore, we shall hereafter adopt the practice of supplying complete lists of variables and parameters before proceeding with the construction of a model.

An asterisk indicates an ex ante value, absence of an asterisk an ex post value. By the ex ante value of an economic variable, say a transaction, is meant its anticipated value or, more precisely, its value as seen from a point of time preceding the transaction. Most practically, that point of time is the beginning of the period during which the transaction takes place. Ex ante variables may be either planned or expected. Their realization in the former case is up to the individual anticipating them; in the latter case, it is up to others. Accordingly, in a buyer's market ex ante purchases are planned, but ex ante sales are expected, for the realization of sales rests with the buyer, not with the seller.

By the ex post value of an economic variable, say a transaction, is meant its value in retrospect or, more precisely, its value as seen from a point of time subsequent to the transaction. Most practically, that point of time is the end of the period during which the transaction takes place.[2]

In our model each transaction (x) must have two subscripts, the first referring to the sector of origin, the last to the sector of destination. For the three sectors, firms, households, and government, the corresponding subscripts are f, h, and g. The trans-

---

[2] The reader may well find himself a bit tired of our distinction between purchases and sales and even more tired of our distinction between ex ante and ex post. After all, in an equilibrium model all four are equal. Two reasons cause us to carry these distinctions through the entire remainder of the present volume. First, they pave the way for the study of disequilibrium, which is involved in our stability test in the last chapter. Second, they provide insight into the nature of equilibrium itself. That such insight is sorely needed is readily apparent from endless arguments that transpire as to whether the equality between supply, say of saving, and demand, say for investment, is an identity, a definition, or an equilibrium condition. Only the careful distinctions made in the text can bring out the correct answers, which may be stated simply as follows: As far as purchases are concerned, ex ante and ex post are equal because of the assumption of a buyer's market in which purchase plans can be carried out. This is true irrespective of whether or not the situation is an equilibrium situation. As far as sales are concerned, ex ante and ex post are equal as a condition for equilibrium. Finally, purchases and sales are equal in the ex post sense only. As Ohlin puts it: What Petterson has bought, Anderson must have sold.

A clarifying discussion of the difference between equations and identities in macroeconomic theory has been provided by Trygve Haavelmo in his "Ligninger vs. identiteter i ökonomisk makroteori," *25 Economic Essays in Honour of Erik Lindahl 21 November 1956* (Stockholm: Ekonomisk Tidskrift, 1956), pp. 68–78.

actions to be considered are shown in Table 4: first, gross private investment $*x_{ff}$; second, household consumption purchases from firms $*x_{fh}$; third, firm purchases of factor services from households $*x_{hf}$; fourth, there are government purchases of goods from firms $*x_{fg}$; fifth, government purchases of factor services from households $*x_{hg}$ (in the United States Department of Commerce

TABLE 4.   Planned Purchases of Goods and Factors

Purchasing from	Purchases Planned by		
	Firms	Government	Households
Firms	$*x_{ff}$	$*x_{fg}$	$*x_{fh}$
Government	—	—	$*x_{gh}$
Households	$*x_{hf}$	$*x_{hg}$	—

terminology $*x_{hg}$ refers to the gross government product); and sixth, taxes $*x_{gh}$ paid by households to government.   Such taxes may, perhaps, be considered as the equivalent to the value of collective goods, such as education and highways, that are transferred from government to households.   Collective goods carry no price, and therefore, their value cannot be expressed as a price times a number of physical units.   Hence $*x_{gh}$, unlike all other x's, is a flow of dollars.   Taxes paid by firms are ignored.

3. THE MODEL, FACTOR PURCHASES

The first transaction to be determined is $*x_{hf}$.   Aggregate planned purchases of factors by firms from households may be written as the following linear function of planned gross private product:

(1) $$*x_{hf} = A_{hf} + a_{hf}*X_f$$

Factor purchase consists of all purchases of labor, land use, and entrepreneurship by firms from households.   It follows that factor purchase is more, and at the same time less, than the cost of production. Such purchase includes first, the cost of selling and distribution and second, dividend payments of corporations as well as profits accruing to owners of noncorporate enterprises. But factor purchase is less than cost in the sense that it does not include depreciation, the dominant item in overhead cost.

The input-output function (1) involves the problem of aggregation. In order to derive a determinate input-output function for business as a whole, one must assume that the distribution of output, both among industries and among individual firms within the same industry, is constant; or one must assume that distribution is a known function of the level of aggregate output; or, finally, one must assume that all firms have the same real marginal propensity to purchase factors (a_{hf}). The use of such assumptions is the price we pay for the convenience of talking in terms of aggregates.

4. THE MODEL, CONSUMPTION PURCHASES

The second transaction to be determined is $*x_{fh}$. Aggregate planned purchases of consumers' goods by households may be written as the following linear function of expected real *disposable* income (where disposable income equals personal income minus tax):

$$(2) \qquad *x_{fh} = A_{fh} + a_{fh} \frac{\pi_h(*\sigma_{hf} + *\sigma_{hg}) - *x_{gh}}{\pi_f}$$

where A_{fh} is autonomous consumption, a_{fh} the marginal propensity to consume expected real disposable income, π_f the price of goods charged by firms, π_h the price of factors charged by households, and $*x_{gh}$ the expected tax payment; such payment is assumed to be the following linear function of expected money income:

$$(3) \qquad *x_{gh} = A_{gh} + a_{gh}\pi_h(*\sigma_{hf} + *\sigma_{hg})$$

where A_{gh} is the autonomous income tax payment and a_{gh} is the marginal income tax rate; both are parameters. Stripping (3) of all three asterisks results in Equation (4), which indicates realized tax payments but is not to be written down explicitly.

The consumption function, like the input-output function, implies a well-known aggregation problem. In order to derive a determinate consumption function for households as a whole, one must assume that first, the distribution of income among them is either constant or a known function of the level of real disposable income, or second, all households have the same real marginal propensity to consume (a_{fh}).

5. PLANNED PURCHASES, PARAMETERS

Finally:

(5) $$*x_{ff} = \text{a parameter}$$

(6) $$*x_{fg} = \text{a parameter}$$

(7) $$*x_{hg} = \text{a parameter}$$

The justification is that if expected gross private investment by firms can be assumed to be a parameter, as it was in the Keynesian model, then a fortiori can government purchase of goods and services likewise be so assumed. Such purchases are motivated by welfare and security, or extraeconomic considerations.

6. ALL PLANS ARE CARRIED OUT

In a buyer's market a unit period can be so selected that plans made at the beginning of a period are not changed until the beginning of the succeeding period. Given such unit periods, at the beginning of the unit period firms announce the price of goods, and households announce the price of factors. Once acquainted with the announced price of factors, firms plan their output and start purchasing factors. Once acquainted with the announced price of goods, households plan their consumption and start purchasing goods. At the end of the unit period, firms will take stock and compare realized sales with expected sales. Likewise households will check realized disposable income against expected disposable income. Thus, all realizations will be checked against corresponding expectations. The difference, if any, will induce changes in future expectations and, in turn, plans. But a methodological requirement of the model is that such changes in plans take place at the transitions *between* unit periods, not *during* a period.[3] Consequently, we can now express the requirement that in a buyer's market, planned purchases within the unit period equal realized purchases within the unit period. Of our five intersector purchases four are planned, but the fifth, $*x_{gh}$ the tax payment, is an expected (dreaded) one, expected according to (3). For each of the four planned purchases we can express the assumption that the plan comes true:

(8) through (11) $$*x_{ij} = x_{ij}$$

where ij represents fh, hf, fg, and hg respectively.

7. PRODUCTION PLANS ARE ALWAYS REALIZED

In a buyer's market it can also be assumed that well-planned production goals will be realized:

(12) $$*X_f = X_f$$

8. WHAT IS PURCHASED IS SOLD

Any sector's realized purchases from another sector constitutes the latter's realized sales to the former. Such correspondence holds for any of the five intersector transactions:

(13) through (17) $$x_{ij} = \sigma_{ij}$$

where ij represents fh, hf, fg, hg, and gh respectively.

[3] Erik Lindahl, *Studies in the Theory of Money and Capital* (London: Allen & Unwin, 1939), pp. 36, 37, 91–92, 125–26; and Bertil Ohlin, "Some Notes on the Stockholm Theory of Savings and Investment," *The Economic Journal*, Vol. XLVII (March, 1937), reprinted in Gottfried Haberler, ed., *Readings in Business Cycle Theory* (Philadelphia: Blakiston, 1944), pp. 96–97.

9. EQUILIBRIUM CONDITIONS

Static equilibrium is defined as the absence of any inherent tendency to change. Obviously, when expectations do not come true, plans are then revised, and this involves change. Therefore, as a static equilibrium condition, economic activity must be self-justifying in the sense that any sector's expected sales to another sector must equal realized sales. Such correspondence holds for any of the five intersector transactions:

(18) through (22) $\qquad *\sigma_{ij} = \sigma_{ij}$

where ij represents fh, hf, fg, hg, and gh respectively.

10. DEFINITIONAL EQUATION

By definition, expected gross private investment is that part of planned gross private product which firms do not expect to sell to households or government:

$$(23) \qquad *x_{ff} = *X_f - (*\sigma_{fh} + *\sigma_{fg})$$

11. SOLUTION

Restating the unknowns, we have: one expected gross investment $*x_{ff}$; five ex ante purchases $*x_{ij}$; five ex post purchases x_{ij}; five expected sales $*\sigma_{ij}$; five realized sales σ_{ij}; one planned output $*X_j$; and one realized output X_j. In order to determine the 23 unknowns we have previously written 23 equations.

Solving for equilibrium gross private product we have:

$$(I) \ X_f = \cfrac{*x_{ff} + *x_{fg} + A_{fh} + a_{fh} \cfrac{\pi_h(A_{hf} + *x_{hg})(1 - a_{gh}) - A_{gh}}{\pi_f}}{1 - a_{fh}a_{hf}(1 - a_{gh})\cfrac{\pi_h}{\pi_f}}$$

The interpretation of this solution is not difficult. Beginning with the denominator, we know that a_{hf} is the physical number of factors purchased by firms per additional unit of output. Multiply by π_h and get the money value of factors purchased by firms per additional unit of output, that is, the money personal income induced per additional unit of firm output. Multiply by $(1 - a_{gh})$ and get money disposable income induced per additional unit of firm output. Divide by π_f and get real disposable income, induced per additional unit of firm output. Finally, multiply by a_{fh}, the marginal propensity to consume real disposable income and get household purchase of consumers' goods induced per additional unit of firm output. Deducting the result from unity, we get community saving and household tax payment induced per additional unit of firm output.

Next the numerator. Here, $A_{hf} + {}^*x_{hg}$ is autonomous private purchase *plus* autonomous government purchase of factors. Multiply by π_h and get the money value of such factor purchases, that is, all money personal income generated autonomously. Multiply by $(1 - a_{gh})$, deduct A_{gh}, and get money disposable income generated autonomously. Divide by π_f and get real disposable income generated autonomously. Finally, multiply by a_{fh} and get household purchase of consumers' goods generated autonomously. Thus we can read (I) as follows. Equilibrium gross private product equals a ratio whose numerator has all the "injections" in it. They are the sum of autonomous expected gross private investment, ${}^*x_{ff}$, autonomous government purchase of goods, ${}^*x_{fg}$, autonomous consumption, A_{fh}, and consumption generated both by autonomous private purchase and autonomous government purchase of factors. The denominator has all the "leakages" in it and includes community saving and household tax payment induced per additional unit of firm output.

12. RESTATEMENT OF THE SYSTEM IN GRAPHICAL FORM

The foregoing algebraic analysis if restated in graphical form is more comprehensible to some readers. In a four-axis diagram, shown in Figure 33, plot planned gross private product $*X_f$ in the western direction. Plot the total of private and government planned purchases of factors from households $*x_{hf} + *x_{hg}$ in the southern direction. Plot expected real disposable income $[\pi_h(*\sigma_{hf} + *\sigma_{hg}) - *x_{gh}]/\pi_f$ in the eastern direction. Finally, plot planned purchases of consumers' goods $*x_{fh}$ in the northern direction. The input-output function (1) will then appear in the

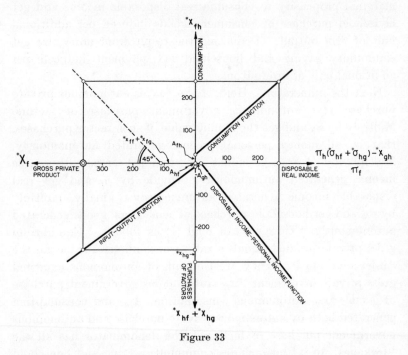

Figure 33

southwestern quadrant. The disposable income-personal income function, emerging after the tax function (3) is deducted from money personal income $\pi_h(*\sigma_{hf} + *\sigma_{hg})$ and the result is deflated by dividing by π_f, will appear in the southeastern quadrant. The consumption function will appear in the northeastern quadrant. In the northwestern quadrant a 45° line has been drawn such that it intersects the gross private product axis at a point whose distance from the origin is the sum of gross investment demand and government demand $*x_{ff} + *x_{fg}$.

The equilibrium value of the gross private product $*X_f$, shown in Figure 33, has the property of inducing merely enough aggregate demand to absorb the gross private product, no more, no less. From the diagram we can see why the value indicated by the double circle is an equilibrium value of the gross private product. If firms plan to produce this output, they will purchase a certain number of factor units $*x_{hf}$, determined by the input-output function and shown on the southern axis. Add the gross government product $*x_{hg}$ and get the entire number of factor units that firms and government plan to purchase. Multiply by the price of factors π_h, deduct the income tax $*x_{gh}$, divide by the price of goods π_f, and get the actual real disposable income. Since our solution is an equilibrium solution, it implies that everybody is happy because his expectations come true. Consequently, actual disposable real income is equal to expected disposable real income, shown on the eastern axis. If households expect this particular disposable real income, they will purchase a certain amount of consumers' goods, determined by the consumption function and shown on the northern axis. To consumption demand add gross investment plus government demand and get aggregate demand. It will be seen that for the value of output selected, the aggregate demand generated will absorb the exact amount of output.

With the slopes and intercepts used in the diagram, no other level of output has this property. After selecting an alternative level of output, the reader working counterclockwise through the four quadrants of the diagram can easily demonstrate that output levels lower than the one shown will generate aggregate demand in excess of output, thus inducing inventory depletion. On the other hand, he can demonstrate that output levels higher than the one shown will generate aggregate demand short of output, thus inducing inventory accumulation. From these demonstrations it follows that gearing output to demand will pull output closer to the equilibrium level, showing the equilibrium to be stable.

13. EMPIRICALLY PLAUSIBLE VALUES OF PARAMETERS

We shall assume the parameters to satisfy the inequalities listed in Table 5.   These assumptions are all empirically plausible: A_{fh}

TABLE 5.   Inequalities Assumed To Be Satisfied by Parameters

$$A_{fh} > 0 \qquad \lambda > 1$$
$$1 > a_{fh} > 0 \qquad \pi_f > 0$$
$$A_{gh} < 0 \qquad \pi_h > 0$$
$$1 > 1 - a_{gh} > 0 \qquad {}^*x_{ff} > 0$$
$$A_{hf} > 0 \qquad {}^*x_{fg} > 0$$
$$1 > a_{hf}\frac{\pi_h}{\pi_f} > 0 \qquad {}^*x_{hg} > 0$$

is autonomous consumption, which is positive at least in the short run; a_{fh} is the marginal propensity to consume expected real disposable income and is a pure number between one and zero; A_{gh} is the autonomous income tax payment and under modern progressive income taxation A_{gh} must be negative; a_{gh} is the marginal income tax rate, a pure number between one and zero (consequently $1 - a_{gh}$ is also a pure number between one and zero); A_{hf} is the autonomous factor purchase by firms and because of tenure is positive; and $a_{hf}\pi_h/\pi_f$ is the money value of additional factor purchase by firms per additional unit of output divided by the price of goods and is a pure number between one and zero. The remaining six inequalities indicate that the mark-up coefficient (to be defined in Section 18) is greater than one, and that prices, gross private investment, government purchases of goods, and gross government product are all positive.

14. APPLICATION OF THE MODEL TO THE THEORY OF PUBLIC POLICY

Our model represents a first and very modest step in the direction of disaggregation of the simplest Keynesian model, in which three parameters could be manipulated: autonomous investment, autonomous consumption, and the marginal propensity to consume. These three parameters are also found in our present model. By successively taking the derivative of output X_f with respect to these parameters: autonomous gross investment $*x_{ff}$, autonomous consumption A_{fh}, and the marginal propensity to consume a_{fh}, the reader can easily demonstrate that the conclusions warranted by the original Keynesian model are in substance warranted by our present model, also. However, the new model should permit of additional conclusions, not possible in the original Keynesian model. It does permit of two sets of such conclusions, the first including factor prices, factor productivities, and goods prices, and the second including fiscal policy.

15. FACTOR PRICES AND FACTOR PRODUCTIVITIES

The derivative of equilibrium gross private product with respect to the price of factors is

(II)
$$\frac{\partial X_f}{\partial \pi_h} =$$
$$\frac{\dfrac{a_{fh}(1 - a_{gh})}{\pi_f}\left[A_{hf} + *x_{hg} + a_{hf}\left(*x_{ff} + *x_{fg} + A_{fh} - a_{fh}\frac{A_{gh}}{\pi_f}\right)\right]}{\left[1 - a_{fh}a_{hf}(1 - a_{gh})\dfrac{\pi_h}{\pi_f}\right]^2}$$

For values of parameters satisfying the inequalities in Table 5 the derivative (II) is positive. A higher price of factors, then, will raise the equilibrium gross private product.

The derivative of equilibrium gross private product with respect to the input-output coefficient a_{hf} is

(III)
$$\frac{\partial X_f}{\partial a_{hf}} =$$
$$\frac{\dfrac{a_{fh}\pi_h(1 - a_{gh})}{\pi_f}\left[*x_{ff} + *x_{fg} + A_{fh} + a_{fh}\dfrac{\pi_h(A_{hf} + *x_{hg})(1 - a_{gh}) - A_{gh}}{\pi_f}\right]}{\left[1 - a_{fh}a_{hf}(1 - a_{gh})\dfrac{\pi_h}{\pi_f}\right]^2}$$

For values of parameters satisfying the inequalities in Table 5 the derivative (III) is positive.   A higher input-output coefficient, then, will raise the equilibrium gross private product.   Feather-bedding practices are examples.   If unions force employers to overstaff, as has happened in respect to diesel engines and printing shops, such overstaffing will actually, according to our assumptions, raise output or keep it higher than it would otherwise have been.   Vice versa, increases in labor productivity that manifest themselves in reducing factor requirements should reduce output. (The reader should keep in mind that at the present time we are manipulating a_{hf} only, prices of factors and goods are assumed constant.)

16. GOODS PRICE POLICY

The derivative of equilibrium gross private product with respect to the price of goods is

(IV) $\dfrac{\partial X_f}{\partial \pi_f} =$

$$-\frac{\dfrac{a_{fh}\pi_h(1 - a_{gh})}{\pi_f{}^2}\left[A_{hf} + {}^*x_{hg} + a_{hf}({}^*x_{ff} + {}^*x_{fg} + A_{fh})\right] - a_{fh}\dfrac{A_{gh}}{\pi_f{}^2}}{\left[1 - a_{fh}a_{hf}(1 - a_{gh})\dfrac{\pi_h}{\pi_f}\right]^2}$$

For values of parameters satisfying the inequalities in Table 5 the derivative (IV) is negative.   A higher price of goods, then, will reduce the equilibrium gross private product.

What kind of market structure are we assuming in our present model?   The use of prices as parameters assumes prices to be administered, pure competition being excluded.   By taking derivatives of our solution with respect to the price parameters, we make it possible to study the macroeconomic effects of price changes in a monopolistic setting.

17. LIMITATIONS OF THE MODEL

Some might call our model a naïve "New Dealish" model: featherbedding practices are always a good thing, raising the price of factors is always a good thing, and raising the price of goods is always a bad thing. (It should be recalled, however, that factor prices include dividend rates.) The crucial assumption is the constancy of aggregate gross investment. More specifically, this assumption implies that aggregate gross investment is not affected by, first, the internal rate of return or, second, the money rate of interest.

Use of featherbedding practices, raising the price of factors, or reducing the price of goods will reduce the internal rate of return to firms and may discourage investment. Furthermore, use of featherbedding practices or raising the price of factors will increase the transaction demand for money. Unless the monetary authorities are willing to expand the money supply, credit restrictions and/or a rising rate of interest will follow, to either of which investment may also be vulnerable.

If, instead of raising the price of factors, we would reduce the price of goods, the effect upon the internal rate of return would be the same; but the transaction demand for money might fall, and the rate of interest might fall with it. In this event unfavorable and favorable effects will set off opposing forces.

18. A QUALIFICATION

Derivative (II) of the present chapter showed that if in a closed economy the price of all factors were to rise at a constant price of goods, the equilibrium gross private product, and with it employment, would rise. We shall now develop the first of five important qualifications of this proposition: repercussions upon the price of goods cannot very easily be ignored. A clue to such repercussions may be found in a widely used pricing practice known as the full-cost principle [4] and frequently mentioned by businessmen. The practice may be described as follows: Let variable labor input per unit of output be a constant. Variable labor cost per unit of output will then be in direct proportion to the wage rate. By profit margin is meant profit per unit of output. This margin, according to the widely used practice, will be in direct proportion to the variable labor cost per unit of output and consequently also in direct proportion to the wage rate. If the profit margin and the wage rate move proportionately π_h may be used to represent both. Moreover, under the widely used practice mentioned, since the allowance for overhead cost per unit is in direct proportion to variable labor cost per unit of output, the price π_f of goods will be in direct proportion to the money value $\pi_h a_{hf}$ of the input of variable factors per unit of output, or

$$(24) \qquad \pi_f = \lambda \pi_h a_{hf}$$

where λ is the mark-up coefficient. Inserting (24) into (I), we may take the derivative of equilibrium gross private product with respect to the price of factors, thus allowing for the repercussion upon the price of goods, and we obtain

$$(V) \qquad \frac{\partial X_f}{\partial \pi_h} = \frac{a_{fh} A_{gh}}{\lambda a_{hf} - a_{fh} a_{hf}(1 - a_{gh})} \frac{1}{\pi_h^2}$$

For values of parameters satisfying the inequalities in Table 5

[4] R. L. Hall and C. J. Hitch, "Price Theory and Business Behaviour," *Oxford Economic Papers* No. 2 (May, 1939) describe the full-cost principle as follows: "Prime (or 'direct') cost per unit is taken as the base, a percentage addition is made to cover overheads . . . , and a further conventional addition (frequently 10 per cent) is made for profit." In *Cost Behavior and Price Policy* (New York: National Bureau of Economic Research, 1943) the Committee on Price Determination for the Conference on Price Research, headed by Edward S. Mason, states that the standard cost calculations of General Motors and International Harvester are "one version of the full cost principle of Hall and Hitch, and it would seem to be in fairly wide use among business firms in this country as well as in England," p. 286.

Needless to say, equation (24) is not incompatible with profit maximization by firms. For its microeconomic counterpart, derived solidly from the premise of profit maximization, see equation (7a) in chapter 17. The λ here and the $e/(1 + e)$ there occupy similar positions.

the derivative (V) is negative. Hence if repercussions upon the price of goods are allowed for, a higher price of factors will reduce the equilibrium gross private product. Derivative (V) may be said to represent what is frequently referred to as "cost-push" inflation. Cost-push inflation is said to originate in labor's pressure for higher wage rates and management's insistence upon "full-cost" pricing. Cost-push inflation may exist at less than full employment; indeed, it may even in itself reduce employment and output. The beneficial effect [see (II)] of a higher price of factors upon employment and output is more than nullified by the unfavorable effect of the ensuing rise in the price of goods. Were it not for the progressiveness of the tax function (3), the beneficial effect would have been *exactly* nullified: if $A_{gh} = 0$ the derivative (V) would assume the value zero. In that case equilibrium gross private product would have remained entirely unaffected by simultaneous and proportional changes in the prices of factors and goods.

19. FISCAL POLICY

In our model the effects of three fiscal-policy parameters upon the equilibrium gross private product deserve special attention, these parameters are government purchase of goods, gross government product, and the marginal income tax rate. The derivative of the equilibrium gross private product with respect to government purchases of goods is

$$(VI) \qquad \frac{\partial X_f}{\partial^* x_{fg}} = \frac{1}{1 - a_{fh}a_{hf}(1 - a_{gh})\dfrac{\pi_h}{\pi_f}}$$

As long as the marginal income tax rate a_{gh} is less than unity, as long as the marginal propensity to consume real disposable income a_{fh} is less than unity, and as long as the money value of factor purchase by firms per additional unit of output divided by the price of goods $(a_{hf}\pi_h/\pi_f)$ is less than unity, derivative (VI) *must be positive and in excess of unity.*

Our second fiscal-policy parameter is gross government product, and the derivative of equilibrium gross private product with respect to it is

$$\text{(VII)} \qquad \frac{\partial X_f}{\partial^* x_{hg}} = \frac{a_{fh}(1 - a_{gh})\dfrac{\pi_h}{\pi_f}}{1 - a_{fh}a_{hf}(1 - a_{gh})\dfrac{\pi_h}{\pi_f}}$$

Again, as long as the marginal income tax rate a_{gh} is less than unity, the marginal propensity to consume real disposable income a_{fh} less than unity, and the money value of factor purchase by firms per additional unit of output divided by the price of goods $(a_{hf}\pi_h/\pi_f)$ less than unity, derivative (VII) is positive.

The last fiscal-policy parameter is the marginal income tax rate, and the derivative of the gross private product with respect to it is

$$\text{(VIII)} \quad \frac{\partial X_f}{\partial a_{gh}} = - \frac{\dfrac{a_{fh}\pi_h}{\pi_f}\left[A_{hf} + {}^*x_{hg} + a_{hf}\left({}^*x_{ff} + {}^*x_{fg} + A_{fh} - a_{fh}\dfrac{A_{gh}}{\pi_f} \right) \right]}{\left[1 - a_{fh}a_{hf}(1 - a_{gh})\dfrac{\pi_h}{\pi_f} \right]^2}$$

For values of parameters satisfying the inequalities in Table 5 derivative (VIII) is negative: increasing the marginal income tax rate will reduce the equilibrium gross private product.

20. THE BALANCED BUDGET

Normally, "congress legislates government expenditure . . . ; but it can never legislate tax receipts. All it can do is legislate tax *rates* which determine the government's net take at each different level (and composition) of national income. Any change in rates will necessarily change income, so that the legislators can never quite know what tax collections will be—without estimating the solution to the simultaneous equations of income determination." [5]   Consequently, the parameters open to government mani-

[5] Paul A. Samuelson, "The Simple Mathematics of Income Determination," *Income, Employment, and Public Policy* (New York: Norton, 1948), p. 143.

pulation are $*x_{fg}$, $*x_{hg}$, and a_{gh}, as used in the preceding sections. However, since much discussion of fiscal policy centers around the balancing of the budget, let us finally assume that the sum total of planned government expenditure minus the sum total of expected tax receipts equals zero:

$$(25) \qquad \pi_f*x_{fg} + \pi_h*x_{hg} - *\sigma_{gh} = 0$$

Obviously, when another equation (25) is added to our already fully determined equilibrium system of 23 equations and 23 unknowns, the result is an overdetermined system: within the system of the original 23 equations the budget would not be balanced unless the choice of parameters was fortuitous. Hence if (25) as well as the original 23 equations are to be satisfied, at least one of the original parameters must be changed, that is, dropped and turned into an unknown.[6] Which parameter is dropped is unimportant from the point of view of determinacy, but practically we should drop the tax rate a_{gh}. Equation (25) will—in conjunction with the other equations in our system— determine the tax rate in such a way that the budget is balanced.

The new system of 24 equations and 24 unknowns can now be solved. Solving again for equilibrium gross private product we have

$$(IX) \qquad X_f = \frac{*x_{ff} + *x_{fg}(1 - a_{fh}) + A_{fh} + a_{fh}A_{hf}\dfrac{\pi_h}{\pi_f}}{1 - a_{fh}a_{hf}\dfrac{\pi_h}{\pi_f}}$$

In this model a_{gh}, no longer a parameter, is not present in (IX). The government has only two parameters: government purchase of goods $*x_{fg}$ and the gross government product $*x_{hg}$. Let us first study the effect of expanding government purchase of goods under

[6] Bent Hansen, *Finanspolitikens ekonomiska teori* (Stockholm: Statens offentliga utredningar 1955:25, 1955), chap. I, pp. 23–45; cf. similar ideas expressed by J. Tinbergen, *On the Theory of Economic Policy* (Amsterdam: North-Holland Publishing Company, 1952).

a balanced budget. Taking the derivative of (IX) with respect
to $*x_{fg}$ we get

(X)
$$\frac{\partial X_f}{\partial *x_{fg}} = \frac{1 - a_{fh}}{1 - a_{fh}a_{hf}\dfrac{\pi_h}{\pi_f}}$$

As long as the marginal propensity to consume real disposable
income a_{fh} is less than unity, and as long as the money value of
factor purchase by firms per additional unit of output divided by
the price of goods $(a_{hf}\pi_h/\pi_f)$ is less than unity, derivative (X) must
be positive but *less than unity*. The derivative is, of course, a new
version of the Haavelmo theorem.[7] With\Haavelmo the balanced-
budget multiplier was always unity. Our derivative (X) would
assume the value unity only if the money value of factor purchase
by firms per unit of output divided by the price of goods $(a_{hf}\pi_h/\pi_f)$
were to assume the value unity, meaning that business depreciation and undistributed profits would be zero. Or, briefly, business
gross saving would have to be zero, a wholly untenable assumption, yet inherent in all strictly Keynesian models—for no
Keynesian model can draw the distinction either between the
goods and the factor market or between household saving and
business saving.

In the interest of simplicity we have ignored taxes paid by

[7] On the Haavelmo theorem, see Jørgen Gelting, "Nogle Bemaerkninger om
Financieringen af offentlig Virksomhed," *Nationaløkonomisk Tidsskrift*, Vol. 79,
No. 5 (1941), pp. 293–299; Trygve Haavelmo, "Multiplier Effects of a Balanced
Budget," *Econometrica*, Vol. 13, No. 4 (Oct., 1945), pp. 311–318; William J.
Baumol and Maurice H. Peston, "More on the Multiplier Effects of a Balanced
Budget," *The American Economic Review*, Vol. XLV, No. 1 (March, 1955),
pp. 141–148; and Alvin H. Hansen, "More on the Multiplier Effects of a Balanced
Budget: Comment," *ibid.*, Vol. XLVI, No. 1 (March, 1956), pp. 157–160, with
reply by Baumol and Peston, pp. 160–162. Further comment by William G.
Bowen, "The Balanced-Budget Multiplier: A Suggestion for a More General
Formulation," *The Review of Economics and Statistics*, Vol. XXXIX, No. 2
(May, 1957), pp. 225–227, and by Erich Schneider, "Zur Frage der Multiplikator-
wirkung eines ausgeglichenen Budgets," *25 Essays in Honour of Erik Lindahl
21 November 1956* (Stockholm: Ekonomisk Tidskrift, 1956), pp. 302–305. On
history of doctrine, see P. Nørregaard Rasmussen, "A Note on the History of the
Balanced-Budget Multiplier," *The Economic Journal*, Vol. LXVIII, No. 269
(March, 1958), pp. 154–156.

business. In the real world, however, corporate net profits are taxed. Taking this fact into account would somewhat reduce the difference between the numerator and the denominator of derivative (X). But as long as business depreciation is not taxed, some difference will remain. This result illuminates the usefulness of substituting the gross private product, as determined here, for the net private product, as customarily determined.

In conclusion: even should the budget be kept in balance an increase in government expenditure on goods would raise the gross private product. But one additional dollar's worth of government expenditure on goods would generate less than one additional dollar's worth of gross private product.

The second policy parameter is the gross government product $*x_{hg}$. The effect of expanding the gross government product upon the gross private product must now be zero. Since $*x_{hg}$ is not present in (IX), we have

$$\frac{\partial X_f}{\partial *x_{hg}} = 0$$

The striking contrast between the effects of expanding government purchase of goods on the one hand and gross government product on the other is, perhaps, intuitively plausible. After all, a tax dollar, if uncollected, would have been partly spent on goods and partly saved.[8] Consequently, if after having collected a tax dollar, the government spends all of it on goods,[9] an ultimate increase in the entire community's propensity to spend on goods results, inducing a rise in the equilibrium output of goods. But

---

[8] In the present model the fact that investment is autonomous rules out the possibility that the tax collection can reduce investment by reducing saving; cf. William J. Baumol and Maurice H. Peston, "More on the Multiplier Effects of a Balanced Budget," *The American Economic Review*, Vol. XLV, No. 1 (March, 1955), p. 146.

[9] In the present model government is assumed to spend its dollar fully on domestically produced goods. In an international model the government might perhaps spend part of its dollar on imported goods. Baumol and Peston, *op. cit.*, allow for this, commenting that if the government has a higher marginal propensity to leak than has the public, then the balanced-budget multiplier will, of course, turn negative.

if instead of spending all of its tax dollar on goods the government spends all of it on factors, purchased from households, that dollar will ultimately be spent on goods no more fully than had it remained uncollected. For we have assumed that all households pay the same marginal income tax rate and have the same marginal propensity to consume disposable income. Consequently, no increase in the entire community's propensity to spend on goods could possibly result from any transfer of dollars from one household to another. Quite another matter, however, is that the expansion of gross government product under a balanced budget, although not raising the output of goods, will raise the community's employment $(*x_{hf} + *x_{hg})$. Private employment $*x_{hf}$ remains constant because the output of goods remains constant, but government employment $*x_{hg}$ climbs.

8

Repressed and Open Inflation

1. REPRESSED INFLATION, THE GAPS

The level of equilibrium gross private product determined by (I) in Chapter 7 is an equilibrium level in the sense that if, according to Equations (8) through (12), all plans of the individual households and firms are carried out (as they can be in a buyers' market), expectations will be self-justifying. But there is no implication that all available factors are employed. Taking availability ("factor supply") into account, we now define two gaps. Denote full employment by $x_{hf}' + {}^*x_{hg}$, a new parameter. The *factor gap* is then defined as the difference $({}^*x_{hf} + {}^*x_{hg}) - (x_{hf}' + {}^*x_{hg})$. Full-employment gross private product is

$$X_f' = \frac{x_{hf}' - A_{hf}}{a_{hf}}$$

and the *gross private product gap* is then defined as ${}^*X_f - X_f'$.

If the gaps are negative, they are called "deflationary gaps," or better, "underemployment gaps," and we have buyers' markets for goods and factors, allowing all plans of households and firms to be carried out, as shown in Equations (8) through (12). Equilibrium defined by solution (I) can then materialize or, which is the same thing, the left-hand terms of the gap differences will materialize.

If the gaps are positive, they are called "inflationary gaps," we have sellers' markets for goods and factors, and the plans of the households and firms cannot be carried out. Equilibrium as defined by (I) cannot materialize, and the right-hand terms of the gap differences will materialize. Should prices of goods and factors be frozen, either by statute or by the voluntary restraint of sellers, the gaps would persist, and we would have the case of repressed inflation, so familiar from World War II and early postwar experience.

2. FLEXIBLE PRICE OF GOODS AND FACTORS ALIKE

Imagine a situation such that at the original values of our parameters π_f and π_h we have repressed inflation. If households try to buy more than is produced, inventory will vanish, and temptation will be strong for firms to raise the price of goods. If they yield to the temptation, open inflation results, a case that can be studied after slight modification of our system of 23 equations and 23 variables.

First, the price of goods charged by firms π_f should be set free to find its equilibrium level. By this we mean a level at which households do not wish to buy more goods than can be produced at full employment. At that price level, then, Equation (8), stating that planned purchases of goods by households equal realized purchases, is satisfied. But if households do not wish to buy more goods than can be produced at full employment, firms will not wish to produce more; consequently, Equation (12) stating that output plans can be carried out, is also satisfied. Finally, the marginal input-output coefficient a_{hf} still holding, Equation (1) will also apply, but a new equation must be added:

$$(26) \qquad\qquad {}^*x_{hf} = x_{hf}{}'$$

where $x_{hf}{}' + {}^*x_{hg}$ is full employment, a new parameter to be added to the list of parameters. If overdetermination is to be avoided, the addition of new equation (26) to our system of 23 equations and 23 variables must be accompanied by the addition of a new variable, which is, of course, the price of goods charged by firms π_f.

Removal of the inflationary gaps by allowing the price of goods to rise to its equilibrium level at constant prices of factors would yield to firms supernormal internal rates of return. Under such circumstances stockholders would be strongly inclined to ask for higher dividend rates and labor for higher wage rates. Firms unwilling to meet such demands could well find themselves raided by firms that were trying to attract entrepreneurship and labor. How far should the former go in granting higher dividend and wage rates as a defense against such raiding? One clue may be found in the widely used pricing practice:[1]

$$(24) \qquad \pi_f = \lambda \pi_h a_{hf}$$

where λ is the mark-up coefficient. If overdetermination of the system is to be avoided, the addition of (24) must be accompanied by the addition of a new variable, the price of factors charged by households π_h. Its value must be determined by the 25 equations in such a way that (1) no inflationary gaps are left in any market and (2) customary ratios between the prices of goods and factors are maintained. Now add (24) and (26) to the system, add x_{hf}' and λ to the list of parameters, remove π_f and π_h from the list of parameters, solve for π_f, and get

$$(XI) \quad \pi_f =$$

$$- \cfrac{a_{fh}A_{gh}}{\cfrac{x_{hf}' - A_{hf}}{a_{hf}} - (*x_{ff} + *x_{fg} + A_{fh}) - \cfrac{a_{fh}}{\lambda a_{hf}}(1 - a_{gh})(x_{hf}' + *x_{hg})}$$

---

[1] Cf. section 18 of chap. 7 and its microeconomic counterpart in equation (7a) of chap. 17.

3. APPLICATION OF THE MODEL

The new model may be applied to a study of the effects of various parameter changes upon the price level under open inflation. The six multipliers are

(XII) $\dfrac{\partial \pi_f}{\partial a_{hf}} = - \dfrac{\dfrac{a_{fh}}{a_{hf}^2} A_{gh}\left[x_{hf}' - A_{hf} - \dfrac{a_{fh}}{\lambda}(1 - a_{gh})(x_{hf}' + *x_{hg})\right]}{m^2}$

(XIII) $\dfrac{\partial \pi_f}{\partial x_{hf}'} = \dfrac{\dfrac{a_{fh}}{a_{hf}} A_{gh}\left[1 - \dfrac{a_{fh}(1 - a_{gh})}{\lambda}\right]}{m^2}$

(XIV) $\dfrac{\partial \pi_f}{\partial *x_{fg}} = - \dfrac{a_{fh}A_{gh}}{m^2}$

(XV) $\dfrac{\partial \pi_f}{\partial *x_{hg}} = - \dfrac{A_{gh}\dfrac{a_{fh}^2}{\lambda a_{hf}}(1 - a_{gh})}{m^2}$

(XVI) $\dfrac{\partial \pi_f}{\partial a_{gh}} = \dfrac{\dfrac{a_{fh}^2}{\lambda a_{hf}} A_{gh}(x_{hf}' + *x_{hg})}{m^2}$

(XVII) $\dfrac{\partial \pi_f}{\partial \lambda} = \dfrac{\dfrac{a_{fh}^2}{\lambda^2 a_{hf}} A_{gh}(x_{hf}' + *x_{hg})(1 - a_{gh})}{m^2}$

In the six multipliers, (XII) through (XVII), m is the denominator of the price solution (XI). For values of parameters satisfying the inequalities in Table 5 in Chapter 7 (which table includes a negative A_{gh}), the multipliers (XIII), (XVI), and (XVII) are negative; all other multipliers are positive. Consequently, the equilibrium price of goods under flexible prices of goods and factors will rise if: (1) the input-output coefficient a_{hf} rises or, in other words, the productivity of factors falls, (2) the physical number of factors available under full employment x_{hf}' falls, (3) government purchases from firms $*x_{fg}$ rises, (4) the gross government product $*x_{hg}$ rises, (5) the marginal income tax rate a_{gh} falls, or (6) the mark-up coefficient λ falls. The six multipliers may be said to represent "demand-pull" inflation.

4. CONCLUSION

We have arrived at the somewhat surprising conclusion that a static equilibrium solution for the price of goods under open inflation does exist. Equation (XI) represents that solution. Since, according to (24), the prices of goods and factors are in fixed proportion, a static equilibrium solution also exists for the price of factors. This fact implies, of course, that the system, if left to itself, would eventually settle down at the solution (XI), inflation eventually dying out.

What causes inflation to die out is the parameter A_{gh}, which was assumed to be negative. If the straight-line tax function (3) has such a negative intercept with the tax axis, the income tax will rise in more than proportion to money income. Consequently, disposable money income will rise in less than proportion to money income. Under open inflation, money income rises exclusively because prices of factors rise; no expansion will occur in physical inputs and outputs. Since disposable money income will rise in less than proportion to factor prices, and since according to (24), factor prices and goods prices are in fixed proportion, disposable real income will fail to keep pace with inflation. The beneficiary is, of course, the government. Without raising a single tax rate, the government will watch its revenue rising in more than proportion to prices.

Government expenditure, on the other hand, will rise only in proportion to prices. Progressively larger government surpluses will develop, and to the politician such large surpluses may seem to warrant tax-rate reduction. Should such reduction be legislated, inflation would gather new momentum. Derivative (XVI) shows that for empirically plausible values of the parameters, including negative A_{gh}, a reduction of the marginal income tax rate a_{gh} will raise the static equilibrium price π_f, toward which the system is tending. The structure of our model exhibits a vulnerability to political pressure and if constantly affected by such pressure, will not ensure the existence of a static equilibrium solution.

But such existence, let us repeat, is dependent in the first place upon the value of the parameter A_{gh}. Were A_{gh} zero, only the trivial solution $\pi_f = 0$ would satisfy our solution (XI). No nonzero price could then represent a static equilibrium value under open inflation. Equally undesirable, were A_{gh} positive, only negative prices could represent a static equilibrium value under open inflation.

9

Nonprice Competition and National Output

1. INTRODUCTION

The Chamberlinian and Keynesian revolutions were entirely unrelated originally and remained so for a long time. To most economists, the theory of monopolistic competition contained interesting propositions relating to resource allocation in a fully employed economy; on the other hand, Keynesianism has contributed to an understanding of an underemployment equilibrium.

Some attention has been paid to the role of price and wage policies in the determination of national output.[1] But price policy is only one aspect of monopolistic competition, and other aspects are equally interesting from the viewpoint of national output determination. A notable feature of the theory of monopolistic competition is its insistence on the product itself and advertising outlay as variables; surely one would expect variations in the

---

[1] Oscar Lange, *Price Flexibility and Employment* (Bloomington, Indiana: The Principia Press, 1944); and Edward S. Mason, "Prices, Costs and Profits," *Money, Trade, and Economic Growth, Essays in Honor of John Henry Williams* (New York: Macmillan, 1951), pp. 177–190.

NOTE: Chaps. 7 and 9 represent a completely rewritten and substantially expanded version of the writer's "Employment, Prices and Monopolistic Competition," *The Review of Economics and Statistics*, Vol. XXIV, No. 4 (Nov., 1952).

product and in advertising outlay to affect the determination of
the national output no less than one would expect price policy to
do so.

2. FIRST HYPOTHESIS

One possible hypothesis is that variations in either advertising
outlay or in the product could affect the consumption function in
such a way that either autonomous consumption would rise or the
marginal propensity to consume would rise, or both.   The effect
of such increases has already been studied, and we have found
that in either case, output will rise: Both derivatives $\partial Y/\partial a$ and
$\partial Y/\partial b$ were found to be positive.[2]

Is such a hypothesis a sound one ?   As a matter of fact we know
very little about this.   General reasoning, not empirical studies,
carried Chamberlin to the conclusion that advertising by members
of a given group does not entirely cancel out within the group, the
reason being that the increased market of a given producer is
derived not alone from the markets of the closest substitutes for
his product, but also from the markets of *other* groups.[3]   At least
one writer has studied the effects of advertising by members of a
group upon demand faced by that group, namely, A. R. Prest.[4]
J. R. N. Stone[5] had made an attempt to determine the demand for
tobacco.   His independent variables included: aggregate real
income, price of tobacco, price level of all other consumers' goods
and services, time, and extent of coupon trading.   In addition to
these independent variables, Prest included press advertising
expenditure and came to the conclusion that "the effect of
advertising is almost negligible though it must be stressed that the

---

[2] Chap. 3, equations (III) and (IV); cf. figures 8 and 9.

[3] Edward H. Chamberlin, *The Theory of Monopolistic Competition* (Cambridge,
Mass.: Harvard University Press, 1933), pp. 151–154.

[4] A. R. Prest, "Some Experiments in Demand Analysis," *The Review of
Economics and Statistics*, Vol. XXXI, No. 1 (Feb., 1949), pp. 33–49.

[5] J. R. N. Stone, "The Analysis of Market Demand," *Journal of the Royal
Statistical Society*, Vol. CVIII, Parts III–IV (1945), pp. 286–382.

series used refers to press advertising expenditure only and therefore may not be too good an indicator of total expenditure." As
a possible explanation of the negligible effect of advertising, Prest
added the observation that "much advertisement is competitive
between the ... *firms* in an industry and therefore the effect of
this factor on the total amount sold by the *industry* may not be so
great."

By analogy, one could say that much advertisement is competitive between the *industries* in an economy, and therefore the effect
of this factor on the total amount of consumers' goods sold in the
economy *as a whole* may not be so great. Extending Chamberlin's
argument one might, of course, observe that since savings are a
substitute for consumers' goods, they are likely to suffer when such
goods are advertised. Hence, advertising of all consumers' goods
is likely to increase aggregate consumption in the economy. But
what if savings are advertised, too? Life and retirement in-
surance advertising in the United States seems impressive indeed,
and the possibility arises, therefore, of advertising by consumption goods industries canceling that by nonconsumption-goods
industries. We simply do not know much about this. Yet
business men [6] and economists have few doubts that advertising
increases consumption for the economy as a whole. In fact, the
opinion of our profession seems almost unanimous. K. W. Rothschild is most categorical in his assertion: "I think it hopeless to
try a quantitative estimate of the effects of total advertising on
total consumption. All we can say is that the habit of advertising
must be responsible for a considerable increase in the propensity
to consume." [7] Lawrence Klein is also sure: "The advertising
industry has certainly had a bad influence on many aspects of our

---

[6] "... In [the] realm of comparative plenty, most people have more money
than they need for subsistence, are 'optional' and therefore arbitrary and erratic
spenders. Advertising and selling provide the only means of persuading them.
And as *Fortune* suggested last April, advertising and selling may provide an
important means of keeping over-all consumption up to production, thus helping
to prevent oversaving and consequent deflation." *Fortune* (June, 1952), p. 192.

[7] K. W. Rothschild, "A Note on Advertising," *Economic Journal*, Vol. LII,
No. 205 (April, 1942), p. 116.

lives . . . but it has also served to maintain consumption at a higher level than it otherwise would have been. Advertising is not the best way to get a high-consumption, low-savings economy, but it is *a* way."[8]   Fellner is more cautious: "The historical behavior of the [consumption] function could be interpreted as being produced in the passage of time by continuous upward shifts of the household budget function. The trendlike upward shift suggested by this hypothesis might be the result of technological innovations which place *new products* on the market, or of other impacts producing a continuous decline in thriftiness. . . . It is conceivable that technological change and the increasing sales effort on the part of producers and retailers tend to produce an upward shift of the consumption function."[9]

3. SECOND HYPOTHESIS

Another possible hypothesis is that product variation and advertising will affect the input-output function in such a way that the propensity to purchase factors rises. The effect has already been studied, and we have found that output will rise: the derivative $\partial X_f / \partial a_{hf}$ was found to be positive.[10]

Is our second hypothesis a reasonable one? Obviously advertising and other forms of selling effort imply the purchase of factors. We know that, as far as this country is concerned, it costs more to distribute goods than it costs to produce them. Not only is personal selling effort a consumer of much manpower, but advertising proper calls for the employment of agency personnel. Also, product development and improvement presumes the employment of high-salaried engineers, industrial designers, and market analysts. If advertising and personal selling effort are essentials of selling goods in a competitive economy, business is

---

[8] Lawrence Klein, *The Keynesian Revolution* (New York: Macmillan, 1947), p. 175.

[9] William Fellner, *Monetary Policies and Full Employment* (Berkeley and Los Angeles: University of California Press, 1947), p. 61.

[10] Chap. 7, equation (III).

forced to purchase more factors at any given level of planned output than it otherwise would have done.

K. W. Rothschild emphasized this fact in his above-mentioned article and compared advertising with the classical weapon against unemployment, that is, public works. In his estimate, annual advertising expenditures in Great Britain around 1934 totaled £100 million. At the same time the central and local governments spent between £14 and £15 millions annually to combat the depression by means of public works.

4. THIRD HYPOTHESIS

Finally, one could formulate the hypothesis that product variation and advertising might increase the investment parameter. We know that if investment rises output will rise: the derivative $\partial Y/\partial I$ was found to be positive.[11]

Is our third hypothesis reasonable? In the second hypothesis we were concerned with the purchase of factors at any *given* level of output planned by business. Our third hypothesis has to do with that part of such output which is called gross investment. In a mature economy a large part of the gross investment is production of durable equipment. At a given capital stock the annual output of durable equipment needed by business will depend upon the useful life of that equipment. When the rate of obsolescence is high, useful life is short, and annual output must likewise be high if capital stock is to be maintained. Product variation is associated with a high rate of obsolescence, not only of the product itself, but also of the durable equipment needed to produce the product, as evidenced by the automobile industry. The frequency of shift in basic models reduces the life span of much durable equipment: "Most of these machines are specialists.

---

[11] In chap. 3, equation (II) and figure 7, investment was net investment; here, the concern is gross investment. The reader, by taking the derivative of X_f with respect to $*x_{ff}$ used in chap. 7 can demonstrate that the derivative of output with respect to *gross* investment is also positive.

They have been built to do a job on a specific motor design. No group of men and other machines can do the job so well. But they are useful only if the job remains the same. When dimensions of cylinder block or crankshaft or transmission are altered materially, as now, these machines are through . . . "[12]

We have seen that firms joining the competitive game are forced to purchase more factors at any given planned output than they otherwise would have done. But could it be that competition is so dangerous that fewer firms would like to join it? If so, investment could suffer in the last analysis, an idea developed by one of the early Keynesians, W. B. Reddaway.[13] He described how demand for luxury and semiluxury goods in a mature capitalistic economy is very hard to predict. Reddaway said: "Demand is likely to be highly erratic. . . . With a market of this type, the potential entrepreneur may have only the haziest idea of the amount he can sell at any given price (or at any price at all), and is faced with very heavy marketing costs, especially at the start. Good will and business connections are half the battle, and here the newcomer inevitably sees himself at a disadvantage; even if his goods are not of a completely new type, there will probably be the need for an expensive advertising campaign to get them on the market . . . and there is the moral certainty that his entry into the field will provoke a rival campaign on the part of established producers." Reddaway's conclusion: "The inevitable instability and imperfection of the market are certain to hamper investment in these spheres, especially where enterprise has got to secure capital by persuading skeptical outsiders."

One objection that could be raised against this line of reasoning is that modern enterprise only infrequently has to secure capital from outsiders. E. S. Mason,[14] in calling attention to the effects

[12] Automobile Manufacturers Association, *What it Takes* (Detroit, Mich.: 1940), p. 11.
[13] W. B. Reddaway, "Special Obstacles to Full Employment in a Wealthy Community," *Economic Journal*, Vol. XLVII, No. 186 (June, 1937), pp. 297–307.
[14] Edward S. Mason, "Various Views on the Monopoly Problem, Introduction," *The Review of Economics and Statistics*, Vol. XXXI, No. 2 (May, 1949), pp. 104–106.

of self-finance upon investment, said: "I . . . would argue that considerations of maintaining the firm probably lead to a higher ratio of investment to output than would be considered optimum on a straight profit-maximization basis. Reinvestment of profits in the firm, e.g., is probably carried to an extent that would be unjustified on a straight profit comparison between external and internal investment opportunities."

Besides being self-financing, the modern large corporation is highly diversified in the sense that it produces, or could easily produce, a large number of products. Both factors make for flexibility. As a matter of fact, innovations frequently originate in established firms rather than in new ones; indeed, most frequently, they originate in the very largest established firms rather than in the smaller ones. In 1945 the 75 largest corporations in the United States accounted for nearly half the total number of professional scientists and engineers employed in industrial research laboratories. M. A. Adelman comments: "It is clear that most of the organized industrial research is carried on by a very tiny fraction of all business firms, or even of all corporations."[15] Thus Reddaway may be right in saying that market imperfections are likely to hamper investment by *small* firms and by *new* firms. But he may not be right that *all* investment is likely to be hampered.

Further light on our problem is shed by Carl Kaysen,[16] who has examined the effect of oligopolistic uncertainty upon investment. Facing an expanding demand for their products, individual oligopolists might strive to outdo one another in adding to capacity in the belief that such activity is less likely to cause reaction by their rivals than would changes in prices. This practice might lead to overinvestment relative to the monopoly optimum. When the oligopolists are facing a declining demand, the position is different. In such a situation tacit price agreements are unlikely

[15] M. A. Adelman, "The Measurement of Industrial Concentration," *The Review of Economics and Statistics*, Vol. XXXIII, No. 4 (Nov., 1951), p. 278.

[16] Carl Kaysen, "A Dynamic Aspect of the Monopoly Problem," *The Review of Economics and Statistics*, Vol. XXXI, No. 2 (May, 1949), pp. 109–113.

to last, because a firm may be willing to increase greatly its risk of further loss for the chance of some gain. Thus a condition of endemic price war will rule. Overinvestment relative to the monopoly optimum is thus less likely.

Reddaway spoke of price and advertising policies only, but Kaysen seems to have only price policies in mind. Both ignore product policies, Kaysen's oligopoly apparently being undifferentiated. Elsewhere the present writer has tried to point out that oligopolists rely on product policies rather than on price policies *and thereby reduce oligopolistic risks*.[17] A fundamental difference between price and product competition lies in the fact that a price variation, if desirable, can be put into action immediately, whereas product variation frequently requires technological research and always requires tooling-up. Since a rival's response to product variation is less prompt than his response to price cuts, the former variation is more attractive than the latter. If this risk-reducing aspect of product variation is included in Kaysen's model we have a good case for a somewhat higher level of oligopolistic investment.

5. CONCLUSION

Our three hypotheses represent three possible ways in which product variation and advertising could raise short-run national output. But the picture is not complete until their long-run effects upon the growth pattern of the economy have been examined. In Chapter 23 we shall find that rapid obsolescence of durable producers' goods and high selling-effort requirements per unit of output may well reduce the proportionate rate of growth of the economy. The contrast between what happens to the level of output and what happens to the time path of output is indeed a striking one.

[17] Hans Brems, *Product Equilibrium under Monopolistic Competition* (Cambridge, Mass.: Harvard University Press, 1951), pp. 234–236.

10

The Balanced Foreign-Trade
Multiplier

1. THE PROBLEM

Recent inquiry [1] has greatly clarified the balanced-budget multiplier. By analogy, is there a balanced foreign-trade multiplier? Stolper and others [2] have examined the multiplier effects of balanced foreign trade using the assumption that a balance is brought about miraculously by two simultaneous shifts: one in the export function and one in the domestic spending function. Miracles aside, suppose that the domestic demand functions for import and for domestically produced goods refuse to shift themselves. In short: assume only one shift, that in the export function. If under such circumstances foreign trade is somehow balanced, is there a balanced foreign-trade multiplier? In real life, the "somehow" has increasingly come to mean fiscal policy.

---

[1] For references see chap. 7, p. 74.

[2] Wolfgang F. Stolper, "The Volume of Foreign Trade and the Level of Income," *The Quarterly Journal of Economics*, Vol. LXI, No. 2 (Feb., 1947), pp. 285–310; and a similar but more rigorous treatment of the same two-shift case, by Preben Munthe, "Multiplikatorvirkning ved en parallel öking av eksport og import," *Festskrift til I. Wedervang* (Oslo: Bedriftsökonomen, 1951), pp. 13–21.

2. THE NEW ROLE OF FISCAL POLICY IN AN OPEN ECONOMY

Applied to analyses of foreign trade and of fiscal policy, the Keynesian model gave early and convincing demonstrations of its power. But fiscal policy was always studied within the framework of a closed economy, and the analysis of foreign trade always ignored government. Recent public policy in Australia and Western Europe, particularly in Britain and the Scandinavian countries, has added great interest to the *joint* study of the two subjects. Quantitative import controls, tariffs, and devaluation being discredited, and the money wage rate being largely beyond control by government, fiscal policy has been increasingly relied upon to balance foreign trade. Therefore, we shall state our problem as follows: If only the export function shifts and if trade is balanced as a result of fiscal policy, is there a balanced foreign-trade multiplier? If so, what is its value in comparison with the conventional foreign-trade multiplier?

3. THE MODEL

In our attempt to provide the answers, we shall make some highly simplifying assumptions. Tax policy will be the only form of fiscal policy considered, and the proportionate personal income tax the only tax considered. Consequently, tax-induced substitution between consumption and saving is excluded, and tax-induced substitution between the consumption of different goods —domestically produced goods and imported goods—is also excluded. As a result, fixed propensities to import and to consume domestically produced goods can be assumed to exist, irrespective of the fiscal policy adopted. Policies other than fiscal policies are not applied as a means of keeping the balance of trade equal to zero.

The notation is essentially the same as that used in Chapter 7 but differs in details. Since we are not interested in this chapter in manipulating prices, we shall assume prices to be constant and shall measure output and transactions in constant-value dollars:

Variables

X_j = output of goods produced by sector j, in constant-value dollars per unit of time

x_{ij} = purchase of product or factor of sector i by sector j, in constant-value dollars per unit of time, except $*x_{ff}$, $*x_{fg}$, $*x_{fH}$, and $*x_{hg}$ which are parameters

σ_{ij} = sale of product or factor of sector i to sector j; dimension same as x_{ij}

Parameters

A_{fh} = autonomous consumption of domestically produced goods

A_{Fh} = autonomous import

a_{fh} = the domestic marginal propensity to consume domestically produced goods out of expected disposable domestic income

a_{Fh} = the domestic marginal propensity to import foreign-produced goods out of expected disposable domestic income

a_{gh} = the income tax rate, a pure number

a_{hf} = dollars' worth of domestic factor purchases by domestic firms per one dollar's worth of domestic gross private product

$*x_{fH}$ = autonomous export

$*x_{ff}$ = domestic expected gross private investment defined as that part of domestic gross private product that domestic firms do not expect to sell to domestic or foreign households or government

$*x_{fg}$ = domestic government purchases of goods from domestic firms

$*x_{hg}$ = domestic government purchases of services from domestic households

The model is a five-sector static equilibrium model. Of the five sectors, the first three are domestic and include firms, government, and households. The subscripts referring to those sectors are, as usual, f, g, and h. The last two sectors are foreign firms and foreign households. The subscripts referring to these new sectors are F and H, respectively. The eight transactions to be considered are tabulated in Table 6. Six of them are purely domestic

TABLE 6.   Planned Purchases of Goods and Factors

Purchasing from	Purchases Planned by				
	Domestic Firms	Domestic Government	Domestic Households	Foreign Firms	Foreign Households
Domestic firms	$*x_{ff}$	$*x_{fg}$	$*x_{fh}$	—	$*x_{fH}$
Domestic government	—	—	$*x_{gh}$	—	—
Domestic households	$*x_{hf}$	$*x_{hg}$	—	—	—
Foreign firms	—	—	$*x_{Fh}$	—	—
Foreign households	—	—	—	—	—

and are treated in Chapter 7. The two new international transactions are purchase of domestically produced goods by foreign households, $*x_{fH}$, and purchase of foreign-produced goods by domestic households $*x_{Fh}$. We are following great precedents in assuming that import and export are for consumption purposes only.

4. DOMESTIC BEHAVIOR EQUATIONS

Three behavior equations determine domestic planned purchases. First, planned purchases of domestic factors by domestic firms are assumed to be in direct proportion to planned domestic gross private product:[3]

$$(1) \qquad\qquad *x_{hf} = a_{hf}*X_f$$

Second, planned purchases of domestic goods by domestic households are stated as the following function:

$$(2) \qquad *x_{fh} = A_{fh} + a_{fh}[(*\sigma_{hf} + *\sigma_{hg}) - *x_{gh}]$$

[3] In order to keep the algebra simple the constant term A_{hf} is now dropped.

where A_{fh} is autonomous consumption of domestically produced goods and a_{fh} the marginal propensity to consume domestically produced goods out of expected disposable income.

Third, planned purchases of foreign goods by domestic households are stated as the following function:

$$(3) \qquad *x_{Fh} = A_{Fh} + a_{Fh}[(*\sigma_{hf} + *\sigma_{hg}) - *x_{gh}]$$

where A_{Fh} is autonomous import and a_{Fh} the marginal propensity to import out of expected disposable income.

In Equations (2) and (3) disposable income equals personal income minus tax, $*x_{gh}$ being the expected tax payment and assumed to be in direct proportion to expected household money income:[4]

$$(4) \qquad *x_{gh} = a_{gh}(*\sigma_{hf} + *\sigma_{hg})$$

where a_{gh} is the income tax rate. Stripping (4) of all three asterisks gives Equation (5), the determination of realized tax payments, not written explicitly.

5. EXPORT, A PARAMETER

Let planned purchase of domestic goods by foreign households be a parameter:

$$(6) \qquad *x_{fH} = \text{a parameter}$$

6. EXPECTED PRIVATE INVESTMENT, A PARAMETER

Expected gross private investment by domestic firms is assumed to be a parameter:

$$(7) \qquad *x_{ff} = \text{a parameter}$$

---

[4] Again dropping the constant term, this time A_{gh}.

7. PLANNED GOVERNMENT PURCHASES, PARAMETERS

Likewise, planned government purchase of goods and services are assumed to be parameters:

(8) $$*x_{fg} = \text{a parameter}$$

(9) $$*x_{hg} = \text{a parameter}$$

8. PURCHASE PLANS ARE ALWAYS REALIZED

In a buyer's market plans made at the beginning of the unit period are carried out during the period.   Of our seven intersector purchases six are planned, but the seventh, $*x_{gh}$ the tax payment, is an expected one, expected according to (4).   For each of the six planned purchases we can express the realization of the plans:

(10) through (15) $$*x_{ij} = x_{ij}$$

where ij represents fh, hf, fH, Fh, fg, and hg, respectively.

9. PRODUCTION PLANS ARE ALWAYS REALIZED

In a buyer's market it can also be assumed that well-planned production goals will be realized:

(16) $$*X_f = X_f$$

10. WHAT IS PURCHASED IS SOLD

Any sector's realized purchases from another sector constitutes the latter's realized sales to the former.   Such correspondences hold for all seven inter-sector transactions:

(17) through (23) $$x_{ij} = \sigma_{ij}$$

where ij represents fh, hf, fH, Fh, fg, hg, and gh, respectively.

11. EQUILIBRIUM CONDITIONS

If equilibrium is to prevail, the activity of the economy must be self-justifying in the sense that any sector's expected sales to another sector must equal realized sales. Such correspondences hold for all seven intersector transactions:

(24) through (30) $\qquad *\sigma_{ij} = \sigma_{ij}$

where ij has the same alternative meanings as in Section 10.

12. DEFINITIONAL EQUATION

By definition, domestic expected gross private investment is that part of domestic planned gross private product which domestic firms do not expect to sell to domestic or foreign households or to government:

(31) $\qquad *x_{ff} = *X_f - (*\sigma_{fh} + *\sigma_{fH} + *\sigma_{fg})$

13. SOLUTION FOR CASE WHERE TRADE BALANCE IS LEFT TO ITSELF

Our 31 unknowns are: one expected gross investment $*x_{ff}$; seven ex ante purchases $*x_{ij}$; seven ex post purchases x_{ij}; seven expected sales $*\sigma_{ij}$; seven realized sales σ_{ij}; one planned output $*X_f$; and one realized output X_f. Solving for equilibrium domestic gross private product X_f, we get

(I) $\qquad X_f = \dfrac{*x_{ff} + *x_{fH} + *x_{fg} + a_{fh}*x_{hg}(1 - a_{gh}) + A_{fh}}{1 - a_{fh}a_{hf}(1 - a_{gh})}$

Having found X_f, we can easily establish the multiplier effect of a change in autonomous export $*x_{fH}$. Taking the derivative of gross private product with respect to autonomous export, we get

(II) $\qquad \dfrac{dX_f}{d*x_{fH}} = \dfrac{1}{1 - a_{fh}a_{hf}(1 - a_{gh})}$

What is the economic interpretation of this multiplier? First, let us interpret the magnitude $a_{fh}a_{hf}(1 - a_{gh})$. According to the parameters, a_{hf} is the dollars' worth of domestic factor purchases by domestic firms per one dollar's worth of domestic gross private product. Or, in other words, the dollars' worth of domestic *personal* income generated per one dollar's worth of domestic gross private product. Multiply by $(1 - a_{gh})$ and get the dollars' worth of domestic *disposable* income generated per one dollar's worth of domestic gross private product. Finally multiply by a_{fh} and get marginal consumption of domestically produced goods generated per one additional dollar's worth of domestic gross private product. The entire magnitude $a_{fh}a_{hf}(1 - a_{gh})$ is, then, the marginal propensity to consume domestically produced goods out of domestic gross private product. Consequently, the magnitude $1 - a_{fh}a_{hf}(1 - a_{gh})$ must be the marginal propensity *not* to consume domestically produced goods out of domestic gross private product. That propensity in turn can be said to be the community's marginal propensity to save, pay taxes, and import out of the gross private product, and the autonomous export multiplier is unity divided by that propensity; this multiplier is positive and in excess of unity.

14. SOLUTION FOR CASE WHERE FOREIGN TRADE IS ALWAYS BALANCED

Let us now turn to the case where foreign trade is always balanced. For this case we must write an additional equation:

$$(32) \qquad {}^*x_{Fh} - {}^*x_{fH} = 0$$

However, adding this new equation (32) to an already fully determined system of 31 unknowns and 31 equations would give us an overdetermined system. To keep our system workable, we must drop one parameter and turn it into an unknown. Which parameter is dropped is unimportant from the point of view of determinacy, but realistically we should drop the tax rate a_{gh}.

Equation (32) will, in conjunction with the other equations in our system, determine a tax rate consistent with the balancing of foreign trade. Our new system of 32 equations can now be solved with respect to equilibrium gross private product X_f. The result is

$$\text{(III)} \quad X_f = {}^*x_{ff} + {}^*x_{fg} + {}^*x_{fH}\left(1 + \frac{a_{fh}}{a_{Fh}}\right) - \frac{a_{fh}}{a_{Fh}}A_{Fh} + A_{fh}$$

We are ready now to establish the multiplier effect of a change in autonomous export ${}^*x_{fH}$. We have assumed that foreign trade is always balanced by way of fiscal policy. Our new multiplier, then, is a balanced foreign-trade multiplier. Its value is simply

$$\text{(IV)} \quad \frac{dX_f}{d^*x_{fH}} = 1 + \frac{a_{fh}}{a_{Fh}}$$

Since both the marginal propensity to consume domestically produced goods a_{fh} and the marginal propensity to import a_{Fh} can be assumed to be positive, multiplier (IV) is positive and always in excess of unity.

15. GRAPHICAL SOLUTION

The hard core of our model is presented graphically in Figure 34, a four-axis diagram. Starting with the first quadrant, we find the rising import function ${}^*x_{Fh}$, the rising total consumption function ${}^*x_{fh} + {}^*x_{Fh}$, and the horizontal export function ${}^*x_{fH}$. The crucial point is the intersection between the import and the export functions, indicated by a double circle. This intersection determines disposable income. At no other level of disposable income will foreign trade be balanced. On the northern axis plot the total amount of consumption, which corresponds to the newly found disposable income. Since export equals import, all consumption generated also equals export ${}^*x_{fH}$ plus consumption of domestically produced goods ${}^*x_{fh}$.

Now move counterclockwise into the second quadrant. The 45° line permits us to transfer the value ${}^*x_{fh} + {}^*x_{fH}$ to the western axis, where we have previously plotted the sum of autonomous investment $*x_{ff}$ and the autonomous government purchase of goods $*x_{fg}$. The sum of all four $*x_{fh} + *x_{fH} + *x_{ff} + *x_{fg}$ must equal the gross private product $*X_f$. Moving on, still counter-clockwise, into the third quadrant, we find the factor purchase function showing the size of personal income that will be generated by the level of output just determined. To personal income generated by firms $*x_{hf}$ add autonomous government purchase of factors $*x_{hg}$. Total personal income $*x_{hf} + *x_{hg}$ appears on the

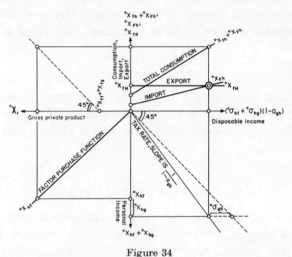

Figure 34

southern axis. All that remains now is to confront the eastern and the southern axis. This is done in the fourth quadrant. On the eastern axis we have disposable income, on the southern personal income. Only one tax rate will make the two levels compatible with one another; it is shown by the thin solid line whose slope is $1/(1 - a_{gh})$, where a_{gh} is the tax rate. The tax revenue $*\sigma_{gh}$ appears as the horizontal distance between the tax-rate line and the 45° broken line in the fourth quadrant. The reader can easily demonstrate that a decrease in autonomous export in the first quadrant will be followed by a decrease in equilibrium output but by a rise in the equilibrium tax rate necessary to make export and import equal and also in equilibrium tax revenue.

16. COMPARISON BETWEEN THE UNBALANCED AND THE BALANCED FOREIGN-TRADE MULTIPLIER

It can be shown algebraically that under empirically plausible assumptions the unbalanced foreign-trade multiplier (II) is smaller than the balanced foreign-trade multiplier (IV). Three assumptions are needed. First, the sum of the marginal propensity to consume domestically produced goods and of the marginal propensity to import is less than unity. Second, the dollars' worth of domestic factor purchases per dollar's worth of gross private product is positive but less than unity. Third, the tax rate is also positive but less than unity. Algebraically,

$$a_{fh} + a_{Fh} < 1$$
$$0 < a_{hf} < 1$$
$$0 < a_{gh} < 1$$

Using these three assumptions, we can prove that

$$\frac{1}{1 - a_{fh}a_{hf}(1 - a_{gh})} < 1 + \frac{a_{fh}}{a_{Fh}}$$

The proof is found in the Appendix to this chapter. Thus, under the said assumptions, the unbalanced foreign-trade multiplier is smaller than the balanced foreign-trade multiplier.

17. THE DIFFERENCE EXPLAINED

The fact that the unbalanced foreign-trade multiplier is normally smaller than the balanced foreign-trade multiplier is easily explained, the explanation emerging once attention is concentrated on the government budget. On the expenditure side of the budget we have $*x_{fg} + *x_{hg}$, each a parameter. The effects of the change in autonomous export upon the budget are confined to the revenue side $*\sigma_{gh}$. Before finding what happens to tax *revenue* we must first find what happens to the tax *rate* a_{gh}. For the balanced foreign-trade case, solving our system of 32 unknowns and 32 equations with respect to the tax rate and then taking the derivative of the tax rate with respect to autonomous export, we get

(V) $$\frac{da_{gh}}{d^*x_{fH}} = - \frac{a_{hf}(^*x_{ff} + \,^*x_{fg} + A_{Fh} + A_{fh}) + \,^*x_{hg}}{a_{Fh}(a_{hf}{}^*X_f + \,^*x_{hg})^2}$$

Since, in perverse cases, the vertical-axis intercepts A_{fh} and A_{Fh} could be negative, they could, if numerically large enough, swamp the $^*x$'s in the numerator, causing the entire derivative to become positive. But normally the intercepts are positive, and the entire derivative negative: should exports fall the tax rate would have to be raised. This result is intuitively very plausible: should autonomous export fall, only an increase in the tax rate would reduce import enough to restore a zero balance of trade. True, falling export will reduce output, personal income, disposable income, and import demand. But many leaks occur in the process of such reductions, and the downward pressure transmitted to the import stage will be greatly reduced. First, there is the business saving leakage (a_{hf} less than one); second, the income tax leakage ($1 - a_{gh}$ less than one); and third, the household saving leakage plus the household consumption of domestically produced goods leakage (a_{Fh} less than one).

What is less obvious is the effect upon tax revenue. Tax revenue is the product of tax rate and personal income. According to (V) the tax rate must go up if and when autonomous export falls. According to (IV) the gross private product, and with it personal income, goes down when autonomous export falls. Will a concurrent higher tax rate and lower personal income produce a higher or a lower tax revenue? Using our system of 32 equations to determine expected government revenue, we take the derivative of the latter with respect to autonomous export, and get

(VI) $$\frac{d^*\sigma_{gh}}{d^*x_{fH}} = \frac{a_{hf}(a_{fh} + a_{Fh}) - 1}{a_{Fh}}$$

In this derivative a_{hf}, the dollars' worth of domestic factor purchases by domestic firms per one dollar's worth of domestic gross private product, is smaller than unity. Furthermore, the sum of $a_{Fh} + a_{fh}$, the marginal propensities, respectively, to import and to consume domestically produced goods, is normally smaller than unity. Since the product of the two propensities is even smaller, the entire numerator must normally be negative. The denominator a_{Fh}, the marginal propensity to import, being positive, the entire derivative (VI) must normally be negative: should autonomous export fall, tax revenue would have to be raised if trade is to be balanced.

18. THE PERVERSE CASE

In our proof (see the Appendix to this chapter) we assume that

$$a_{fh} + a_{Fh} < 1$$

Should this assumption not be fulfilled, it is possible that the unbalanced foreign-trade multiplier may turn out to be *larger* than that for balanced foreign trade. And, should the assumption not be fulfilled, it is possible that derivative (VI) may become *positive* —if exports fall, tax revenue may also fall. Furthermore, it is likely that very large values of a_{fh} and a_{Fh} would be accompanied by negative values of the intercepts A_{fh} and A_{Fh}. In such cases derivative (V) might become *positive*, too—if exports fall, the tax rate may also fall. Figure 35 shows a "perverse" case in point. How likely are such cases?

As long as import is used for consumption only, such cases are not likely. The slope $a_{fh} + a_{Fh}$ of the total consumption function is normally less than unity, and its intercept $A_{fh} + A_{Fh}$ is normally positive. But should the assumption that import is only for consumption purposes be relaxed, a foreign-trade accelerator could conceivably make import a very rapidly rising function of gross private product, the slope of the function being the capital coefficient with respect to *imported* capital goods.

An inspection of the econometrics of international trade is rather illuminating. Table 7 reproduces Polak's findings for the early part of the interwar period that preceded the large-scale adoption of quantitative import controls. Of his 25 countries,

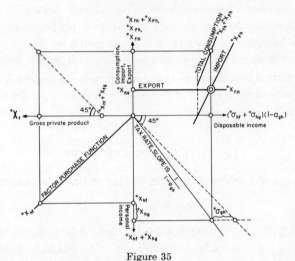

Figure 35

only the six included in Table 7 had marginal propensities to import in excess of one-half. All six economies are, of course, small. With the exception of Norway they are all characterized

TABLE 7.   Marginal Propensities to Import in Early Part of Interwar Period

Denmark	0.73
Finland	0.93
Indonesia	0.62
New Zealand	0.65
Norway	0.67
Union of South Africa	0.57

SOURCE: J. J. Polak, *An International Economic System* (Chicago: The University of Chicago Press, 1953), pp. 156–157.

by Polak as primary producers. Except for Indonesia, they could also be characterized, perhaps, as highly developed primary producers needing and importing durable capital goods. For such primary producers, import of durable capital goods should be allowed for, and in such cases the propensity to import could conceivably be high enough to produce the "perverse" effects described above.

19. CONCLUSION

We have found that the balanced foreign-trade multiplier is normally larger than the unbalanced foreign-trade multiplier, the reason being that the balanced foreign-trade multiplier *incorporates* the multiplier effect of any change in taxation that is necessary to keep foreign trade balanced. Such a change will *normally* reinforce the effect of a change in autonomous export: falling autonomous export will normally be accompanied by a higher tax revenue. The perverse case described in Section 18 represents an exception.

APPENDIX: A PROOF

Assume that

$$a_{fh} + a_{Fh} < 1$$
$$0 < a_{hf} < 1$$
$$0 < a_{gh} < 1$$

Then

$$a_{hf}(1 - a_{gh})(a_{fh} + a_{Fh}) < 1$$
$$a_{hf}(1 - a_{gh}) < \frac{1}{a_{fh} + a_{Fh}}$$

Multiply both sides by minus one and reverse the inequality sign. Then multiply both sides by a_{fh} (positive), and finally add plus one to each side:

$$1 - a_{fh}a_{hf}(1 - a_{gh}) > 1 - \frac{a_{fh}}{a_{fh} + a_{Fh}}$$

Turning this inequality upside down, and reversing the inequality sign, we get

$$\frac{1}{1 - a_{fh}a_{hf}(1 - a_{gh})} < 1 + \frac{a_{fh}}{a_{Fh}}$$

a comparison of our two multipliers. On the left-hand side of the inequality sign we have the unbalanced foreign-trade multiplier (II), and on the right-hand side the balanced foreign-trade multiplier (IV). We observe that the former is less than the latter.

11

Employment and Money Wages Under Balanced Foreign Trade

1. THE PROBLEM

Prices, too important to be overlooked, have been ignored in our preceding foreign-trade models for the sake of simplification. Our present purpose is to study the effects of raising the price of domestic factors in a country whose government applies fiscal policy to keep the balance of trade equaling zero.[1] (Quantitative controls, higher tariffs, and devaluation will not be applied.) Such a study is highly topical for economies such as certain

[1] A surprisingly large number of analyses of the wage-employment relationship assumes a closed economy. Analyses that do not so assume ignore the need for balancing foreign trade and do not usually mention the foreign-trade elasticities, e.g., Keynes' *General Theory* (London: Macmillan, 1936), p. 263, and James Tobin, "Money Wage Rates and Employment," *The New Economics* (New York: Knopf, 1950), pp. 586–587. But two fine beginnings have been made: by Jan Tinbergen, "De Betekenis van de Loonpolitiek voor de Werkgelegenheid," *De Economist* (March, 1950), translated as "The Significance of Wage Policy for Employment," *International Economic Papers*, No. 1 (1951), pp. 186–194, and by D. B. J. Schouten, "Loonshoogte, Werkgelegenheid en de Economische Structuur," *Economie*, Vol. 15, No. 7 (April, 1951), translated as "The Wage Level, Employment, and the Economic Structure," *International Economic Papers*, No. 2 (1952), pp. 221–232.

NOTE: The present chapter is a revision of the author's "Employment and Money Wages Under Balanced Foreign Trade," *Econometrica*, Vol. 25, No. 2 (April, 1957).

Western European ones which are subjected to a threefold pressure emanating from powerful labor unions asking for higher wages, from the Organization for European Economic Cooperation or the Common Market asking for freer trade, and finally from ever-present international competition.

2. THE MODEL

The model to be used is a five-sector model having exactly the same sectors and exactly the same table of transactions as those described in Chapter 10. The model as treated in Chapter 11 represents an attempt to "marry" the elasticity and the absorption approaches to international trade theory. The former approach traditionally has ignored output variations, the latter relative price variations. A marriage of the two, then, is almost bound to become quite complicated, even though the model should be kept as simple as possible in all details.

Notation is essentially the same as that in Chapters 7 and 10. Since the present chapter is a study of price effects, prices will re-emerge, and output and transactions will once again be measured in physical units. The notation follows.

Variables

X_j = output of goods produced by sector j, in physical number of goods per unit of time

x_{ij} = purchase of product or factor of sector i by sector j, in physical number of goods or factors per unit of time, except $*x_{ff}$, $*x_{fg}$, and $*x_{hg}$ which are parameters

σ_{ij} = sale of product or factor of sector i to sector j. Dimension: same as x_{ij}

a_{gh} = the income tax rate, in tax dollars paid per dollar's worth of household money income

π_f = the price of domestic goods charged by domestic firms

Parameters

a_{fh} = the domestic propensity to consume domestically produced goods out of money disposable domestic income when $\pi_f = \pi_F\rho = 1$ and $e_{fh} + E_{fh} = 1$

a_{Fh} = the domestic propensity to import foreign-produced goods out of money disposable domestic income when $\pi_f = \pi_F\rho = 1$ and $e_{Fh} + E_{Fh} = 1$

a_{fH} = the foreign propensity to import domestically produced goods out of money disposable foreign income when $\pi_F = \pi_f/\rho = 1$ and $e_{fH} + E_{fH} = 1$

a_{hf} = physical number of domestic factors purchased by domestic firms per physical unit of domestic output

e_{ij} = the elasticity of demand for goods produced by sector i, demanded by sector j with respect to real disposable income of sector j in terms of domestic goods

E_{ij} = the elasticity of demand for goods produced by sector i, demanded by sector j with respect to real disposable income of sector j in terms of foreign goods

π_h = the price of domestic factors charged by domestic households

π_F = the price of foreign goods charged by foreign firms

ρ = the exchange rate, in number of domestic monetary units per foreign monetary unit

λ = the mark-up coefficient by which the money value $\pi_h a_{hf}$ of the input of factors per unit of output should be multiplied

*x_{ff} = domestic gross private investment defined as that part of domestic gross private product that domestic firms do not expect to sell to domestic or foreign households or government

*x_{fg} = domestic government purchases of goods from domestic firms

*x_{hg} = domestic government purchases of services from domestic households

*y = money disposable foreign income

3. DOMESTIC PURCHASE EQUATIONS

The first dilemma to be resolved is the amount of international trade to include in the model. If import were used for investment as well as for consumption purposes, substitution in production as well as in consumption would have to be considered. An increase in the price of domestic factors would induce producers to switch to inputs of foreign origin and consumers to switch to foreign-produced consumers' goods. To the extent producers switch, the increase in cost per unit of domestic output is checked, for inputs of foreign origin are assumed to have constant prices. Consequently, the increase in price per unit of domestic output is checked, and the incentive for consumers to switch to foreign-produced consumers' goods is weakened. Since in this sense international substitution of input and international substitution in consumption are alternatives, we need include only one. In the short run, the substitution in consumption is likely to be greater; in fact, in the long run even many producers' goods imported by an industrialized economy are likely to be raw materials and fuels for which no domestic substitutes exist. Concentrating upon essentials, we shall assume that international substitution in consumption is not only the dominant but the sole substitution, the easiest way being to follow tradition in theory and assume import to be for consumption purposes only.[2] For values of the elasticities of foreign trade (in consumers' goods only) in our theoretical model we shall use estimates of the actual elasticities of foreign trade (in *all* goods) of the countries to which our model is applied. To the manipulation of the price of factors, then, the theoretical model should respond in essentially the same way as would actual foreign trade.

[2] The assumption that import is for consumption purposes only goes back to Lloyd A. Metzler, "Underemployment Equilibrium in International Trade," *Econometrica*, Vol. 10, No. 2 (April, 1942), pp. 97–112, or his "The Transfer Problem Reconsidered," *The Journal of Political Economy*, Vol. L, No. 3 (June, 1942), pp. 397–414, reprinted in *Readings in the Theory of International Trade*, Howard S. Ellis and Lloyd A. Metzler, eds. (Philadelphia: Blakiston, 1949), pp. 179–197.

Our assumptions give us three domestic purchase equations. First, planned purchases of domestic factors by domestic firms are assumed to be in direct proportion to planned domestic gross private product:

$$(1) \qquad *x_{hf} = a_{hf}*X_f$$

where a_{hf} is the proportionality factor representing the physical number of domestic factors purchased by domestic firms per unit of domestic gross private product.

Turning to consumption demand, we shall assume it to be a function of real disposable income, as carefully defined below. Absence of money illusions in consumers, which seems to be the best first approximation is not, of course, incompatible with presence of money illusions in labor union members in the sense that their representatives are bargaining primarily for higher *money* wage rates. For one thing, under decentralized bargaining a single industrial union may rightly ignore the simultaneous pressure that is possible from other unions. For another, even under centralized national bargaining of the Scandinavian type, a national labor union may rightly ignore the simultaneous pressure possible from other countries' unions. In an open economy very real gains from money wage increases are to be expected if prices of foreign-produced consumers' goods do not change.

A careful definition of real income in an open economy must distinguish between real income in terms of domestic goods and real income in terms of foreign goods. This distinction is made by assuming that planned purchases of domestic goods by domestic households are the following function:

$$(2) \quad *x_{fh} = a_{fh}\left[\frac{\pi_h(*\sigma_{hf} + *\sigma_{hg}) - *x_{gh}}{\pi_f}\right]^{e_{fh}}\left[\frac{\pi_h(*\sigma_{hf} + *\sigma_{hg}) - *x_{gh}}{\pi_F\rho}\right]^{E_{fh}}$$

where ρ is the exchange rate in number of domestic monetary units per foreign monetary unit, π_f the price of domestic goods charged by domestic firms, π_h the price of domestic factors charged by domestic households, π_F the price of foreign goods charged by foreign firms, e_{fh} the elasticity of domestic demand for domestic goods with respect to expected real disposable domestic income in terms of domestic goods, and E_{fh} the elasticity with respect to expected real disposable domestic income in terms of foreign goods. The elasticity with respect to expected money disposable income [the numerator of the bracketed expressions in (2)] is $e_{fh} + E_{fh}$. The domestic propensity to consume domestically produced goods out of money disposable domestic income is a_{fh} when $\pi_f = \pi_F \rho = 1$, and $e_{fh} + E_{fh} = 1$.

Third, planned purchases of foreign goods by domestic households are assumed to be the following function:

$$(3)\quad {}^*x_{Fh} = a_{Fh}\left[\frac{\pi_h({}^*\sigma_{hf} + {}^*\sigma_{hg}) - {}^*x_{gh}}{\pi_f}\right]^{e_{Fh}}\left[\frac{\pi_h({}^*\sigma_{hf} + {}^*\sigma_{hg}) - {}^*x_{gh}}{\pi_F \rho}\right]^{E_{Fh}}$$

where the elasticity of domestic demand for foreign goods is e_{Fh} with respect to expected real disposable domestic income in terms of domestic goods, and E_{Fh} with respect to expected real disposable domestic income in terms of foreign goods. The elasticity with respect to expected money disposable income is $e_{Fh} + E_{Fh}$. The domestic propensity to import foreign-produced goods out of money disposable domestic income is a_{Fh} when $\pi_f = \pi_F \rho = 1$, and $e_{Fh} + E_{Fh} = 1$.

The result that the money income elasticity is the sum of the two real income elasticities in terms of domestic and foreign goods, respectively, is a consequence of our eradicating the money illusion. In order to make this consequence perfectly clear to himself, the reader may wish, perhaps, to perform the three following hypothetical operations.

First, reducing the price π_f of domestic goods by one percent will result in an increase of one percent in domestic real disposable income in terms of domestic goods. According to (2) domestic demand for domestically produced goods ${}^*x_{fh}$ will then change by e_{fh} percent, and according to (3) domestic demand for foreign-produced goods ${}^*x_{Fh}$ will change by e_{Fh} percent.

Second, reducing the price π_F of foreign goods by one percent will result in an increase of one percent in domestic real disposable income in terms of foreign goods. According to (2) domestic demand for domestically produced goods $*x_{fh}$ will then change by E_{fh} percent, and according to (3) domestic demand for foreign-produced goods $*x_{Fh}$ will change by E_{Fh} percent.

Third, suppose that we had not reduced the price of domestic or foreign goods but instead had raised the domestic money disposable income by one percent while keeping all prices constant. Domestic real disposable income in terms of foreign, *as well as* domestic, goods would then have risen by one percent. According to (2) domestic demand for domestically produced goods $*x_{fh}$ would then have risen by $e_{fh} + E_{fh}$ percent, and according to (3) domestic demand for foreign-produced goods $*x_{Fh}$ would have risen by $e_{Fh} + E_{Fh}$ percent.

4. DOMESTIC FISCAL POLICY

The second dilemma to be resolved is the amount of fiscal policy to include in the model. Rather drastic simplification seems both possible and desirable. Tax policy is the only variation of fiscal policy considered. For balance of trade equalization the essential function of a tax is to absorb and destroy excess purchasing power, and for this purpose the personal income tax is as effective as any. If we are interested in the aggregate absorption and destruction of purchasing power rather than in its distribution among income brackets, the proportionate personal income tax is as useful as a progressive tax. Consequently, in our model the proportionate personal income tax will be the only tax considered. If the reader prefers, he may think of the rate a_{gh} of a proportionate household money income tax as being, in effect, a weighted average of all tax rates (one for each individual income bracket) included in a progressive income tax.

In Equations (2) and (3) expected disposable income equals expected personal income minus expected tax, where $*x_{gh}$ is expected tax payment, assumed to be in direct proportion to expected household money income:

$$(4) \qquad *x_{gh} = a_{gh}\pi_h(*\sigma_{hf} + *\sigma_{hg})$$

where a_{gh} is the income tax rate. Stripping (4) of all three asterisks will give Equation (5) determining realized tax payments, not written explicitly.

The fiscal policy of our economy is assumed to equalize the balance of trade:

$$(6) \qquad \pi_F\rho*x_{Fh} - \pi_f*x_{fH} = 0$$

where again ρ is the exchange rate and π_F and π_f the prices of foreign- and domestic-produced goods, respectively.

5. DOMESTIC PRICE POLICY

The third dilemma to be resolved is the dependence of the price of domestic goods upon the price of domestic factors. Again, we wish to keep our hypothesis simple yet realistic. For the moment, disregard the inputs of raw materials. Let labor input per unit of output be a constant, as assumed in (1). For the manufacturing industry such an assumption is undoubtedly realistic. Labor cost per unit of output will be in direct proportion to the wage rate. By profit margin is meant profit per unit of output. This margin, according to a widely used pricing practice,[3] will be in direct proportion to the labor cost per unit of output and consequently also in direct proportion to the wage rate. If the profit margin and the wage rate move proportionately, π_h may be used to represent both. Moreover, under the widely used practice mentioned, since the allowance for overhead cost per unit of output is in direct proportion to labor cost per unit of output, the price π_f of goods will be in direct proportion to the money value $\pi_h a_{hf}$ of the input of factors per unit of output, or

$$(7) \qquad \pi_f = \lambda\pi_h a_{hf}$$

---

[3] Cf. section 18 of chap. 7 and its microeconomic counterpart in equation (7a) of chap. 17.

where λ is the mark-up coefficient. Now let us take the inputs of raw materials into account. Since all raw materials used by domestic firms have been assumed to be of domestic origin their prices will be determined by the same formula, i.e., the full-cost principle, as the prices of the goods described above. Raw material cost per unit of output, then, is also in direct proportion to the wage rate, and the inclusion of raw material inputs will not necessitate any modification of Equation (7).

6. A FOREIGN PURCHASE EQUATION

The only foreign behavior equation in which we are interested is the demand equation for the domestically produced goods exported by the country to which we apply the model. Let planned purchases of domestic goods by foreign households be the following function:

$$(8) \qquad *x_{fH} = a_{fH} \left[\frac{*y}{\frac{\pi_f}{\rho}} \right]^{e_{fH}} \left[\frac{*y}{\pi_F} \right]^{\mathrm{E}_{fH}}$$

where $*y$ is expected money disposable foreign income (a parameter), and where the elasticity of foreign demand for domestic goods is e_{fH} with respect to expected real disposable foreign income in terms of domestic goods and E_{fH} with respect to expected real disposable foreign income in terms of foreign goods. The foreign propensity to import domestically produced goods out of money disposable foreign income is a_{fH} when $\pi_F = \pi_f/\rho = 1$, and $e_{fH} + E_{fH} = 1$.

To domestic and foreign consumers alike, domestic and foreign goods are assumed to be substitutes. Consequently, the elasticities e_{fh}, E_{Fh} and e_{fH}, are always positive, income and substitution effects pulling in the same direction. The elasticities E_{fh}, e_{Fh}, and E_{fH} may be positive or negative since income and substitution effects pull in opposite directions.

7. PRIVATE INVESTMENT AND GOVERNMENT PURCHASES

Expected gross private investment by domestic firms is assumed to be a parameter:

(9) $*x_{ff}$ = a parameter

Likewise, the planned government purchase of goods and of services, respectively, are assumed to be parameters:

(10) $*x_{fg}$ = a parameter

(11) $*x_{hg}$ = a parameter

8. EX ANTE–EX POST RELATIONSHIPS

In a buyer's market plans made at the beginning of the period are carried out during the period. Of our seven intersector purchases six are planned, but the seventh, the tax payment $*x_{gh}$, is expected—according to (3). For each of the six planned purchases we can express the realization of the plans:

(12) through (17) $*x_{ij} = x_{ij}$

where ij represents fh, hf, fH, Fh, fg, and hg, respectively.

In a buyer's market it can also be assumed that well-planned production goals will be realized:

(18) $*X_f = X_f$

Any sector's realized purchases from another sector constitutes the latter's realized sales to the former, a correspondence holding for all seven intersector transactions:

(19) through (25) $x_{ij} = \sigma_{ij}$

where ij represents fh, hf, fH, Fh, fg, hg, and gh respectively.

If equilibrium is to prevail, the activity of the economy must be self-justifying in the sense that any sector's expected sales to another sector must equal the former's realized sales, a correspondence holding for all seven intersector transactions:

(26) through (32) $\qquad *\sigma_{ij} = \sigma_{ij}$

where ij has the same alternative meanings as in (19) through (25).

9. DEFINITIONAL EQUATION

By definition, the domestic expected gross private investment is that part of the domestic gross private product which domestic firms do not expect to sell to domestic or foreign households or to government:

(33) $\qquad *x_{ff} = *X_f - (*\sigma_{fh} + *\sigma_{fH} + *\sigma_{fg})$

10. SOLUTION

Our unknowns are: one expected gross investment $*x_{ff}$, seven ex ante purchases $*x_{ij}$; seven ex post purchases x_{ij}; seven expected sales $*\sigma_{ij}$; seven realized sales σ_{ij}; one planned output $*X_f$; one realized output X_f; one price of domestically produced goods π_f; and one tax rate a_{gh}. In order to determine these 33 unknowns we have written 33 equations, some of which are nonlinear. Solving for equilibrium gross private product is difficult but possible, the mechanics being set out in the Appendix to this chapter. The solution is

(I) $\quad X_f = m_1 \pi_h^{(1 - e_{fH} - E_{Fh}) \frac{e_{fh} + E_{fh}}{e_{Fh} + E_{Fh}} + E_{fh}} + m_2 \pi_h^{-e_{fH}} + *x_{ff} + *x_{fg}$

where the coefficients m_1 and m_2 are the following agglomerations of our parameters:

$$m_1 = a_{fh} \left[\frac{a_{fH}}{a_{Fh}} *y^{e_{fH} + E_{fH}}\right]^{\frac{e_{fh} + E_{fh}}{e_{Fh} + E_{Fh}}} \left[\lambda a_{hf}\right]^{(1 - e_{fH} + e_{Fh}) \frac{e_{fh} + E_{fh}}{e_{Fh} + E_{Fh}} - e_{fh}}$$

$$\times \rho^{(e_{fH} - 1 + E_{Fh}) \frac{e_{fh} + E_{fh}}{e_{Fh} + E_{Fh}} - E_{fh}} \pi_F^{(-E_{fH} - 1 + E_{Fh}) \frac{e_{fh} + E_{fh}}{e_{Fh} + E_{Fh}} - E_{fh}}$$

$$m_2 = a_{fH} *y^{e_{fH} + E_{fH}} \left[\lambda a_{hf}\right]^{-e_{fH}} \rho^{e_{fH}} \pi_F^{-E_{fH}}$$

Taking the derivative of X_f with respect to π_h we get

$$(\text{II}) \quad \frac{dX_f}{d\pi_h} =$$

$$m_1 \left[(1 - e_{fH} - E_{Fh}) \frac{e_{fh} + E_{fh}}{e_{Fh} + E_{Fh}} + E_{fh} \right] \pi_h^{(1-e_{fH}-E_{Fh})\frac{e_{fh}+E_{fh}}{e_{Fh}+E_{Fh}}+E_{fh}-1}$$
$$- m_2 e_{fH} \pi_h^{-e_{fH}-1}$$

11. ELASTICITY MEASUREMENTS, GENERAL

The crucial elasticities appearing in (II) are E_{fh}, E_{Fh}, e_{fh}, e_{Fh}, and e_{fH}. Beginning with E_{Fh} and e_{fH}, we note that they have not been studied directly, although certain observations have been made of related elasticities. If the domestic demand elasticity of import with respect to domestic real income in terms of foreign goods is defined as we have defined it, as E_{Fh}, we can write the simple price elasticity of domestic demand for import as $-E_{Fh}$; likewise, we can write the price elasticity of foreign demand for imports as $-e_{fH}$. These two magnitudes have been studied quite intensively if not successfully.

Chang, in an article in the *Review of Economic Studies*,[4] estimated the elasticity of real import with respect to real income (or what we would call $e_{Fh} + E_{Fh}$) and the elasticity of real import with respect to relative price of import $-E_{Fh}$. In another article, this one in the *Review of Economics and Statistics*,[5] he estimated the elasticity of real export with respect to the relative price of export $-e_{fH}$. Orcutt[6] has argued convincingly that the Chang estimates are substantially under the numerical value of the export and import price elasticities. Brown[7] applied confluence analysis and

[4] Tse Chun Chang, "International Comparison of Demand for Imports," *The Review of Economic Studies*, Vol. XIII (2), No. 34 (1945–1946), pp. 53–67.

[5] Tse Chun Chang, "A Statistical Note on World Demand for Export," *The Review of Economics and Statistics*, Vol. XXX, No. 2 (May, 1948), pp. 106–116.

[6] Guy H. Orcutt, "Measurement of Price Elasticities in International Trade," *The Review of Economics and Statistics*, Vol. XXXII, No. 2 (May, 1950), pp. 117–132.

[7] A. J. Brown, "The Fundamental Elasticities in International Trade," *Oxford Studies in the Price Mechanism* (Oxford: Clarendon Press, 1951), pp. 91–106.

also demonstrated the inherent unreliability of Chang's estimates. Unlike Orcutt, Brown found the elasticity of substitution a more promising tool, one that Chang had used in his article in the *Review of Economics and Statistics*. More elasticities of substitution were estimated by Kubinski[8] and by Polak,[9] the latter having little faith in his own findings. Orcutt was not specific in his rejection of the elasticity of substitution, but Morgan and Corlett[10] delivered it a devastating blow. Furthermore, they applied the simultaneous equations approach developed by the Cowles Commission to this field but found it unsatisfactory. An equally convincing critique of the use of the elasticity of substitution in general was offered by Morrissett.[11]

The least negative conclusion to be drawn from the work of the several investigators seems to be that the Chang price elasticities were numerically too low.[12]

12. ELASTICITY MEASUREMENTS APPLIED TO OUR DERIVATIVE (II)

In establishing the sign of derivative (II) let us consider its two terms separately. Since m_2, e_{fH}, and π_h are always positive, the value of the last term of (II), which is preceded by a minus, is always negative. Next the first term. Since m_1 and π_h are

[8] Z. Kubinski, "The Elasticity of Substitution Between Sources of British Imports, 1921–1938," *Yorkshire Bulletin of Economic and Social Research*, Vol. 2, No. 1 (January, 1950), pp. 17–29, giving the estimates; and his "Measurements of Elasticity of Substitution in International Trade," *The South African Journal of Economics*, Vol. 22, No. 2 (June, 1954), pp. 210–222, devoted to methodology.

[9] J. J. Polak, *An International Economic System* (Chicago: The University of Chicago Press, 1953).

[10] D. J. Morgan and W. J. Corlett, "The Influence of Price in International Trade: A Study in Method," *Journal of the Royal Statistical Society*, Vol. CXIV, Part III (1951), pp. 307–358.

[11] Irving Morrissett, "Some Recent Uses of Elasticity of Substitution—A Survey," *Econometrica*, Vol. 21, No. 1 (Jan., 1953), pp. 41–62.

[12] Cf. Gottfried Haberler, *A Survey of International Trade Theory* (Princeton, Princeton University Press, 1955), p. 40; and Howard S. Ellis, *The Economics of Freedom, The Progress and Future of Aid to Europe* (New York: Harper, 1950), pp. 83–84.

always positive, the value of the first term of (II), which is preceded by a plus, will be negative if

$$(1 - e_{fH} - E_{Fh}) \frac{e_{fh} + E_{fh}}{e_{Fh} + E_{Fh}} + E_{fh} < 0$$

Deduct E_{fh} on both sides, divide on both sides by $e_{fh} + E_{fh}$, which is always positive, and get

(III) $$\frac{1 - e_{fH} - E_{Fh}}{e_{Fh} + E_{Fh}} < -\frac{E_{fh}}{e_{fh} + E_{fh}}$$

Realizing that the Chang price elasticities were numerically too low, using them for minima we calculate the left-hand side of the inequality (III). Table 8 contains such calculations for five countries of the type to which the present Chapter should apply—

TABLE 8.   Values of $\dfrac{1 - e_{fH} - E_{Fh}}{e_{Fh} + E_{Fh}}$

Based upon Chang's Elasticity
Estimates

Australia	− 0.12
Denmark	− 0.04
Norway	− 0.28
Sweden	+ 0.16
U.K.	+ 0.29

countries very dependent upon foreign trade and whose labor unions are capable of exerting a very powerful pressure upon the money wage rate.   Table 8 indicates that with the exception of Sweden and the United Kingdom the left-hand side of our inequality is negative but numerically small.   For Sweden and the United Kingdom it is positive but still numerically small.   Since the Chang estimates were probably too low, it seems fair to conclude that the true values would in all cases be negative and numerically larger than those shown in Table 8.   Values smaller than minus one should by no means be considered implausible.

In the absence of any empirical measurements, even unsuccessful ones, what can be said about the right-hand side of our inequality? First, the denominator $e_{fh} + E_{fh}$ is the elasticity of domestic demand for domestically produced goods with respect to expected money disposable domestic income. Dismissing without hesitation the possibility that domestic output as a whole is an inferior good, we can safely say that this income elasticity must be positive. But what is its numerical value? Let us go back to Chang. With the exception of the United Kingdom, he found the income elasticities of import $e_{Fh} + E_{Fh}$ to be rather high—around $+2.00$. Although his income elasticities may be on the high side, they appear to be much more reliable than are his price elasticities. Should import be for consumption purposes only, as we have assumed, the income elasticity of domestic output $e_{fh} + E_{fh}$ would be correspondingly low, for the income elasticity of *all* consumption (of imported as well as of domestically made goods) must be one or just below one. Since e_{fh} is known to be always positive and since $e_{fh} + E_{fh}$ must be one or just below one, the conclusion can be drawn that E_{fh} must be either positive while considerably smaller than one or negative. E_{fh} was the elasticity of domestic demand for domestic goods with respect to expected real disposable domestic income in terms of foreign goods. If in the domestic market the income effect is large relative to the substitution effect, E_{fh} would be positive: a falling price of foreign-produced goods would *raise* the domestic consumption of domestically produced goods. If, on the other hand, the income effect were small relative to the substitution effect, E_{fh} would be negative: a falling price of foreign-produced goods would *reduce* the domestic consumption of domestically produced goods.

When the income effect is relatively small in comparison with the substitution effect, the right-hand side of our inequality (III) will be positive, the inequality then being easily satisfied. In such a case, both terms of (II) are negative: if wages rise, output falls. However, when the income effect is large relative to the substitution effect, we cannot be so sure. Since E_{fh} is then positive, the entire right-hand side is negative.   Both sides being then negative, the sign of (II) would depend upon numerical values.   If positive, E_{fh} is numerically smaller than one.   If the income elasticity of domestic output $e_{fh} + E_{fh}$ is not too low, the right-hand side of our inequality can still be numerically low enough to satisfy the inequality.   But our assumption is that imports are for consumption purposes only.   Once that assumption is relaxed and durable producers' goods constitute a large proportion of imports, it is possible that imports will be an extremely steep function of national output.[13]   In such cases a high income elasticity of import, $e_{Fh} + E_{Fh}$, would not necessarily be accompanied by a low income elasticity of domestically produced goods, $e_{fh} + E_{fh}$; both could be high.   And E_{fh}, if positive, would not have to be considerably smaller than one; consequently, on the right-hand side of our inequality (III) we might have a rather high numerical value of E_{fh} divided by a rather high value of $e_{fh} + E_{fh}$.   Whether these values would satisfy our inequality (III) cannot be known a priori.   But even if they did not, the sign of the entire derivative (II) might still, of course, be minus because the second term of (II) is always negative.

In summary, when in the domestic market the income effect is small relative to the substitution effect and when the foreign-trade accelerator effect must be modest, we have a clear answer—raising the price of factors must reduce output and employment.   Given conditions other than these, there is a remote possibility that output and employment may rise.

13. CONCLUSION

Derivative (II) of Chapter 7 shows that in a closed economy should the price of all factors rise at constant price of goods, the equilibrium gross private product, and with it employment, would rise.   As we have said, at least five important qualifications of this proposition must be made.   The first was that the price of goods

---

[13] Cf. chap. 24, pp. 292–293.

will rise with the price of factors. Our second qualification, developed in the present chapter, simply applies the first to the case of an open economy. Here, the price of *domestically* produced goods will rise as a consequence of an increase in the price of domestic factors just as in a closed economy. But the price of *foreign*-produced goods will not rise as long as the price of foreign factors does not rise. Hence the threatening substitution by domestic households, labor households among them, of foreign-produced goods for domestically produced ones. Far from implying that our conclusion—raising the price of factors in an open economy is likely to affect employment adversely—is infallible, we submit it as a first approximation to reality and invite further study of this important problem.

APPENDIX: THE MECHANICS OF FINDING THE SOLUTION (I)

Using (12) through (32) and taking (1), (2), (4), and (6) together we get:

$$x_{fh} = a_{fh}[(a_{hf}X_f + x_{hg})(1 - a_{gh})]^{e_{fh}+E_{fh}} \pi_h{}^{E_{fh}} (\lambda a_{hf})^{-e_{fh}} (\pi_F \rho)^{-E_{fh}}$$

Taking (1), (3), (4), (6), and (7) together, inserting into (5), we get:

$$[(a_{hf}X_f + x_{hg})(1 - a_{gh})]^{e_{Fh}+E_{Fh}}$$
$$= \frac{a_{fH}}{a_{Fh}} *y^{e_{fH}+E_{fH}} \pi_h{}^{1-e_{fH}-E_{Fh}} (\lambda a_{hf})^{1-e_{fH}+e_{Fh}} \rho^{e_{fH}-1+E_{Fh}} \pi_F{}^{-E_{fH}-1+E_{Fh}}$$

Take the $(e_{Fh} + E_{Fh})$th root on each side of this equation, insert the value of $(a_{hf}X_f + x_{hg})(1 - a_{gh})$ thus found into the equation found above for x_{fh}; use the auxiliary symbol m_1 and write

$$x_{fh} = m_1 \pi_h{}^{(1-e_{fH}-E_{Fh})\frac{e_{fh}+E_{fh}}{e_{Fh}+E_{Fh}}+E_{fh}}$$

the first term of (I). Using (6) and the auxiliary symbol m_2, next write equation (7) as

$$x_{fH} = m_2 \pi_h{}^{-e_{fH}}$$

the second term of (I). The values found for x_{fh} and x_{fH} inserted into (11) with (8) and (9) give the complete Equation (I).

12

The Static Open Leontief Model

1. INTERINDUSTRY ARITHMETIC

To visualize the allocation problem in its most simple form, let us disregard the government and imagine an economy with only three sectors: manufacturing, agriculture, and households. The output in this economy will consist of two different categories of goods, manufactured goods and agricultural goods or, as we may briefly call them, "manufactures" and "produce." Manufactures are absorbed by households for purposes of consumption, and let us assume that the number needed for this purpose is 40. Manufactures are also absorbed by agriculture in the form of inputs (fuels, implements, etc.); let us assume that for each unit of output of produce agriculture will absorb 0.5 units of manufactures as inputs. Produce is absorbed by households for purposes of consumption; let the number needed for this purpose be 16. Produce is also absorbed by manufacturing industry as an input (cotton, hides, etc.); for each unit of output of manufactures let 0.4 units of produce be absorbed as inputs. Under these assumptions what will be the equilibrium outputs of our two industries?

The answer is that the economy must produce 60 units of manufactures and 40 units of produce. The proof follows. Of the 60 units of manufactures produced, households take 40, 20 remaining. Since each of the 40 units of produce requires 0.5 units of manufactures as input, the total agricultural demand for manufactured inputs will be exactly the 20 units of manufactures that remain. Manufacturing industry sells 40 units to households and 20 units to agriculture; accordingly, manufacturing inventories will neither rise nor fall, and equilibrium is achieved. Agriculture produces 40 units; households take 16 of these, leaving 24 units for manufacturing industry, exactly the number manufacturing industry needs, because for each of the 60 units of manufactures produced, 0.4 unit of produce is required as input. Agriculture sells its 40 units of produce: 16 to households and 24 to manufacturing industry; thus inventory is neither accumulated nor depleted, and again equilibrium is achieved.

If the outputs of our two industries are any different, equilibrium cannot be reached. For example, suppose merely 50 units of manufactures are produced but that the output of produce is still 40. Households take, as before, 40 units of manufactures, leaving only 10 for agriculture instead of the 20 needed (0.5 times 40). Supplying the difference, available only from inventory, causes manufacturing industry to suffer an inventory depletion of 10, disequilibrium resulting. Nor is there equilibrium in agriculture. Of the 40 units of output of produce, households take 16, leaving 24 units, a surplus of 4 units, for manufacturing industry, which needs merely 0.4 times 50 which is 20. Agricultural inventory accumulates 4 units. The over-all result, then, is that manufacturing industry is underproducing and agriculture overproducing. Obviously, disequilibrium must result in *both* industries as soon as the outputs are not exactly 60 units of manufactures and 40 units of produce.

2. THE ALGEBRA OF INTERINDUSTRY RELATIONS

When disaggregation is carried to its logical end, the Leontief input-output model emerges: consider an $(m + 1)$-sector model of stationary equilibrium. Let the $m + 1$st sector be entrepreneur households; the mth sector labor households, and the remaining $m - 1$ sectors firm sectors. Each firm sector produces only one product. This product is demanded, first by the firm sectors using it for an input, second by the household sectors consuming it. Output must equal total demand for every product. The labor household sector is selling man-hours to the $m - 1$ firm sectors. The remuneration, the wage bill, constitutes income from the point of view of the labor households. But from the point of view of the firms, the wage bill constitutes an element of cost. The other elements of cost are the money values of inputs absorbed from firms. To any firm sector the difference between its revenue and cost constitutes its profit earnings, to be distributed as dividends to the entrepreneur household sector. The peculiarity of the open Leontief model is that household demand for consumers' goods is a parameter. More specifically, demand is *not* a function of household income. The notation follows:

Variables

c_j = the number of dollars of cost incurred annually by industry j

p_j = the number of dollars of profits earned annually by industry j

X_j = output of goods produced by sector j, in physical number of goods per unit of time

x_{ij} = purchase of product or factor of sector i by sector j, in physical number of goods or factors per unit of time, except $*x_{jm}$ and $*x_{j(m+1)}$

σ_{ij} = sale of product or factor of sector i to sector j. Dimension: same as for x_{ij}

Parameters

a_{ij} = the number of physical units of the product of industry i absorbed per physical unit of product of industry j

π_j = the price of the output produced by industry j

$*x_{jm}$ = autonomous labor household demand

$*x_{j(m+1)}$ = autonomous entrepreneur household demand

3. INTERFIRM INPUT-OUTPUT TRANSACTIONS

Let any firm sector absorb inputs from all firm sectors, including itself. Since the input-output coefficient a_{ij} is the number of physical units of the product of industry i to be absorbed per unit of product of industry j, we have the $(m - 1)^2$ equations:

$$(1) \qquad *x_{ij} = a_{ij}*X_j \qquad \text{for} \qquad i, j = 1 \cdots m - 1$$

4. LABOR INPUT

Let any firm sector absorb inputs of man-hours from the labor household sector. Since input-output coefficient a_{mj} is the number of man-hours absorbed per unit of product of industry j, we have the $m - 1$ equations:

$$(2) \qquad *x_{mj} = a_{mj}*X_j \qquad \text{for} \qquad j = 1 \cdots m - 1$$

5. ENTREPRENEUR INPUT

Let any firm sector absorb inputs of entrepreneur service from the entrepreneur household sector. In quantitative terms such inputs can be expressed only as dividends received by entrepreneurs in return. Thus we have the $m - 1$ equations:

$$(3) \qquad *x_{(m+1)j} = *p_j \qquad \text{for} \qquad j = 1 \cdots m - 1$$

6. LABOR HOUSEHOLD DEMAND

Let labor households consume the output of any firm sector, and let the physical quantity of each output demanded be a parameter. We get $m - 1$ equations:

$$(4) \qquad *x_{jm} = \text{a parameter} \qquad \text{for} \qquad j = 1 \cdots m - 1$$

7. ENTREPRENEUR HOUSEHOLD DEMAND

Entrepreneur households, too, consume the output of any firm sector. Let the physical quantity of each output demanded be a parameter. Again we obtain $m - 1$ equations:

$$(5) \qquad *x_{j(m+1)} = \text{a parameter} \qquad \text{for} \qquad j = 1 \cdots m - 1$$

8. DEFINITION OF PROFITS

In Equation (3) expected profits served as the independent variable. Applying the familiar microeconomic definition of profits as revenue minus cost, we have the $m - 1$ ex ante definitions:

$$(6) \qquad *p_j = \pi_j \sum_{i=1}^{m+1} *\sigma_{ji} - *c_j \qquad \text{for} \qquad j = 1 \cdots m - 1$$

Removing the asterisks, we get another set of $m - 1$ ex post definitions of profits, constituting the system (7), not written.

9. DEFINITION OF COST

In Equation (6) planned cost served as the independent variable. Applying the familiar microeconomic definition of cost as the money value of all inputs, we have the $m - 1$ ex ante definitions:

$$(8) \qquad *c_j = \sum_{i=1}^{m} (\pi_i *x_{ij}) \qquad \text{for} \qquad j = 1 \cdots m - 1$$

Removing the asterisks, we get another set of $m - 1$ ex post definitions of cost, constituting the system (9), not written.

10. ABSENCE OF EXPECTED INVENTORY CHANGE

If expected inventory is neither to accumulate nor be depleted, output of any sector must equal the demand for this output. We get the $m - 1$ equations:

$$(10) \qquad *X_j = \sum_{i=1}^{m+1} *\sigma_{ji} \qquad \text{for} \qquad j = 1 \cdots m - 1$$

11. PRODUCTION PLANS ARE ALWAYS REALIZED

In Equation (10) planned output served as the dependent variables. Assuming that production plans are always realized, we have the following $m - 1$ equations:

(11) $$*X_j = X_j \qquad \text{for} \qquad j = 1 \cdots m - 1$$

12. OTHER EX ANTE—EX POST RELATIONSHIPS

There are another three ex ante—ex post relationships. First, purchase plans are always realized, second, what is purchased is sold, and third (if equilibrium is to prevail) expected sales must equal realized sales. Three groups of equations correspond:

(12) $$*x_{ij} = x_{ij}$$
(13) $$x_{ij} = \sigma_{ij}$$
(14) $$*\sigma_{ij} = \sigma_{ij}$$

Each of the three groups (12) through (14) includes $(m - 1)^2 + 4(m - 1)$ equations: Every firm sector absorbs inputs from all firm sectors, giving us $(m - 1)^2$ transactions. Furthermore, the firm sector absorbs inputs from both household sectors, such inputs constituting an additional $2(m - 1)$ transactions. Finally, either of the two household sectors consumes the output of any firm sector, resulting in an additional $2(m - 1)$ transactions.

13. COUNTING EQUATIONS AND UNKNOWNS

Groups of equations (1) through (14) contain in total $4(m - 1)^2 + 22(m - 1)$ equations. The number of unknowns is as follows. There are $(m - 1)^2 + 4(m - 1)$ transactions within each of the four categories $*x_{ij}$, x_{ij}, $*\sigma_{ij}$, and σ_{ij}. There are $m - 1$ variables in each of the six categories $*X_j$, X_j, $*p_j$, p_j, $*c_j$, and c_j. Consequently, within the present system, the total number of unknowns equals the total number of equations.

14. SOLUTION

Using equations (1), (4), (5), (11), (12), (13), and (14) upon (10), the latter can be written as shown in Table 9 or in more compact

TABLE 9. System of $(m - 1)$ Equations Determining the $(m - 1)$ Outputs X_j

$$+ (1 - a_{11})X_1 - a_{12}X_2 \quad - \cdots - a_{1(m-1)}X_{m-1} \quad = *x_{1m} \quad + *x_{1(m+1)}$$

$$- a_{21}X_1 \quad + (1 - a_{22})X_2 - \cdots - a_{2(m-1)}X_{m-1} \quad = *x_{2m} \quad + *x_{2(m+1)}$$

$$\cdots \cdots \cdots \cdots \cdots \cdots \cdots \cdots$$

$$- a_{(m-1)1}X_1 \quad - a_{(m-1)2}X_2 \quad - \cdots + [1 - a_{(m-1)(m-1)}]X_{m-1} = *x_{(m-1)m} + *x_{(m-1)(m+}$$

matrix notation as

$$\mathbf{AX} = \mathbf{y}$$

where $\mathbf{A}$ is the $(m - 1)(m - 1)$ square matrix whose non-diagonal elements are $-a_{ij}$, and whose diagonal elements are $1 - a_{jj}$. The latter are assumed to be positive; indeed, since Leontief's own definition of net output excluded x_{jj}, $a_{jj} = 0$. All other elements are nonpositive.[1] As to the other terms, $\mathbf{X}$ is a column vector of $m - 1$ variables X_j and $\mathbf{y}$ a column vector of the parameters $*x_{jm} + *x_{j(m+1)}$. The square matrix $\mathbf{A}$ is assumed to be of the rank $m - 1$; consequently a unique solution for outputs X_j exists.[2]

Having solved for outputs, we now solve for employment and incomes. Equation (2) determines employment. Employment multiplied by the wage rate π_m is the wage bill. Equations (1)

[1] An element may have the value zero. If $a_{ij} = 0$, industry j does not use industry i's product for an input. Indeed, in the Bureau of Labor Statistics input-output-coefficients matrix for the year 1947, in which $m - 1 = 45$, no less than 633 out of the 2,025 coefficients were zero; see W. Duane Evans and Marvin Hoffenberg, "The Interindustry Relations Study for 1947," *The Review of Economics and Statistics*, Vol. XXXIV, No. 2 (May, 1952), Table 5, p. 142.

[2] On linear equations and their solution, see R. G. D. Allen, *Mathematical Economics* (London: Macmillan, 1956), pp. 453–461; or D. W. Bushaw and R. W. Clower, *Introduction to Mathematical Economics*, chap. 11, section 6 (Homewood, Ill.: Irwin, 1957).

and (2) inserted into (8), and (8) and (10) then inserted into (6) disclose the amount of profits earned in each firm sector; the total of all such amounts is the aggregate of profit. Since further simplification may be useful, let us consider the simplest possible case of the static open Leontief model.

15. TWO FIRM SECTORS, TWO HOUSEHOLD SECTORS

The simplest possible case is that of $m = 3$, indicating only two firm sectors and two household sectors. Further simplifying, assume each industry's demand for its own output per unit of output (a_{jj}) to be zero. The solution for outputs is

$$\text{(I)} \qquad X_1 = \frac{{}^*x_{13} + {}^*x_{14} + a_{12}({}^*x_{23} + {}^*x_{24})}{1 - a_{12}a_{21}}$$

$$\text{(II)} \qquad X_2 = \frac{{}^*x_{23} + {}^*x_{24} + a_{21}({}^*x_{13} + {}^*x_{14})}{1 - a_{12}a_{21}}$$

The solution for employment is

$$\text{(III)} \qquad x_{31} = a_{31}X_1$$

$$\text{(IV)} \qquad x_{32} = a_{32}X_2$$

The solution for the wage bill is, of course, $\pi_3(x_{31} + x_{32})$. The solution for profits is

$$\text{(V)} \qquad p_1 = X_1(\pi_1 - \pi_2 a_{21} - \pi_3 a_{31})$$

$$\text{(VI)} \qquad p_2 = X_2(\pi_2 - \pi_1 a_{12} - \pi_3 a_{32})$$

In solutions (V) and (VI) the three prices π_1, π_2, and π_3 are parameters, upon which certain restrictions must be imposed. Taking technology and autonomous demand for granted and assuming that both outputs X_1 and X_2 are positive and finite, we shall find such restrictions for the price ratios π_1/π_3 and π_2/π_3. We are using the wage rate π_3 as the *numéraire*; no restrictions exist for the absolute prices.

16. RELATIVE PRICE BOUNDARIES: NONNEGATIVE PROFITS

The two price ratios must be such that the profits of the two firm sectors are nonnegative.   Setting $p_1 \geqq 0$ and $p_2 \geqq 0$ one finds the following pair of conditions: If the first firm sector's profits are to be nonnegative, the following must hold:

$$(15) \qquad \frac{\pi_1}{\pi_3} \geqq a_{21}\frac{\pi_2}{\pi_3} + a_{31}$$

If the second firm sector's profits are to be nonnegative, the following must hold:

$$(16) \qquad \frac{\pi_1}{\pi_3} \leqq \frac{1}{a_{12}}\frac{\pi_2}{\pi_3} - \frac{a_{32}}{a_{12}}$$

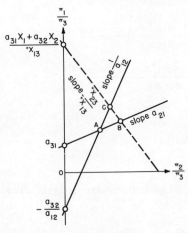

Figure 36

Conditions (15) and (16) can be shown graphically as follows. In Figure 36 (15) is observed to be satisfied by all points lying upon or above the straight line through A and B, and condition (16) by all points lying upon or below the straight line through A and C.   Consequently, if both firm sectors are to have nonnegative profits, the price ratios π_1/π_3 and π_2/π_3

will have to be combined at a point lying inside the cone CAB. Will a cone like CAB always exist in the first quadrant?   A closer examination of the intercepts and the slopes of AB and AC will produce an affirmative answer. AB has the positive intercept a_{31} with the vertical axis and has the positive slope a_{21}. AC has the negative intercept $-a_{32}/a_{12}$ with the vertical axis and has the positive slope $1/a_{12}$.   For positive and finite outputs X_1 and X_2 their common denominator must be positive, i.e., $1 - a_{12}a_{21} > 0$.

Hence $1/a_{12} > a_{21}$; therefore, AC is steeper than AB. The steeper line having a negative intercept and the flatter line having a positive intercept, the two can only intersect in the first quadrant.

Conditions (15) and (16) accord fully with Leontief tradition. Leontief assumed the value of the output of each industry to be equal to the value of *all* goods and services absorbed by that industry. However, some services were absorbed from households in the form of "capital and entrepreneurial services," and Leontief explicitly refused to distinguish between interest payments, entrepreneurial returns, monopolistic revenue, and windfall profits.[3] Thus Leontief never committed himself to any particular assumption about market structure and most certainly did not assume competition to be pure.

17. NONNEGATIVE SAVING WITHIN EACH HOUSEHOLD SECTOR?

If we begin with the strong requirement that within each particular household sector savings must be nonnegative, the total wage bill minus labor's autonomous consumption demand must also be nonnegative:

$$(17) \qquad \pi_3(a_{31}X_1 + a_{32}X_2) - (*x_{13}\pi_1 + *x_{23}\pi_2) \geqq 0$$

and total profits minus entrepreneurial autonomous consumption demand also must be nonnegative:

$$(18) \qquad p_1 + p_2 - (*x_{14}\pi_1 + *x_{24}\pi_2) \geqq 0$$

Into (18) insert the definitions (V) and (VI), use the familiar Leontief equilibrium condition that the output of any industrial sector equals the sum of the demands for it, and prove that inequality (18) is identical to inequality (17) with the inequality

---

[3] Wassily W. Leontief, *The Structure of American Economy, 1919–1929* (Cambridge, Mass.: Harvard University Press, 1941), or enlarged edition (New York: Oxford University Press, 1951), pp. 25 and 36 in both editions.

sign of the latter reversed. But if so, their equality signs must hold, their inequality signs ignored, indicating that both household sectors must have zero saving. In (17), divide through by the *numéraire* π_3, ignore the inequality sign, and get

$$(17a) \qquad \frac{\pi_1}{\pi_3} = - \frac{{}^*x_{23}\pi_2}{{}^*x_{13}\pi_3} + \frac{a_{31}X_1 + a_{32}X_2}{{}^*x_{13}}$$

Condition (17a) can be shown graphically as follows. In Figure 36 (17a) is seen to be satisfied by all points lying upon the straight broken line through B and C. BC has the positive intercept $(a_{31}X_1 + a_{32}X_2)/{}^*x_{13}$ with the vertical axis and has the negative slope $-{}^*x_{23}/{}^*x_{13}$. In the graph as drawn it is possible to satisfy all three conditions: Any point on the line BC between the points B and C satisfies them. On the other hand, there may be no point satisfying all three conditions. If BC had intersected the two positively sloped lines AB and AC *below* their intersection point A, there would have existed no point which would have satisfied all three conditions. Such a possibility of nonexistence is not surprising. It would have been absurd indeed to have expected a set of positive relative prices always to exist, guaranteeing firms against losses and households against deficits, irrespective of the productivity of labor and irrespective of the size of autonomous consumption demand. But let us now relax our requirement a bit.

18. ZERO HOUSEHOLD SAVING FOR BOTH HOUSEHOLD SECTORS, TAKEN TOGETHER

Since the requirement that household saving must be zero within each household sector may seem much too strong, let us replace it by the requirement that *taken together*, all household sectors must have zero saving, thus permitting one household sector to dissave while the other would save an equivalent amount. Consequently, add the left-hand sides of (17) and (18) and set the total equal to zero. Then, by using the definitions (V) and (VI) and the equality between output of any industrial sector and the sum of the demands for such output, the identity $0 = 0$ is found; we see that any set of π_1/π_3 and π_2/π_3 will satisfy our new and weaker requirement, and we are left with merely conditions (15) and (16). As we have seen, a comfortably large space within the first quadrant will always be available to satisfy those conditions.

19. APPLICATION: TECHNOLOGICAL PROGRESS IN THE OPEN MODEL

The Leontief model as an interindustry demand model is admirably suited to the analysis of technological progress. Technological progress may be thought of as a reduction of an input-output coefficient a_{ij} meaning that the jth industry has now organized its production or distribution processes more efficiently, producing the same output with less input absorbed from industry i. What is the effect of such technological progress upon outputs X_1 and X_2? Examine the derivatives:

$$\text{(VII)} \qquad \frac{dX_1}{da_{12}} = \frac{X_2}{1 - a_{12}a_{21}}$$

$$\text{(VIII)} \qquad \frac{dX_2}{da_{12}} = \frac{a_{21}X_2}{1 - a_{12}a_{21}}$$

What are the signs of these derivatives? First, let us observe that for positive and finite outputs X_1 and X_2 their common denominator in (I) and (II) must be positive, i.e., $1 - a_{12}a_{21} > 0$. Second, that an input-output coefficient like a_{21} is always positive. Hence, both derivatives (VII) and (VIII) are unquestionably positive. Hence a reduction of the input-output coefficient a_{12} resulting from technological progress will reduce both outputs X_1 and X_2.

A reduction of a_{12} causes $1/a_{12}$, the slope of AC (the steepest of the two lines in Figure 36) to rise. Hence the area satisfying conditions (15) and (16) increases. If relative prices π_1/π_3 and π_2/π_3

satisfied the stated conditions before the technological progress occurred, they would continue to do so afterwards. In our application of the open model to technological progress we may, therefore, ignore the relative price boundaries. The result that technological progress unequivocally reduces all output is peculiar to the open model. In Chapter 13 we shall close the model and render that result invalid.

20. A CRITIQUE OF THE STATIC OPEN LEONTIEF MODEL

The theory of general economic interdependence was first developed by Walras.[4] However, the theory in its Walrasian form was characterized by a very large number of variables between which relationships were postulated but not specified. Thus it was long on generality, short on substance.

Walras himself never thought of putting his model to practical use by estimating its parameters empirically, a mission later accomplished by Leontief.[5] But before Leontief could succeed, heroic simplification was necessary: (1) input-output functions were assumed to be linear and homogeneous; (2) supply limits were ignored; (3) price was suppressed as a variable; and (4) that great Keynesian discovery, the consumption function, found no

[4] Leon Walras, *Eléments d'économie politique pure* (Lausanne: Corbaz, 1874), translated by W. Jaffe and published as *Elements of Pure Economics* (Homewood, Ill.: Irwin, 1954).

[5] Wassily W. Leontief, *The Structure of American Economy, 1919–1929* (Cambridge, Mass.: Harvard University Press, 1941), or enlarged edition (New York: Oxford University Press, 1951); Wassily Leontief, "Static and Dynamic Theory," Part I of *Studies in the Structure of the American Economy* (New York: Oxford University Press, 1953); Robert Dorfman, "The Nature and Significance of Input-Output," *The Review of Economics and Statistics*, Vol. XXXVI, No. 2 (May, 1954), pp. 121–133; and Leonid Hurwicz, "Input-Output Analysis and Economic Structure," *The American Economic Review*, Vol. XLV, No. 4 (Sept., 1955), pp. 626–636. For further analysis of the Leontief model, see R. G. D. Allen, *Mathematical Economics* (London: Macmillan, 1956), chap. 11; and Robert Dorfman, Paul A. Samuelson, and Robert M. Solow, *Linear Programming and Economic Analysis* (New York: McGraw-Hill, 1958), chaps. 9 and 10.

place in the open Leontief model, because nonindustry demand, called the "final bill of goods," was assumed to be independent of employment and output. The lack of generality in each of these respects was the price to be paid, at least in the early stage of the inquiry, for a model whose parameters could be estimated statistically.

13

Closing the Open Leontief Model

1. TYING TOGETHER TWO LOOSE ENDS OF THE OPEN MODEL

The model developed in the previous chapter has two loose ends. One is labor and entrepreneur household incomes as determined by Equations (2) and (3), the other labor and entrepreneur consumption demand as determined by Equations (4) and (5). These two ends could be connected if labor household demand for the various goods were to be made a function of employment and entrepreneur household demand for the various goods similarly a function of entrepreneur income (profits). Income, to be sure, is not the only variable determining household demand, but it may well be the most important one. Other variables are goods prices, fashion changes, age distribution, and marital status of the population, etc., all of which we shall ignore.[1]

2. INDUCED LABOR HOUSEHOLD DEMAND

Replace Equation (4) in the preceding chapter by

$$(4a) \quad {}^*x_{jm} = A_{jm} + a_{jm} \sum_{j=1}^{m-1} {}^*\sigma_{mj} \quad \text{for} \quad j = 1 \cdots m - 1$$

[1] Ignoring relative goods prices is more objectionable in the consumption sphere than in the production sphere. Substitution in the former is far more important

where A_{jm} is the autonomous labor household demand for the jth commodity, a_{jm} the marginal propensity of labor households to consume the jth commodity, and $*\sigma_{mj}$ the total employment expected by labor households. Using (12) through (14) and (2), we write (4a) as follows:

$$(4b) \quad *x_{jm} = A_{jm} + a_{jm} \sum_{j=1}^{m-1} (a_{mj}*X_j) \quad \text{for} \quad j = 1 \cdots m - 1$$

3. INDUCED ENTREPRENEUR HOUSEHOLD DEMAND

Replace Equation (5) in the preceding chapter by

$$(5a) \quad *x_{j(m+1)} = A_{j(m+1)} + a_{j(m+1)} \sum_{j=1}^{m-1} *p_j \quad \text{for} \quad j = 1 \cdots m - 1$$

where $A_{j(m+1)}$ is the autonomous entrepreneur household demand for the jth commodity, $a_{j(m+1)}$ the marginal propensity of entrepreneur households to consume the jth commodity, and $*p_j$ the amount of profits expected by entrepreneur households [defined by Equation (6) in the preceding chapter]. After inserting (1) and (2) into (8) and both the outcome and Equation (10) into (6), we write (5a) as follows:

$$(5b) \quad *x_{j(m+1)} = A_{j(m+1)} + a_{j(m+1)} \left\{ *X_1\left[\pi_1 - \sum_{i=1}^{m} (\pi_i a_{i1})\right] \right.$$

$$+ *X_2\left[\pi_2 - \sum_{i=1}^{m} (\pi_i a_{i2})\right]$$

$$\cdot$$
$$\cdot$$
$$\cdot$$

$$\left. + *X_{m-1}\left[\pi_{m-1} - \sum_{i=1}^{m} (\pi_i a_{i(m-1)})\right]\right\}$$

$$\text{for} \quad j = 1 \cdots m - 1$$

---

than in the latter, as pointed out by James S. Duesenberry and Helen Kistin in "The Role of Demand in the Economic Structure," *Studies in the Structure of the American Economy*, Leontief, ed. (New York: Oxford University Press, 1953), pp. 452–453.

4. SOLUTION

The closed model now under scrutiny contains exactly the same number of equations and unknowns as included in the open model discussed in the preceding chapter, the only difference being that the two equations (4) and (5) have been replaced by new equations

TABLE 10.   System of $(m-1)$ Equations Determining the $(m-1)$ Outputs X_j

$$
\begin{aligned}
\alpha_{11}X_1 + \alpha_{12}X_2 + \cdots + \alpha_{1(m-1)}X_{m-1} &= A_{1m} + A_{1(m+1)} \\
\alpha_{21}X_1 + \alpha_{22}X_2 + \cdots + \alpha_{2(m-1)}X_{m-1} &= A_{2m} + A_{2(m+1)} \\
\cdots \qquad\qquad\qquad\qquad\qquad\qquad & \\
\alpha_{(m-1)1}X_1 + \alpha_{(m-1)2}X_2 + \cdots + \alpha_{(m-1)(m-1)}X_{m-1} &= A_{(m-1)m} + A_{(m-1)(m+1)}
\end{aligned}
$$

TABLE 11.   Definitions of the α's

$$
\alpha_{11} = 1 - a_{11} - a_{1m}a_{m1} - a_{1(m+1)}\left[\pi_1 - \sum_{i=1}^{m}(\pi_i a_{i1})\right]
$$

$$
\alpha_{12} = -a_{12} - a_{1m}a_{m2} - a_{1(m+1)}\left[\pi_2 - \sum_{i=1}^{m}(\pi_i a_{i2})\right]
$$

$$
\alpha_{1(m-1)} = -a_{1(m-1)} - a_{1m}a_{m(m-1)} - a_{1(m+1)}\left[\pi_{m-1} - \sum_{i=1}^{m}(\pi_i a_{i(m-1)})\right]
$$

$$
\alpha_{21} = -a_{21} - a_{2m}a_{m1} - a_{2(m+1)}\left[\pi_1 - \sum_{i=1}^{m}(\pi_i a_{i1})\right]
$$

$$
\alpha_{22} = 1 - a_{22} - a_{2m}a_{m2} - a_{2(m+1)}\left[\pi_2 - \sum_{i=1}^{m}(\pi_i a_{i2})\right]
$$

$$
\alpha_{2(m-1)} = -a_{2(m-1)} - a_{2m}a_{m(m-1)} - a_{2(m+1)}\left[\pi_{m-1} - \sum_{i=1}^{m}(\pi_i a_{i(m-1)})\right]
$$

$$
\alpha_{(m-1)1} = -a_{(m-1)1} - a_{(m-1)m}a_{m1} - a_{(m-1)(m+1)}\left[\pi_1 - \sum_{i=1}^{m}(\pi_i a_{i1})\right]
$$

$$
\alpha_{(m-1)2} = -a_{(m-1)2} - a_{(m-1)m}a_{m2} - a_{(m-1)(m+1)}\left[\pi_2 - \sum_{i=1}^{m}(\pi_i a_{i2})\right]
$$

$$
\alpha_{(m-1)(m-1)} = 1 - a_{(m-1)(m-1)} - a_{(m-1)m}a_{m(m-1)} - a_{(m-1)(m+1)}\left[\pi_{m-1} - \sum_{i=1}^{m}(\pi_i a_{i(m-1)})\right]
$$

(4a) and (5a) which contain no new unknowns. After suitable substitutions are made, Equation (10) can be written as a system of $m - 1$ equations in the $m - 1$ unknowns X_1 through X_{m-1}. In each equation the variable terms may appear on the left-hand side and the terms consisting of parameters only on the right-hand side, as shown in Tables 10 and 11. Although in principle the new system looks very much like the old, the coefficients of the X's now contain not only technological input-output coefficients but also profit margins and marginal propensities to consume, a difference that is highly important from the economic point of view, as we shall presently see (the equations will, in general, still have a solution).

5. THE SIMPLEST POSSIBLE CASE

Like the open model, the present closed model can be handled much more easily if we set $m = 3$ and $a_{jj} = 0$. The solution for outputs is then

$$\text{(I)} \qquad X_1 = \frac{\alpha_{22}(A_{13} + A_{14}) - \alpha_{12}(A_{23} + A_{24})}{\alpha_{11}\alpha_{22} - \alpha_{12}\alpha_{21}}$$

$$\text{(II)} \qquad X_2 = \frac{\alpha_{11}(A_{23} + A_{24}) - \alpha_{21}(A_{13} + A_{14})}{\alpha_{11}\alpha_{22} - \alpha_{12}\alpha_{21}}$$

where

$$\alpha_{11} = 1 - a_{13}a_{31} - a_{14}(\pi_1 - \pi_2 a_{21} - \pi_3 a_{31})$$

$$\alpha_{12} = - a_{12} - a_{13}a_{32} - a_{14}(\pi_2 - \pi_1 a_{12} - \pi_3 a_{32})$$

$$\alpha_{21} = - a_{21} - a_{23}a_{31} - a_{24}(\pi_1 - \pi_2 a_{21} - \pi_3 a_{31})$$

$$\alpha_{22} = 1 - a_{23}a_{32} - a_{24}(\pi_2 - \pi_1 a_{12} - \pi_3 a_{32})$$

The solutions for employment, the wage bill, and profits may be written in the forms (III) through (VI) presented in the preceding chapter, X_1 and X_2 now standing for our new solutions, of course.

6. RELATIVE PRICE BOUNDARIES

Price ratios must be such that profits of the two firm sectors are nonnegative, yielding conditions (15) and (16), conditions exactly alike in the open and the closed model. In Figure 36 our price combination would again have to lie inside the cone CAB.

In respect to household saving, the first requirement, a strong one, is that it should be nonnegative within each household sector, the result being condition (17a) of the preceding chapter. Allowing for the peculiarities of the closed model [see Equation (4a)], condition (17a) should now be rewritten as

$$(17b) \quad \frac{\pi_1}{\pi_3} = -\frac{\pi_2}{\pi_3} \frac{a_{23} + \dfrac{A_{23}}{a_{31}X_1 + a_{32}X_2}}{a_{13} + \dfrac{A_{13}}{a_{31}X_1 + a_{32}X_2}} + \frac{1}{a_{13} + \dfrac{A_{13}}{a_{31}X_1 + a_{32}X_2}}$$

When graphed, condition (17b) is represented by a line whose intercept is the last term on the right-hand side, always positive, and whose slope is the coefficient of π_2/π_3, always negative.

The second requirement, a weaker one, is that household saving should be zero for the economy as a whole. When this requirement is expressed formally, the identity $0 = 0$ results, and no restrictions upon π_1/π_3 and π_2/π_3 remain other than conditions (15) and (16). A comfortably large area will always exist within the first quadrant to satisfy those conditions, and technological progress increases that area even more, as we saw in Chapter 12, Section 19. In our application of the closed model, to follow, we may therefore again ignore the relative price boundaries.

7. APPLICATION: TECHNOLOGICAL PROGRESS IN THE CLOSED MODEL

The certainty with which we were formerly able to predict the effect of technological progress upon outputs in the open model is now gone. There, technological progress reduced interindustry demand, nothing more. Household demand, being autonomous, remained unaffected. However, in the closed model household demand has an induced part. Therefore, when a_{12} is reduced, industry 2, in order to produce one unit of its own output, needs less of industry 1's output, and industry 2's profit margin must rise. The necessary rise in entrepreneur household demand ensuing constitutes an offsetting tendency vis-à-vis the reduction in interindustry demand. Which of the two tendencies is stronger? Even for the simplest possible case where $m = 3$ and $a_{jj} = 0$, details become quite complicated. Again taking the derivatives of X_1 and X_2 with respect to a_{12}, we get

$$(III) \qquad \frac{dX_1}{da_{12}} = \frac{\alpha_{12}\pi_1 a_{24} - \alpha_{22}(\pi_1 a_{14} - 1)}{\alpha_{11}\alpha_{22} - \alpha_{12}\alpha_{21}} X_2$$

$$(IV) \qquad \frac{dX_2}{da_{12}} = -\frac{\alpha_{11}\pi_1 a_{24} - \alpha_{21}(\pi_1 a_{14} - 1)}{\alpha_{11}\alpha_{22} - \alpha_{12}\alpha_{21}} X_2$$

What signs will the two derivatives have? First, all autonomous consumption A_{13}, A_{14}, A_{23}, and A_{24} may be assumed to be positive. Second, as we shall see presently, α_{11} and α_{22} would probably be positive, but α_{12} and α_{21} must always be negative. Hence, the numerators of (I) and (II) must be positive. If outputs X_1 and X_2 are to be positive and finite, the denominators of (I) and (II) $\alpha_{11}\alpha_{22} - \alpha_{12}\alpha_{21}$ must be positive. Being identical to the denominators of (I) and (II), the denominators of (III) and (IV) must also be positive. But the numerators of (III) and (IV) may be positive or negative, as we shall soon see.

8. ECONOMIC INTERPRETATION OF THE α's

If output X_1 rises by one physical unit, employment will rise by a_{31} man-hours, and labor household demand for the first commodity will rise by $a_{13}a_{31}$ physical units of that commodity. Profits will rise by $\pi_1 - \pi_2 a_{21} - \pi_3 a_{31}$ dollars, and entrepreneur household demand for the first commodity will rise by $a_{14}(\pi_1 - \pi_2 a_{21} - \pi_3 a_{31})$ physical units of that commodity. Hence α_{11} is simply one minus the rise in labor household demand minus the rise in entrepreneur household demand for the first commodity. The dimension of α_{11} is one minus the number of additional physical units of the first commodity demanded per additional physical unit of the first commodity produced. We should expect α_{11} ordinarily to be positive.

If output X_2 rises by one physical unit, the input of the first commodity will then rise by a_{12} physical units of that commodity. Employment will rise by a_{32} man-hours, and labor household demand for the first commodity will rise by $a_{13}a_{32}$ physical units of that commodity. Profits will rise by $\pi_2 - \pi_1 a_{12} - \pi_3 a_{32}$ dollars, and entrepreneur household demand for the first commodity will rise by $a_{14}(\pi_2 - \pi_1 a_{12} - \pi_3 a_{32})$ physical units of that commodity. Hence α_{12} is simply minus the rise in interindustry demand minus the rise in labor household demand minus the rise in entrepreneur demand for the first commodity. The dimension of α_{12} is minus the number of additional physical units of the first commodity demanded per additional physical unit of the second commodity produced. Hence, α_{12} must always be negative.

If output X_1 rises by one physical unit, the input of the second commodity will then rise by a_{21} physical units of that commodity. Employment will rise by a_{31} man-hours, and labor household demand for the second commodity will rise by $a_{23}a_{31}$ physical units of that commodity. Profits will rise by $\pi_1 - \pi_2 a_{21} - \pi_3 a_{31}$ dollars, and entrepreneur household demand for the second commodity will rise by $a_{24}(\pi_1 - \pi_2 a_{21} - \pi_3 a_{31})$ physical units of that commodity. Hence α_{21} is simply minus the rise in interindustry demand minus the rise in labor household demand minus the rise in entrepreneur demand for the second commodity. The dimension of α_{21} is minus the number of additional physical units of the second commodity demanded per additional physical unit of the first commodity produced. Hence, α_{21} must always be negative.

If output X_2 rises by one physical unit, employment will rise by a_{32} man-hours, and labor household demand for the second commodity will rise by $a_{23}a_{32}$ physical units of that commodity. Profits will rise by $\pi_2 - \pi_1a_{12} - \pi_3a_{32}$ dollars, and entrepreneur household demand for the second commodity will rise by $a_{24}(\pi_2 - \pi_1a_{12} - \pi_3a_{32})$ physical units of that commodity. Hence α_{22} is simply one minus the rise in labor household demand minus the rise in entrepreneur household demand for the second commodity. The dimension of α_{22} is one minus the number of additional physical units of the second commodity demanded per additional physical unit of the second commodity produced. We should expect α_{22} ordinarily to be positive.

In summary, α_{11} and α_{22} are each equal to one minus the entire direct increase in the demand for a commodity generated by a unit increase in the output of that commodity. And α_{12} and α_{21} are each equal to minus the entire direct increase in demand for one commodity generated by a unit increase in the output of the other commodity.

9. ECONOMIC INTERPRETATION OF THE REMAINING MAGNITUDES

Besides the α's, two magnitudes π_1a_{24} and $(\pi_1a_{14} - 1)$ are also contained in the numerators of the two derivatives (III) and (IV). a_{24} is the number of additional physical units of the second commodity purchased by entrepreneur households per additional profit dollar, which (ignoring inferior goods) is positive. a_{14} is the number of additional physical units of the first commodity purchased by entrepreneur households per additional profit dollar. Multiply by the price of the first commodity and get π_1a_{14} which is the additional dollar expenditure on the first commodity by entrepreneur households per additional profit dollar. Should these households spend any amount on any other item, π_1a_{14} would be less than one, and, consequently $\pi_1a_{14} - 1$ must always be negative.

10. CONCLUSION

The conclusion may be presented in more vivid terms. Let sectors 1 and 2 be "agriculture" and "manufacturing," respectively and their output "produce" and "manufactures," respectively. Technological progress causes less produce to be needed to produce one unit of manufactures. Technological progress substituting synthetics like rayon or nylon for nature-given raw materials like cotton would be examples in point.

We can now see that the two derivatives (III) and (IV) may conceivably be negative. If α_{12} were numerically large relative to α_{22}, and if $\pi_1 a_{24}$ were numerically large relative to $(\pi_1 a_{14} - 1)$, dX_1/da_{12} could be negative. Consequently, despite technological progress, the output of produce may rise if (1) the additional number of physical units of produce demanded per additional physical unit produced of manufactures is still high, even though reduced; (2) the number of additional physical units of manufactures demanded per additional physical unit produced of manufactures is high; and/or (3) out of an additional profit dollar earned, entrepreneur households buy a large number of physical units of manufactures and of produce. Satisfaction of these three conditions is tantamount to maximization of the repercussions from the increase in household demand resulting from the higher profit margin within the manufacturing industry. A high a_{12} even if somewhat reduced represents the only hope for the output of agriculture to be pulled ahead by the output of manufactures.

If α_{11} were numerically large relative to α_{21}, and if $\pi_1 a_{24}$ were numerically large relative to $(\pi_1 a_{14} - 1)$, dX_2/da_{12} could be negative. Output of manufactures may rise if (1) the number of additional physical units of produce demanded per additional physical unit produced of produce is low; (2) the number of additional physical units of manufactures demanded per additional physical unit produced of produce is low; and/or (3) out of an additional profit dollar earned, entrepreneur households will buy a large number of physical units of manufactures and of produce. Satisfaction of the first two conditions is tantamount to minimization of the repercussions from the reduction in firm demand resulting from reduced input requirements within manufacturing. The two conditions express the hope that a reduction of demand for produce will not damage too severely the demands for produce and manufactures.

CONCLUSIONS

In Part II modification of the Keynesian model in a number of respects enables us to draw further policy conclusions. By differentiating firm, household, and government sectors, we can distinguish between output and employment and between the gross private product and the gross government product. By including prices of factors and goods in Chapter 7, we showed that in an underemployed economy, raising the price of factors, insisting upon featherbedding practices, or reducing the price of goods would have beneficial effects upon output and employment, all only preliminary results, of course. Further aspects of the wage-employment relationship were studied in Chapter 11 on an open economy, and more will be studied in Chapters 16, 17, and 19 of Part III. Next, we saw that in an underemployed economy, raising government purchases of goods, raising the gross government product, or reducing the marginal income tax rate would have beneficial effects upon output and employment. Even should the budget remain balanced, simultaneous increases of both sides of it might have such beneficial effects.

But what if the economy were not underemployed? By a simple interchange of certain parameters and variables we changed the underemployment model into an inflation model and in Chapter 8 showed that inflation would be accelerated by an increase in the input-output coefficient, by a reduction of the factor supply, by an increase in government purchases, by an increase in the gross government product, by a reduction of the marginal income tax rate or by a reduction of the mark-up coefficient.

Price policy is not the only kind of competitive policy. Non-price competition has been studied as a microeconomic phenomenon traditionally, but in Chapter 9 we examined some of its macroeconomic aspects, which can be summarized, perhaps, by saying that so-called wastes of monopolistic competition (advertising, frequent style changes, etc.) may have beneficial effects in an underemployed economy. The parallel between such wastes and featherbedding practices suggests itself.

In the Keynesian model import and taxes alike are leakages, export and investment alike injections. Just as we showed that the balanced budget is usually not neutral in its effect upon output and employment, we showed in Chapter 10 that balanced foreign trade may also not be neutral.

The models used in Part II are characterized by increasing disaggregation. Disaggregation carried to its logical end is seen in the Leontief interindustry transactions model. For purposes of comparison with the Keynesian model, such an interindustry transactions model is sketched, the open and closed forms appearing in Chapters 12 and 13, respectively. When applied to the analysis of technological progress, the open model shows that such progress will always reduce equilibrium output, while in the closed model equilibrium output may or may not fall.

PART III

The Demand for Input

The sluggard does not plow in the autumn;
he will seek at harvest and have nothing.
THE PROVERBS OF SOLOMON

No less important than the determination of aggregate output is the determination of the inputs going into it. Indeed, the models presented in Part II all explicitly determined inputs as well as output, but usually assumed them to be in direct proportion. By contrast Keynes believed that as an economy was approaching full employment, employment must rise in more than proportion to output because of diminishing marginal productivity of labor.

To a closer examination of the demand for input and the underlying "law" of diminishing marginal productivity Part III is devoted. In Chapter 14 the neoclassical theory of the firm is briefly reproduced. In Chapter 15 the neoclassical theory of wages and rent is briefly reproduced. Replacing the neoclassical theory with modern linear programming Chapter 16 develops the demand for input at constant product quality, while in Chapter 17 the analysis is extended to the case of variable product quality.

Until now the capital aspect of input-output relationships was ignored. However, the neoclassical theory of wages and capital is presented and criticized in Chapter 18 on the grounds that this theory may be incompatible with modern technology. In Chapter 19 a modern restatement is attempted. The restatements attempted in Chapters 17 and 19 appear to salvage at least one cornerstone of neoclassical doctrine, namely, that a lower relative price of an input induces entrepreneurs to use more of said input.

14

Neoclassical Theory of the Firm

1. THE MODEL

Neoclassical theory successfully determined the optimum time rates of all inputs needed within the firm. Selling effort was ignored, and no attempt was made to manipulate the product quality parameters. The notation follows:

Variables

c_j = the number of dollars' worth of cost incurred annually by a firm in industry j

p_j = the number of dollars' worth of profits earned annually by a firm in industry j

π_j = the price of the output produced by a firm in industry j

X_j = the number of physical units of product produced annually by a firm in industry j

σ_j = the number of physical units of product sold annually by a firm in industry j

Parameters

π_i = the price of the input absorbed from industry i, a parameter not to be manipulated

x_{ij} = the number of physical units of the product of industry i absorbed annually by a firm in industry j, to be manipulated

153

The neoclassicists saw input as the parameter to be manipulated by the firm, "the parameter of action." Hence their chain of causation is this: Input is fixed by the firm; output is a function of input; sales are a function of output; and price of product is a function of sales. (Every variable is an ex ante variable and as usual will carry an asterisk.)

The firm in industry j is assumed to produce only one product and to absorb as inputs the products of industry i, i representing m industries, including labor but not including industry j itself. The prices at which such inputs are purchased are beyond the control of the firm. One fundamental equation needed in our analysis states the demand faced by the firm:

$$(1) \qquad *\pi_j = *\pi_j(*\sigma_j)$$

that is, the price obtained by the firm depends upon the quantity sold by the firm. The demand equation (1) is assumed continuous and differentiable.

The second equation is the definition of cost:

$$(2) \qquad *c_j = \sum_{i=1}^{m} (\pi_i x_{ij})$$

that is, cost is the sum of m products, each product being obtained by multiplying price by the quantity of input.

The third fundamental equation states the production function:

$$(3) \qquad *X_j = *X_j(x_{1j}, \cdots, x_{mj})$$

that is, output is a function of all m inputs, which are assumed substitutable and fully divisible. Like the demand function, the production function is assumed continuous and differentiable.

The fourth equation is the definition of profit:

$$(4) \qquad *p_j = *\pi_j *\sigma_j - *c_j$$

Ignoring inventory problems, we shall assume that annual sales expected by the firm equal annual output planned by the firm:

$$(5) \qquad *\sigma_j = *X_j$$

2. MANIPULATING ONE INPUT

Let us now vary the ith input x_{ij} in isolation, taking the partial derivative of profits $*p_j$ with respect to the ith input. Inserting (1), (2), (3), and (5) into (4) and differentiating, we get:

$$\frac{\partial *p_j}{\partial x_{ij}} = *\pi_j \frac{\partial *X_j}{\partial x_{ij}} + *X_j \frac{\partial *\pi_j}{\partial x_{ij}} - \pi_i$$

But

$$\frac{\partial *\pi_j}{\partial x_{ij}} = \frac{d *\pi_j}{d *X_j} \frac{\partial *X_j}{\partial x_{ij}}$$

Consequently,

$$(6) \qquad \frac{\partial *p_j}{\partial x_{ij}} = \left(*\pi_j + *X_j \frac{d *\pi_j}{d *X_j} \right) \frac{\partial *X_j}{\partial x_{ij}} - \pi_i$$

The derivative of profits with respect to the ith input is seen to equal marginal revenue *times* the physical marginal productivity of the ith input *minus* the price of the ith input. A necessary[1] condition for the profit maximum is that (6) equal zero or

$$(7a) \qquad \pi_i = \left(*\pi_j + *X_j \frac{d *\pi_j}{d *X_j} \right) \frac{\partial *X_j}{\partial x_{ij}}$$

Equation (7a) reads: for profits to be maximized, input price should equal input marginal-revenue productivity, which is the general case. A special case is pure competition; here the price of the product $*\pi_j$ is a constant, (7a) reducing to

$$(7b) \qquad \pi_i = *\pi_j \frac{\partial *X_j}{\partial x_{ij}}$$

Equation (7b) states that if profits are to be maximized under pure competition, input price must equal input *marginal-value* productivity.

---

[1] Necessary conditions alone are considered. Part III of this volume is devoted to a study of the demand for input, which is seen as an implication of profit maximization by firms. Such implications are set out in the form of *necessary* conditions for profit maximization. Hence the existence of a maximum is postulated. For *sufficient* conditions, see chap. IV of Paul A. Samuelson, *Foundations of Economic Analysis* (Cambridge, Mass.: Harvard University Press, 1947).

A second necessary condition for the profit maximum is that the second derivative of profits with respect to the ith input be negative. Taking the derivative of (6) we have:

(8) $\dfrac{\partial^{2*}p_j}{\partial x_{ij}{}^2} =$

$$\left({}^*\pi_j + {}^*X_j \frac{d^*\pi_j}{d^*X_j} \right) \frac{\partial^{2*}X_j}{\partial x_{ij}{}^2} + \left(\frac{\partial^*X_j}{\partial x_{ij}} \right)^2 \frac{d\left({}^*\pi_j + {}^*X_j \dfrac{d^*\pi_j}{d^*X_j} \right)}{d^*X_j} < 0$$

Accordingly, the second derivative of profits equals marginal revenue *times* the derivative of physical marginal productivity with respect to the ith input *plus* physical marginal productivity squared *times* the derivative of marginal revenue with respect to output.[2]   Marginal revenue, if not positive would not satisfy (7a). As long as inputs are fully divisible and substitutable, physical marginal productivity is meaningful and positive.   Under the law of diminishing returns, the *derivative* of physical marginal productivity with respect to input is negative.   Furthermore, since the marginal revenue curve is usually a declining one, the derivative of marginal revenue with respect to output also is usually negative.   Therefore, the entire second derivative of profits is usually negative.

3. MANIPULATING ANY INPUT

While manipulating not one but all inputs we must insist that Equation (7a) hold simultaneously for *any i*, and we may write it as

(7c) $\dfrac{\pi_i}{\dfrac{\partial^*X_j}{\partial x_{ij}}} = {}^*\pi_j + {}^*X_j \dfrac{d^*\pi_j}{d^*X_j}$ for $i = 1 \cdots m$

which holds for any i.   Accordingly, the ratio between the price

[2] When taking the derivative of marginal revenue with respect to the ith input, first take the derivative of marginal revenue with respect to output, then multiply by the derivative of output with respect to the ith input (the function-of-function rule).

of the ith input and the physical marginal productivity of the ith input must be equal to marginal revenue, such ratio holding simultaneously for any i. Consequently,

(7d)
$$\frac{\pi_1}{\dfrac{\partial *X_j}{\partial x_{1j}}} = \frac{\pi_2}{\dfrac{\partial *X_j}{\partial x_{2j}}} = \cdots = \frac{\pi_m}{\dfrac{\partial *X_j}{\partial x_{mj}}}$$

that is, a necessary condition for maximization of profits is that inputs must be combined in such a way that the ratio between price and physical marginal productivity is the same for all inputs.

4. CONCLUSION

The neoclassical theory of the firm made it possible to draw an important conclusion about the effect of a rising price of input upon the demand for that input. The conclusion may be stated as follows. Suppose that the price of the ith input, π_i, would rise. Then the left-hand side of (7a) as written above would rise. If nothing happened to π_j and $*X_j$, the right-hand side would remain constant. The two factors of the product on the right-hand side of (7a) could be made to rise by reducing x_{ij}. In the first place, since the marginal revenue curve is usually declining, such a reduction would raise the value of the entire parenthesis on the right-hand side of (7a). In the second place, since physical marginal productivity is assumed to be positive although diminishing, a reduction of x_{ij} will cause $\partial *X_j/\partial x_{ij}$ to rise. For both reasons, then, (7a) can be restored. In (7b) only the last of the two effects of reducing x_{ij} would materialize. But whether competition is pure or not, the conclusion is that raising the price of an input will reduce the demand for that input.

15

Neoclassical Theory of Wages, Rent, and Output

1. THE MODEL

The neoclassical marginal-productivity theory of distribution was firmly based upon the theory of the firm, discussed in Chapter 14. In the interest of utmost simplicity, let us ignore the time element of production, assume only one output and only two inputs, labor and land, with both inputs of uniform quality. Further, let us assume pure competition in the product market [Equation (7b) of Chapter 14 thus holding], and also pure competition in the input markets. Consequently, the wage rate will be such as to clear the labor market, and the rent of land will be such as to clear the market for land. Let the total labor force and the total available amount of land be parameters. We shall consider two alternative institutional frameworks, one with landlords, the other with labor, as entrepreneurs.

2. LANDLORDS AS ENTREPRENEURS

First, assume the landlords to be entrepreneurs hiring labor input until their rent income is at a maximum. Labor will then be hired until the aforementioned equation (7b) is satisfied.

Geometrically this may be shown in a diagram like Figure 37 in which labor input x_{1j} is plotted in the horizontal direction, and the marginal value productivity $*\pi_j \partial *X_j/\partial x_{1j}$ of labor is plotted in the vertical direction. The marginal value productivity curve is negatively sloped. In Figure 37, the aggregate input of labor x_{1j} equals the entire labor force, for the labor market is assumed to be cleared. The wage rate at which it is cleared is π_1 equaling the marginal value productivity of the last man in the labor force. Should the wage rate be any lower, competition

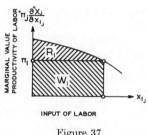

Figure 37

among landlords would force it up; should it be higher, competition among workers would force it down. The total wage bill is $W_1 = \pi_1 x_{1j}$, and total rent the residual R_1.

3. WORKERS AS ENTREPRENEURS

Second, assume the workers to be the entrepreneurs hiring land input until their wage income is at a maximum. Land will then be hired until the aforementioned equation (7b) is satisfied. Geometrically this may be shown in a diagram like Figure 38 in which land input x_{2j} is plotted in the horizontal direction, and the marginal value productivity $*\pi_j \partial *X_j/\partial x_{2j}$ of land is plotted in the vertical direction. The marginal value productivity curve is negatively sloped. In Figure 38, the aggregate input of land x_{2j} equals the entire acreage of

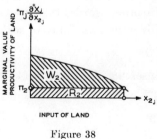

Figure 38

arable land, for the land market is assumed to be cleared. The rate of rent at which it is cleared is π_2 equaling the marginal value productivity of the last acre in the economy. Should the rate of rent be any lower, competition among the workers would force it up; should it be higher, competition among landlords would force it down. The total rent bill is $R_2 = \pi_2 x_{2j}$, and total wages the residual W_2.

4. EULER'S THEOREM

Since R_1 and W_2 are residuals, we know that $W_1 + R_1 = {}^*\pi_j {}^*X_j$ and that $W_2 + R_2 = {}^*\pi_j {}^*X_j$. But do we also know that $W_1 + R_2$ would be equal to ${}^*\pi_j {}^*X_j$? If so, $W_1 = W_2$ and $R_1 = R_2$, and the institutional framework of the economy would be irrelevant: whether landlords or workers were the entrepreneurs, the distributive shares would be the same. Is it possible to prove $W_1 + R_2 = {}^*\pi_j {}^*X_j$?

Let the labor force rise by dx_{1j}, and the acreage of land by dx_{2j}. The differential of output is then defined as

$$(1) \qquad d^*X_j = \frac{\partial^* X_j}{\partial x_{1j}}\, dx_{1j} + \frac{\partial^* X_j}{\partial x_{2j}}\, dx_{2j}$$

Now assume that

$$(2) \qquad dx_{1j} = a x_{1j}$$

$$(3) \qquad dx_{2j} = a x_{2j}$$

In other words, the inputs of *both* labor and land rise a times. Given no economies of scale, output will also rise a times; hence

$$(4) \qquad d^*X_j = a^*X_j$$

Inserting (2), (3), and (4) into (1) and dividing through by a, we get

$$(5) \qquad {}^*X_j = \frac{\partial^* X_j}{\partial x_{1j}}\, x_{1j} + \frac{\partial^* X_j}{\partial x_{2j}}\, x_{2j}$$

According to (7b) we have

$$(6) \qquad \frac{\partial^* X_j}{\partial x_{1j}} = \frac{\pi_1}{{}^*\pi_j}$$

(7)
$$\frac{\partial^* X_j}{\partial x_{2j}} = \frac{\pi_2}{{}^*\pi_j}$$

Inserting (6) and (7) into (5) and multiplying through by ${}^*\pi_j$, we get

(I)
$${}^*\pi_j{}^*X_j = \pi_1 x_{1j} + \pi_2 x_{2j}$$

or more briefly, ${}^*\pi_j{}^*X_j = W_1 + R_2$. Wicksell,[1] the first to apply Euler's theorem (5) to distributive shares, proved that in the absence of economies of scale the sum of the distributive shares of labor and land will exactly exhaust the value of the total product. Conversely, if diseconomies of scale exist, output will rise less than a times, hence $d^*X_j < a^*X_j$. In Equation (5), the equality sign should then be replaced by a "greater than" sign, and the sum of the distributive shares will *fall short of* the pie to be distributed. The extra profits will attract new firms, thus decreasing the size of the individual firm until Equation (I) is satisfied.

In the third and more practical case—when economies of scale exist—output will rise more than a times, that is, $d^*X_j > a^*X_j$. Accordingly, the equality sign in Equation (5) is replaced by a "less than" sign, and the sum of the distributive shares *exceeds* the pie to be shared. Any firm smaller than the size at which such economies have ceased to be obtainable must pay more for its inputs than warranted by the value of that firm's total product. Obviously such firms would succumb in competition with larger and more efficient firms capable of paying to each his own. Consequently, if economies of scale were considerable, the size of firms would have to grow to a point where the initial assumptions of pure competition would have to be abandoned. To that case we now turn.

---

[1] Knut Wicksell, *Lectures on Political Economy, Volume One, General Theory* (London: Routledge and Kegan Paul, 1934), pp. 124–133. The original edition was first published in Swedish in 1901. On the development of Euler's theorem, see Joseph A. Schumpeter, *History of Economic Analysis* (New York: Oxford, 1954), p. 1033, especially footnote 19.

5. NO ECONOMIES OF SCALE, NO PURE COMPETITION

Assume economies of scale to be absent and the assumption of pure competition abandoned.   According to (7a), we have

$$(8) \qquad \frac{\partial {}^*X_j}{\partial x_{1j}} = \frac{\pi_1}{{}^*\pi_j + {}^*X_j \dfrac{d{}^*\pi_j}{d{}^*X_j}}$$

$$(9) \qquad \frac{\partial {}^*X_j}{\partial x_{2j}} = \frac{\pi_2}{{}^*\pi_j + {}^*X_j \dfrac{d{}^*\pi_j}{d{}^*X_j}}$$

Inserting (8) and (9) into (5), we get

$$(II) \qquad {}^*X_j\left({}^*\pi_j + {}^*X_j \frac{d{}^*\pi_j}{d{}^*X_j}\right) = \pi_1 x_{1j} + \pi_2 x_{2j}$$

Since $d{}^*\pi_j/d{}^*X_j$ is negative

$${}^*\pi_j {}^*X_j > \pi_1 x_{1j} + \pi_2 x_{2j}$$

We observe that the sum of the two distributive shares is smaller than the pie to be distributed.   The difference, profits, accrue to entrepreneurs as a third distributive share.

16

Linear Programming Within the Firm

1. ZERO MARGINAL PRODUCTIVITIES IN THE THEORY OF THE FIRM

The neoclassical theory of the firm relies heavily on the assumption of a positive but diminishing marginal productivity of inputs,[1] a requirement not normally satisfied in manufacturing. Modern manufacturing production processes may be more easily studied if broken down into their component stages. For example, in one stage of automobile manufacturing, in which sheet metal is stamped into body panels, the inputs required are stamping-press-hours, man-hours required to operate the press, the flow of energy required to operate the press, and the flow of sheet metal to be stamped. To obtain a given quality of the stamped body panel, a given speed of operation is maintained. Increasing the speed (if possible) would cause quality to deteriorate; decreasing the speed might either improve quality or waste time. At the given speed, then, the addition of one more man or of more sheet metal per hour would not increase output.

To generalize: As a first approximation to a realistic isoquant map for the stage we shall treat, let us assume the isoquants to be L-shaped, as in Figure 39. This figure represents what the neoclassicists called joint demand with rigid proportions. If waste were permitted, it would be physically possible, for example, to

[1] Cf. chap. 14.

produce in a point on the solid vertical line above the point Q, letting some of the first input go to waste. Moving slightly upwards from the point Q, then, would be possible, but the partial derivative of output with respect to the first input would be zero. Alternatively, one could produce in a point on the solid horizontal

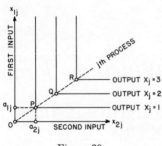

Figure 39

line to the right of the point Q, in which event some of the second input would be going to waste. Moving slightly right from the point Q, then, would be possible, but the partial derivative of output with respect to the second input would be zero. Consequently, along the line $OPQR$ and for a given quality of product, the marginal productivity of any input is zero! Such a statement is indeed remarkable—and a serious indictment of neoclassical theory. Ultimately, of course, the empirical basis of neoclassical theory is an agricultural production function, in particular the response of a crop to increasing inputs of fertilizer, water, or labor.

2. THE PROCESS CONCEPT

In the one-output, several-inputs case, a process may be defined as a production program within which every input is in direct proportion to output. According to Dorfman,[2] who has so aptly expressed the difference between a process and the neoclassical production function, the latter is a family of processes that uses identical inputs and produces identical products. If we find, when comparing any two points on a production surface, that the

[2] Robert Dorfman, *Application of Linear Programming to the Theory of the Firm* (Berkeley and Los Angeles: University of California Press, 1951), pp. 14–15. The word "activity," formerly used as a synonym of "process," is now used to refer to a point on the process line rather than to the line itself; see Tjalling C. Koopmans, *Three Essays on the State of Economic Science* (New York: McGraw-Hill, 1957), pp. 76–77.

ratios of every input to output at the two points are the same, the points are said to represent different levels of the same process. If, on the other hand, the ratios are not the same, the two points represent two different processes.

In Fig. 39 the broken line through zero *OPQR* clearly represents one process. But might there not be additional processes? Each of them would pass through the origin, and once chosen would make all marginal productivities equal to zero. True, modern technology frequently offers a choice from among a finite number of processes. The processes may not use the same inputs; in any process some of the inputs may be zero. For example, the inputs used in an earth-moving job may be (1) shovel-hours, (2) pick-hours, (3) bulldozer-hours, and (4) man-hours. Of the two alternative processes, one includes inputs (1), (2), and (4), the other only inputs (3) and (4). Another example: the inputs used in a computing job may be (1) calculator-hours, (2) electronic digital computer-hours, and (3) man-hours. One of the two alternative processes includes inputs (1) and (3), the other (2) and (3). The emphasis here is first on the absence of substitution between inputs within the same process and second on the presence of substitution between processes. It is reasonable to ask how perfect this substitution really is. More specifically, will not quality of product differ among processes? Would not a bulldozer wreak a flowerbed? Although the Alaska Highway might have had the same quality had it been built by men armed with nothing but picks and shovels, could it have been finished in 1942? Or, in our second example, the man operating the desk calculator is surely more error-prone than is the electronic computer. But whatever the significance of quality differences, they are usually ignored in linear programming.

3. THE MODEL

Linear programming permits the determination of the best processes available within the firm. Selling effort is usually ignored,[3] nor is any attempt made to manipulate demand by manipulating product quality.[4] The notation follows:[5]

Variables

c_j = the number of dollars' worth of cost incurred annually by the firm in its jth process

μ_j = the number of dollars' worth of profit earned per unit of output of the jth process; μ_j is called the "profit margin"

p_j = the number of dollars' worth of profit earned annually by the firm in its jth process

σ_j = the number of physical units of product sold annually by the firm in its jth process

x_{ij} = the number of physical units of the ith input absorbed annually by the firm in its jth process

Parameters

a_{ij} = the number of physical units of the ith input absorbed per physical unit of output in the jth process, a parameter not to be manipulated

π_i = the price of the ith input, a parameter not to be manipulated

[3] One exception is the determination of the optimal composition of a hypothetical television show that includes commercial time and comedy time; see John G. Kemeny, J. Laurie Snell, and Gerald L. Thompson, *Introduction to Finite Mathematics* (Englewood Cliffs, N. J.: Prentice-Hall, 1957), pp. 259–263.

[4] Linear programming refers to the quality of output much more explicitly than did neoclassical theory. But quality appears as a certain minimum requirement among the constraints. For example, the diet problem is solved under the constraints that the diet contain total amounts of calories, niacin, vitamin D, etc., which are greater than or equal to respective specified annual amounts; cf. Robert Dorfman, Paul A. Samuelson, and Robert M. Solow, *Linear Programming and Economic Analysis* (New York: McGraw-Hill, 1958), chap. 2. The gasoline blending problem is solved under the constraints that the octane rating be greater than or equal to a certain number and that the vapor pressure be smaller than or equal to a certain number; cf. A. Charnes, W. W. Cooper, and B. Mellon, "Blending Aviation Gasolines—A Study in Programming Interdependent Activities in an Integrated Oil Company," *Econometrica*, Vol. 20, No. 2 (April, 1952), pp. 135–159. The emphasis is on meeting certain minimum quality standards, and the effect upon consumer demand of varying such standards is no part of the problem.

[5] Linear programming and Leontief input-output analysis are members of the same family, the notation used in this volume reflecting this fact.

π_0 = the price of output, a parameter not to be manipulated

X_j = the number of physical units of product produced annually by the firm in its jth process, a parameter to be manipulated

In linear programming levels of output in a finite number of processes serve as the parameters to be manipulated and optimized by the firm. The chain of causation may be thought of as composed of these links: In each process the level of output is fixed by the firm; in each process input is in proportion to output; and in each process sales equal output. The price at which output is sold and the prices at which all inputs are purchased are beyond the control of the firm. All variables are ex ante variables and as usual will carry asterisks.

Let us now be more rigorous in our examination. Assume the firm produces only one product in n different processes and absorbs m different inputs. In any one of the n processes, one or more of the m inputs may be zero. Within any process cost is conventionally defined as the money value of all inputs absorbed in that process:

$$(1) \qquad *c_j = \sum_{i=1}^{m} (\pi_i * x_{ij}) \qquad \text{for} \qquad j = 1 \cdots n$$

Replacing the neoclassical production function, linear programming states that within any process every input is in direct proportion to output; indeed, as we saw in Section 2, that is the very definition of a process.

$$(2) \qquad *x_{ij} = a_{ij} X_j \qquad \text{for} \qquad i = 1 \cdots m \text{ and } j = 1 \cdots n$$

Within any process, profits are defined as revenue minus cost:

$$(3) \qquad *p_j = *\pi_0 *\sigma_j - *c_j \qquad \text{for} \qquad j = 1 \cdots n$$

Ignoring inventory problems, we assume that within any process sales expected by the firm equal output:

$$(4) \qquad *\sigma_j = X_j \qquad \text{for} \qquad j = 1 \cdots n$$

For the firm as a whole, profits are defined as the sum total of the profits made within each of the processes:

$$(5) \qquad *p = \sum_{j=1}^{n} *p_j$$

For our purposes an alternative expression of firm profits will be useful. Inserting (2) into (1), (1) into (3), dividing the result by (4), we get the profit margin of the jth process:

$$(6) \qquad *\mu_j = \pi_0 - \sum_{i=1}^{m} (\pi_i a_{ij}) \qquad \text{for} \qquad j = 1 \cdots n$$

Equation (6) permits us to write firm profits as

$$(5a) \qquad *p = \sum_{j=1}^{n} (*\mu_j X_j)$$

In other words, total profits can be thought of as the total of weighted profit margins of all individual processes, the individual weights being the levels of output within the respective processes.

4. MAXIMIZATION OF FIRM PROFIT; NO INPUT CONSTRAINTS

Assume that the firm can sell the total amount X_0. Hence the sum of the outputs within the individual processes must add up to X_0:

$$(7) \qquad X_0 = \sum_{j=1}^{n} X_j$$

Furthermore, assume that no other constraints are imposed upon the firm. Assume that one of the processes, say the jth process, carries a positive and higher profit margin $*\mu_j$ than that of any of the remaining $n - 1$ processes. Assume finally that the output in one of the latter, say the ith process, is positive.

Reducing the output X_i of the ith process by one unit, and expanding the output X_j of the jth process by one unit, we lose $*\mu_i$ but gain $*\mu_j$; but, since by assumption, $*\mu_i < *\mu_j$, a net gain is realized. As long as any of the $n - 1$ processes other than the jth process has a positive output this operation can be repeated. The firm maximizes its profits, then, by concentrating all its output in the jth process, setting $X_j = X_0$ and setting all other X's equal to zero.

In the special case where two processes carry an identical profit margin that is higher than the profit margin of any of the remaining processes, the firm will concentrate all its output in the two former processes but be indifferent to the allocation of output between the two.

5. INPUT CONSTRAINTS

Things become far less simple if constraints affect some inputs. Assume that there is no constraint on output. Assume, too, that out of the m inputs, f inputs are available in fixed quantities only, which for durable plant and equipment will often be the case. Let the fixed quantity available of the ith input be the parameter x_i. The total amount of the ith input absorbed in all processes must be equal to or smaller than x_i, a condition that must hold for every one of the f inputs:

$$(8) \qquad a_{11}X_1 + a_{12}X_2 + \cdots + a_{1n}X_n \leqq x_1$$
$$a_{21}X_1 + a_{22}X_2 + \cdots + a_{2n}X_n \leqq x_2$$
$$\cdots\cdots\cdots\cdots\cdots\cdots\cdots\cdots\cdots\cdots\cdots\cdots$$
$$a_{f1}X_1 + a_{f2}X_2 + \cdots + a_{fn}X_n \leqq x_f$$

In (8) all outputs X_j must be nonnegative. But it would be desirable to transform system (8), now a system of inequalities, into a system of equations. The introduction of disposal processes will make such a transformation possible.

6. DISPOSAL PROCESSES

Assume $*x_{i(n+i)}$ to be the difference between the quantity of the ith input absorbed (appearing on the left-hand side of inequalities (8)) and the fixed quantity available of that input (appearing on the right-hand side of the inequalities). Then $*x_{i(n+i)}$ may be said to be the quantity of the ith input disposed of as waste or idling in a new so-called "disposal process." In contrast, the first n processes, discussed earlier, are called "active processes." An active process has an output as well as several inputs, and its level is measured in terms of its output Xj. A disposal process has no output, merely one input, and its level is measured in terms of that input $*x_{i(n+i)}$, assumed to be nonnegative. The introduction of the disposal processes will make it possible to rewrite system (8):

$$\begin{aligned}
(9) \quad a_{11}X_1 + a_{12}X_2 + \cdots + a_{1n}X_n + *x_{1(n+1)} &= x_1 \\
a_{21}X_1 + a_{22}X_2 + \cdots + a_{2n}X_n + *x_{2(n+2)} &= x_2 \\
\cdots\cdots\cdots\cdots\cdots\cdots\cdots\cdots\cdots\cdots\cdots\cdots\cdots\cdots\cdots \\
a_{f1}X_1 + a_{f2}X_2 + \cdots + a_{fn}X_n + *x_{f(n+f)} &= x_f
\end{aligned}$$

At this point we hasten to make the assumption that the column of the x's on the right-hand side of (9) is linearly independent of every set of $f - 1$ columns of a's on the left-hand side of (9), an assumption known as the "nondegeneracy" assumption.[6]

The addition of the f disposal processes, disposing of waste, has converted system of inequalities (8) into system of f equations (9) that has the $n + f$ unknowns X_j and $*x_{i(n+i)}$, where $j = 1 \cdots n$ and $i = 1 \cdots f$. The conversion of (8) into (9) is an important achievement, equations being much easier to handle than inequalities.

---

[6] A simple example of degeneracy, where $n = 3$ and $f = 2$, follows:

$$\begin{aligned}
4X_1 + 2X_2 + 6X_3 + x_{14} &= 20 \\
3X_1 + 5X_2 + 2X_3 + x_{25} &= 50
\end{aligned}$$

The column (20, 50) on the right-hand side is linearly dependent on one column of coefficients on the left-hand side [the second column (2, 5)]. Column (20, 50) may be obtained by multiplying column (2, 5) by ten.

7. BASIC SOLUTIONS

The price to be paid for changing inequalities into equations is the introduction of f additional unknowns. Where n is a positive integer, a system of f equations in $n + f$ unknowns will normally not have a unique solution. But it is the very multiplicity of solutions that makes our problem one of maximization: multiplicity provides a choice from among possible alternatives and in this way opportunity for profit maximization. How much choice do we actually have? Let us see step by step.

In a system of f equations in $n + f$ unknowns, we could arbitrarily set any n of the unknowns equal to zero, leaving a system of f equations in f unknowns. Under certain circumstances such a system would have a unique solution. The number n can be picked from the number $n + f$ in

$$\binom{n + f}{n}$$

different ways representing the number of possible unique solutions involving no more than f unknowns. Such a solution is called a "basic" solution, and the collection of processes involved in it is called a "basis."

8. BASIC FEASIBLE SOLUTIONS

Some basic solutions may involve negative values of X_j and $*x_{i(n+i)}$. Rejecting such solutions leaves us with the so-called "basic feasible" solutions, defined as solutions involving no more than f unknowns and involving nonnegative values of outputs X_j and of disposals of inputs $*x_{i(n+i)}$.

9. FIRM PROFITS IN THE DISPOSAL PROCESSES

Within any process Equation (3) defines profits as revenue minus cost. Within the $n + i$th process the disposal of the quantity

$*x_{i(n+i)}$ of the ith input is the sole activity. Since no other input is absorbed in the disposal process, according to equation (1) $*c_{n+i} = \pi_i*x_{i(n+i)}$. Since no output results from the disposal process, $X_{n+i} = 0$, and according to Equation (4), $*\sigma_{n+i}$ also is zero. According to (3) the profits of a disposal process are then $*p_{n+i} = -\pi_i*x_{i(n+i)}$.[7] The level of a disposal process is measured in terms of its input; its profit margin may therefore be found by dividing through by that input $*x_{i(n+i)}$:

(10) $$*\mu_{n+i} = -\pi_i \quad \text{for} \quad i = 1 \cdots f$$

Firm profits as defined by (5a) must be rewritten to include the negative profits made in disposal processes:

(11) $$*p = \sum_{j=1}^{n} (*\mu_j X_j) + \sum_{i=1}^{f} (*\mu_{n+i}*x_{i(n+i)})$$

10. COULD A NONBASIC FEASIBLE SOLUTION BE BETTER THAN THE BEST BASIC FEASIBLE ONE?

A fundamental theorem of linear programming is that no non-basic feasible solution can be more profitable than the most profitable basic feasible solution. Proving it for the simplest possible case where $m = 2$, $n = 2$, and $f = 1$,[8] we maximize

(11a) $$*p = *\mu_1 X_1 + *\mu_2 X_2 + *\mu_3 *x_{13}$$

where

(6a) $$*\mu_1 = \pi_0 - \pi_1 a_{11} - \pi_2 a_{21}$$

(6b) $$*\mu_2 = \pi_0 - \pi_1 a_{12} - \pi_2 a_{22}$$

(10a) $$*\mu_3 = -\pi_1$$

---

[7] In other words, whether certain inputs are fixed or not, we are still using the same profit definition, equation (3). If an input is fixed, the *cost* of that input is a fixed one, but the cost will still have to be deducted from revenue before net profit is arrived at. As we shall see in section 14, fixed cost is irrelevant to the choice between processes. The use of net profits here differs from conventional linear programming practice, which mostly uses gross profits.

[8] Adapted from Sven Danö, "Lineär programmering," *Nordisk Matematisk Tidsskrift*, Bind 4 (1956), pp. 121–138.

and where Equation (11a) is subject to the constraint

(9a) $$a_{11}X_1 + a_{12}X_2 + {}^*x_{13} = x_1$$

where $X_1 \geqq 0$, $X_2 \geqq 0$, and ${}^*x_{13} \geqq 0$, and where a_{11}, a_{12}, x_1, ${}^*\mu_1$, and ${}^*\mu_2$ are positive but ${}^*\mu_3$ negative.

Our system is seen to be one with one equation (9a) in three unknowns. The number of basic solutions is

$$\binom{3}{2} = 3$$

The three basic solutions are

(12) $$X_1 = \frac{x_1}{a_{11}}, \qquad X_2 = 0, \qquad {}^*x_{13} = 0$$

(13) $$X_1 = 0, \qquad X_2 = \frac{x_1}{a_{12}}, \qquad {}^*x_{13} = 0$$

(14) $$X_1 = 0, \qquad X_2 = 0, \qquad {}^*x_{13} = x_1$$

From our assumption that a_{11}, a_{12}, and x_1 are positive, it follows that these three basic solutions are also feasible. Of nonbasic feasible solutions there are infinitely many, but they may all be written as

(15) $$X_1 = \omega_1 \frac{x_1}{a_{11}}, \qquad X_2 = \omega_2 \frac{x_1}{a_{12}}, \qquad {}^*x_{13} = \omega_3 x_1$$

where $\omega_1 + \omega_2 + \omega_3 = 1$, where ω_1, ω_2, and ω_3 are nonnegative, and where at most one of them is equal to zero. From the latter three assumptions it follows that the nonbasic solutions described by (15) are feasible. Using (9a) to express X_1 in terms of X_2, ${}^*x_{13}$, and x_1, we get

(16) $$X_1 = \frac{x_1 - a_{12}X_2 - {}^*x_{13}}{a_{11}}$$

Inserting (16) into (11a), we get

(17) $${}^*p = \left({}^*\mu_2 - {}^*\mu_1 \frac{a_{12}}{a_{11}}\right)X_2 + \left({}^*\mu_3 - {}^*\mu_1 \frac{1}{a_{11}}\right){}^*x_{13} + {}^*\mu_1 \frac{x_1}{a_{11}}$$

If in (16) $X_2 = *x_{13} = 0$, we have $X_1 = x_1/a_{11}$, that is, our basic solution (12).   That solution will give us the amount of firm profits $*\mu_1 x_1/a_{11}$.   Can firm profits be raised by letting X_2 and $*x_{13}$ rise above zero?   It is immediately seen that $*x_{13}$ ought not to rise above zero, for—since $*\mu_3$ is negative, $*\mu_1$ positive and a_{11} positive—the coefficient of $*x_{13}$ in equation (17) is negative. How about letting X_2 rise above zero, then?   Three possibilities offer themselves.   First, if $*\mu_2 < *\mu_1 a_{12}/a_{11}$ the coefficient of X_2 in (17) is negative, and X_2 ought not to be greater than zero.   Second, if $*\mu_2 = *\mu_1 a_{12}/a_{11}$ the coefficient of X_2 in (17) is zero, and firm profits $*p$ will remain unaffected by an increase in X_2 above zero. Third, if $*\mu_2 > *\mu_1 a_{12}/a_{11}$ the coefficient of X_2 in (17) is positive, and X_2 ought definitely to be raised as far as possible above zero. But how far can it be raised?   From (16) it follows that if X_2 is raised beyond x_1/a_{12}, X_1 will become negative, which is inadmissible.   Consequently, X_2 should be set equal to x_1/a_{12}, X_1 becoming zero.   This is our basic solution (13).

The conclusion is that the value of firm profits $*p$ corresponding to a nonbasic feasible solution, defined by (15), can in no case be greater than the highest value of $*p$ corresponding to one of the basic feasible solutions (12) or (13).   Our proof, based on the assumption that $n = 2$ and $f = 1$, can easily be generalized.[9] For a larger number of processes and a larger number of constraints, it is still possible to think of each nonbasic feasible solution as a positive weighted average of the values of the corresponding variables of basic feasible solutions.   Because of the linear form of profits, Equation (11), the profits of a nonbasic feasible solution may be thought of as the weighted average (with the same positive weights) of the values of profits corresponding to basic feasible solutions.   Hence the profits earned in a nonbasic feasible solution cannot exceed the highest profits earned in one of the basic feasible solutions.   The optimum solution, conse-

[9] Dorfman, Samuelson, and Solow, *op. cit.*, pp. 67–80.   Robert Dorfman, *Application of Linear Programming to the Theory of the Firm* (Berkeley and Los Angeles: The University of California Press, 1951), pp. 28–30.

quently, must be found among the basic feasible solutions. The firm may confine itself to an examination of basic feasible solutions, whose number is fortunately finite.

11. THE SIMPLEX CRITERION

To proceed with such an examination of the basic feasible solutions, let us still assume that $m = 2$, $n = 2$, and $f = 1$ but now assign numerical values to the parameters used in the preceding section:

$$x_1 = 20 \qquad a_{22} = 5$$
$$a_{11} = 4 \qquad \pi_1 = 2$$
$$a_{12} = 2 \qquad \pi_2 = 3$$
$$a_{21} = 3 \qquad \pi_0 = 20$$

It follows that

$$*\mu_1 = 3$$
$$*\mu_2 = 1$$
$$*\mu_3 = -2$$

Equations (11a) and (9a) may now be written

(11a) $$*p = 3X_1 + X_2 - 2*x_{13}$$

(9a) $$4X_1 + 2X_2 + *x_{13} = 20$$

Our problem is to maximize (11a) subject to the constraint (9a), X_1, X_2, and $*x_{13}$ being nonnegative, as usual. Let us experiment a bit with Equations (11a) and (9a).

First, using (9a) to express $*x_{13}$ in terms of X_1 and X_2, inserting the result into (11a), we get

(18) $$*p = 11X_1 + 5X_2 - 40$$

From Equation (18) we conclude that X_1 or X_2 could profitably be raised above zero, for both have positive coefficients—the basis $*x_{13}$ is undesirable.

Second, using (9a) to express X_2 in terms of X_1 and $^*x_{13}$, inserting the result into (11a), we get

$$(19) \qquad\qquad ^*p = X_1 - 2\frac{1}{2}\,^*x_{13} + 10$$

From Equation (19) we conclude that $^*x_{13}$ should be zero, for it has a negative coefficient. On the other hand, X_1 could profitably be raised above zero, for it has a positive coefficient—the basis X_2 is less favorable than the best solution.

Third, using (9a) to express X_1 in terms of X_2 and $^*x_{13}$, inserting the result into (11a), we get

$$(20) \qquad\qquad ^*p = -\frac{1}{2}X_2 - 2\frac{3}{4}\,^*x_{13} + 15$$

Equation (20) has in it all the information contained in (9a) and (11a); no information has been lost, no new assumptions have been added. Thus (20) represents our problem in a nutshell. Combine it with our knowledge that an optimum solution, if existing, must be found among the basic feasible ones, i.e., those solutions that involve only one process, the remaining two processes being operated at zero levels. The beauty of Equation (20) is that it instantly shows us which processes ought to be operated at zero levels: X_2 and $^*x_{13}$, for both have negative coefficients. Indeed, should either of these two unknowns have values higher than zero, firm profits, according to (20), would be lower than if both of them were to have zero values. Negativity of the coefficients is called the "simplex criterion," a criterion that has now helped us see that the basis X_1 must be the best possible. That basis corresponds to our solution (12) above.

Our luck was bad, and we had to go through all three experiments. Had we reversed the order of our experiments, we should have immediately arrived at (20), which would have told us all we wanted to know. We should not have needed to find (18) or (19).

12. THREE ACTIVE PROCESSES, TWO INPUT CONSTRAINTS

In our last example let us make $m = 2$, $n = 3$, and $f = 2$ and specify the following numerical values of the parameters:

$$
\begin{array}{ll}
x_1 = 20 & a_{21} = 3 \\
x_2 = 30 & a_{22} = 5 \\
a_{11} = 4 & a_{23} = 2 \\
a_{12} = 2 & \pi_1 = 2 \\
a_{13} = 6 & \pi_2 = 3 \\
\multicolumn{2}{c}{\pi_0 = 20}
\end{array}
$$

It follows that

$$
\begin{array}{ll}
*\mu_1 = 3 & *\mu_3 = 2 \\
*\mu_2 = 1 & *\mu_4 = -2 \\
\multicolumn{2}{c}{*\mu_5 = -3}
\end{array}
$$

The profit equation is

(11b) $\qquad *p = 3X_1 + X_2 + 2X_3 - 2*x_{14} - 3*x_{25}$

The two constraints are

(9b) $\qquad 4X_1 + 2X_2 + 6X_3 + *x_{14} = 20$
$\qquad\qquad 3X_1 + 5X_2 + 2X_3 + *x_{25} = 30$

Our problem is to maximize (11b) subject to the constraints (9b), X_1, X_2, X_3, $*x_{14}$, and $*x_{25}$ being nonnegative, as usual. Using (9b) to express X_1 and X_2 in terms of X_3, $*x_{14}$, and $*x_{25}$, inserting the outcome into (11b), we get

(21) $\qquad *p = \dfrac{90}{7} - \dfrac{20}{7} X_3 - \dfrac{20}{7} *x_{14} - \dfrac{20}{7} *x_{25}$

This time we are having better luck than last time: Equation (21) satisfies the simplex criterion that all coefficients be negative. Should any one of the three unknowns X_3, $*x_{14}$, or $*x_{25}$ have values higher than zero, firm profits, according to (21), would be lower than if all three of them were to have zero values. The basis X_1 and X_2 is found to be the best possible (and thanks to our luck we do not have to try out the other possible basic solutions). It remains merely to find the numerical values of X_1 and X_2 and to make sure they are nonnegative. Setting X_3, $*x_{14}$, and $*x_{25}$ equal to zero and using (9b), we get

$$(22) \qquad\qquad X_1 = \frac{20}{7}$$

$$(23) \qquad\qquad X_2 = \frac{30}{7}$$

which satisfy the nonnegativity requirement. The solution represented in Equations (22) and (23) is the basic, feasible, and optimal solution.

13. COMPUTATION

The search for a profit expression which satisfies the simplex criterion may be a tedious one, if one has neither luck nor electronic computer. We have seen that in a problem involving n active processes and f input constraints, the number of basic solutions is $\binom{n + f}{n}$. To be true, some of these will be nonfeasible.[10] Furthermore, in the examination of the $\binom{n + f}{n}$ basic solutions short cuts may be taken. In one of them, the simplex method, developed by Dantzig,[11] an arbitrary basic solution is selected as a starting

[10] Sven Danö in "Linear Programming in Ice Cream Making," *Nordisk Tidsskrift for Teknisk Ökonomi*, No. 42 (Dec., 1955), pp. 151–177, has solved an actual problem involving the optimal blending of ingredients: each ingredient defines a process and contains one or more constituents (corresponding to our "inputs"). The number of basic solutions was 330, a large number of which was not feasible however. The remarkable fact was that the firm in question (Hendrie's Ice Cream Co., Milton, Mass.) had been able to establish the least-cost solution without knowing the simplex method, or even the formal apparatus of linear programming. The firm did have a "hunch" that the consideration of basic feasible solutions would be sufficient.

[11] G. B. Dantzig, "Maximization of a Linear Function of Variables Subject to Linear Inequalities," *Activity Analysis of Production and Allocation*, T. C. Koopmans, ed. (New York: Wiley, 1951). An elementary and very illuminating exposition of the simplex method is that given by John S. Chipman in "Computational Problems in Linear Programming," *The Review of Economics and Statistics*, Vol. XXXV, No. 4 (Nov., 1953), pp. 342–349.

point. At each of several successive stages the simplex criterion is applied. Since firm profit improves with every stage, it is impossible to slip back to an earlier stage.[12] Even so, without good luck one may find the amount of computational work involved in solving a practical linear-programming problem to be formidable. Fortunately, the use of electronic digital computers may accelerate the computational work very substantially. For example, a linear-programming routine prepared for the University of Illinois digital computer has a capacity of $4(f + n + 1) + fn = 712$, where n is the number of active processes and f the number of input constraints. In one actual problem, $n = 11$ and $f = 19$. The number of basic solutions, all not necessarily feasible, was then $\binom{30}{11} = 54.6$ million. In another problem, where $n = 25$ and $f = 18$, basic solutions numbered $\binom{43}{25} = 608.4$ billion. The computer required only 8 and 20 minutes, respectively, for solving the two problems.

14. CRITICAL PRICES OF INPUT

To apply our model to the theory of the demand for input, let us return to the simple case of $m = 2$, $n = 2$, and $f = 1$, which we studied in Sections 10 and 11. Using the simplex criterion, we found the basis X_1 to be the best possible. The question now arises: how sensitive is this result to manipulations of the price parameters of our model? The clue is found in Equation (17), where the coefficient of X_2 was

$$*\mu_2 - *\mu_1 \frac{a_{12}}{a_{11}} = \frac{\pi_0 - 7\pi_2}{2}$$

[12] In case of degeneracy the simplex method may not operate smoothly; slipping back to an earlier stage is possible. Degeneracy, ruled out by assumption at the time we set up system (9) of equations, does occur in economic problems. For example, in solving the aviation gasoline blending problem, Charnes, Cooper, and Mellon, *op. cit.*, encountered degeneracy. For remedies, see A. Charnes, "Optimality and Degeneracy in Linear Programming," *Econometrica*, Vol. 20, No. 2 (April, 1952), pp. 160–170; and Dorfman, Samuelson, and Solow, *op. cit.*, pp. 92–93.

and the coefficient of $*x_{13}$ was

$$*\mu_3 - *\mu_1 \frac{1}{a_{11}} = \frac{-\pi_0 + 3\pi_2}{4}$$

If the simplex criterion is to be satisfied, both coefficients must be negative:

(24) $$\frac{\pi_0}{7} < \pi_2 < \frac{\pi_0}{3}$$

The first thing to notice is that Inequality (24) includes π_0 and π_2 but not π_1, the price of the first input, the reason of course being that in the coefficients of X_2 and $*x_{13}$ in (17) price π_1 has disappeared.   Absence of π_1 shows that the satisfaction or non-satisfaction of the simplex criterion is independent of the value of price π_1 of the first input.   A moment's reflection reveals the sound economic meaning of this mathematical result.   It follows from constraint (9a) that the first input, available in the fixed quantity x_1, is *always* completely "used up," whether in active processes or in the disposal process.   Consequently, the total cost of the first input is fixed, and its particular value, dependent upon price π_1, is irrelevant to the choice from among processes.

15. THE DEMAND FOR INPUT

Inequality (24) does permit interesting conclusions to be drawn relative to the prices π_0 and π_2.   Inequality (24) indicates two boundaries for π_2.   What happens if π_2 "crosses" either of these two critical boundaries?   First, let π_2 be smaller than $\pi_0/7$.   The coefficient of X_2 in (17) becoming positive, the simplex criterion will no longer be satisfied.   The basis X_1 is no longer the best, but which basis will replace it?   Using (9a) to express X_2 in terms of X_1, $*x_{13}$, and x_1, inserting the result into (11a), using (6a), (6b), and (10a), we get

(25) $$*p = (-\pi_0 + 7\pi_2)X_1 + \frac{-\pi_0 + 5\pi_2}{2} *x_{13} + *\mu_2 \frac{x_1}{a_{12}}$$

From (25) we see that should π_2 be smaller than $\pi_0/7$, the coefficients of both X_1 and $*x_{13}$ would be negative. Thus (25) satisfies the simplex criterion, and the best basis is now X_2. To summarize: When π_2 becomes smaller than $\pi_0/7$, the optimal solution switches from (12) to (13). Under (12) the total demand for the second input was $*x_{21} = a_{21}X_1 = a_{21}x_1/a_{11} = 15$. Under (13) the total demand for the second input is $*x_{22} = a_{22}X_2 = a_{22}x_1/a_{12} = 50$.

What if π_2 crosses the opposite boundary in (24)? Should π_2 be larger than $\pi_0/3$, the coefficient of $*x_{13}$ in (17) would be positive. It can easily be shown that the best basis is now $*x_{13}$ and the optimal solution now (14). Since nothing is produced, the entire available supply of the first input is wasted in the disposal process. Of the second input, nothing is used at all, which is as it should be—under the new high price of the second input, the price of output from both active processes falls short of the cost of the second input alone. Under such circumstances none of the active processes should be operated.

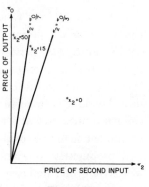

Figure 40

cumstances none of the active processes should be operated.

Our findings can be summarized in Figure 40 and as follows:

π_2	$*x_2$
$\pi_2 < \dfrac{\pi_0}{7}$	50
$\dfrac{\pi_0}{7} < \pi_2 < \dfrac{\pi_0}{3}$	15
$\pi_2 > \dfrac{\pi_0}{3}$	0

Like the neoclassical theory of the firm, linear programming makes it possible to draw the important conclusion that raising the price of an input will reduce the demand for it.   But the price rise may have to be considerable before a reduction follows.   The demand curve, which may be said to be discontinuous, is stairway-shaped, a curve form contrasting markedly with the neoclassical smooth demand curve for inputs.

16. CONCLUSION

Derivative (II) of Chapter 7 shows that if in a closed economy the price of *all* factors rises at a constant price of goods, the equilibrium gross private product, and with it employment, also rises.   Of this macroeconomic proposition there were, we said, at least five important qualifications, the third of which we have now developed: in certain critical areas, if the price of *one* factor, the ith input, rises at a constant price of output, the result is that within the firm the total input $*x_i$ will be reduced.

Consequently, one and the same thing, a rising price of input will strengthen macroeconomic demand, while weakening microeconomic demand, for input.   It seems almost unnecessary to point out that strengthened macroeconomic demand is fully compatible with weakened microeconomic demand.   What we have found in Chapter 16 is not a refutation of the macroeconomic proposition but rather a microeconomic qualification of that proposition.[13]

17. A CRITIQUE OF LINEAR PROGRAMMING

Linear programming represents a climax of the trend toward more substance and more operational significance in economic theory.   Neoclassical analysis was able to find certain properties

[13] This micro-macro distinction is one example of economic theory as a sequence of models, of which Tjalling C. Koopmans speaks in his *Three Essays on the State of Economic Science* (New York: McGraw-Hill, 1957), pp. 142–144.

of a solution, for instance, that to achieve maximization of profits, inputs must be combined in such a way that the ratio between price and physical marginal productivity is the same for every input. But linear programming accomplishes much more. It represents an explicit, simple, and workable instruction of *how to find* the solution, the simplicity being made possible by the linearity of the entire model. But we have bought high operational significance at the expense of generality. To be true, a finite number of processes, within each of which linearity as expressed by input-output equation (2) will hold, may represent a very good approximation to real-world production engineering. But does linearity as expressed by profit-output equation (3) represent an equally good approximation to real-world marketing? Is it not to be feared that in precisely those industries in which the input-output equations will be linear the profit-output equations will be nonlinear, the reason being that the price at which output is sold will not be beyond the control of the firm? Manufacturing industries are precisely the industries in which competition is less than pure. Needless to say, solutions may exist and may be found in such cases, but the explicit solution methods so successfully applied by linear programming will no longer serve.[14]

The reader may well wonder why competition should be less than pure in industries within which a linear input-output equation like (2) will hold. Is it not precisely the economies of scale that force firms to grow to a size where pure competition is no longer possible? And does not an input-output equation like (2) exclude economies or diseconomies of scale? Taken by itself, it does, but the input constraints are yet to be allowed for. Input constraints reflect the fact that durable plant and equipment are frequently available only in a fixed quantity. A process may always be operated below the capacity of the fixed quantity of plant and equipment, in which case, waste or idling is involved, hence the introduction of the disposal processes. The important thing to remember is that input constraints may reflect not merely

[14] See Dorfman, Samuelson, and Solow, *op. cit.*, chap. 8.

the trivial fact that in the short run plant and equipment are fixed, but also the long-run fact that plant and equipment of a certain type simply are available in certain minimum sizes. If scaled down below the minimum size, displacements may become too small relative to surfaces, and surfaces too small relative to lengths (reduce length to one-half, surfaces will reduce to one-fourth, and displacements will reduce to one-eighth). Hence small sizes might be uneconomical. When a small firm employs plant and equipment, it must accept minimum or larger sizes available and must accept the consequent waste or idling involved. If so, the small firm might eventually succumb in competition with larger firms, and pure competition would cease to exist. In this sense, the input constraints and the disposal processes lend a touch of realism to the entire model.

17

A Modern Restatement of the Theory of the Firm

1. SELLING EFFORT AND PRODUCT QUALITY AS PARAMETERS TO BE MANIPULATED

Taking for granted all prices of input and output, all input-output coefficients, and all input constraints, linear programming could determine the optimum levels of output in a finite number of processes. Presumably any output could be sold at the given price of output, advertising and selling effort being ignored. The possibility that quality of output might differ among processes was ignored, thus precluding any study of the effects upon consumer demand of varying the quality of output. The neoclassical theory of the firm, too, ignored selling effort and product quality as parameters to be manipulated. It has now long been recognized that the nonprice parameters are at least as important as the price parameter. But the road to a satisfactory quantitative treatment of those parameters has been blocked by the following dilemma. Some aspects of product quality and selling effort are thought of as being nonquantitative. As far as selling effort is concerned,

---

NOTE: The first six sections of the present chapter represent a revised version of the author's "Input-Output Coefficients as Measures of Product Quality," *The American Economic Review*, Vol. XLVII, No. 1 (March, 1957).

this difficulty traditionally has been overcome by using not selling effort itself but selling-effort expenditure, always quantitative, as the parameter to be optimized. If satisfactory, this approach could obviously be used for nonquantitative aspects of product quality, too. But it is not satisfactory for selling effort any more than for product quality, for both are multidimensional. Moreover, from the point of view of demand, alternative dimensions are substitutable. For example, the quantity sold may rise if the input of aluminum is substituted for the input of steel, or if television advertising is substituted for magazine advertising. It is not enough, then, to seek the optimal total expenditure. Somewhere in the firm, a decision-maker must know exactly how far to go in every particular dimension of quality and selling effort.[1]

The present chapter suggests that certain assumptions developed

[1] Most of the literature fails to answer the question of "how far shall we go?" Chamberlin in his *Monopolistic Competition*, was the first to ask it, but he thought that the answer would be hampered by the small extent to which quality might be reduced to quantitative terms. He now thinks that the extent was definitely underestimated in *Monopolistic Competition*; cf. his "The Product as an Economic Variable," *Quarterly Journal of Economics*, Vol. LXVII, No. 1 (Feb., 1953), p. 8. Five other prominent contributions have assumed either that both quality and selling effort are alike one-dimensional or that the expenditure on quality variation and selling effort can be taken to represent quality itself or selling effort itself, i.e., F. Zeuthen, "Effect and Cost of Advertisement from a Theoretic Aspect," *Nordisk Tidsskrift for Teknisk Økonomi*, Vol. I, No. 1 (1935), pp. 62–72; Heinrich von Stackelberg, "Theorie der Vertriebspolitik und der Qualitätsvariation," *Schmollers Jahrbuch für Gesetzgebung, Verwaltung und Volkswirtschaft im Deutschen Reiche* 63. Jahrgang Heft 1 (1939), pp. 43–85; Lawrence Abbott, "Vertical Equilibrium under Pure Quality Competition," *The American Economic Review*, Vol. XLIII, No. 5 (Dec., 1953), pp. 830–831; Robert Dorfman and Peter O. Steiner, "Optimal Advertising and Optimal Quality," *The American Economic Review*, Vol. XLIV, No. 5 (Dec., 1954), pp. 827 and 832; and Arne Rasmussen, *Pristeori eller parameterteori* (Copenhagen: Einar Harck, 1955), pp. 195 and 203. But Stackelberg and Dorfman-Steiner clearly saw and solved the substitution problem as between quality as a whole and selling effort as a whole. A refined graphical solution of the substitution problem as between different advertising media was offered 22 years ago by Børge Barfod in his *Reklamen i teoretisk-økonomisk Belysning* (Copenhagen: Einar Harck, 1937). Two contributions have solved the substitution problem as between all the dimensions of quality and selling effort: T. Scitovsky, *Welfare and Competition* (Chicago: Irwin, 1951), p. 259; and the author's *Product Equilibrium under Monopolistic Competition* (Cambridge, Mass.: Harvard University Press, 1951), chap. 5.

by Leontief for entirely different purposes may provide a satisfactory solution to the dilemma just described. Quality and selling effort can be defined simply as a complete specification both of the production and of the distribution process of the product in question, the complete specification consisting of two elements. First, a specification of the following form. To produce and sell the physical quantity $*X_j$ per unit of time of the product of the jth industry requires the input of the physical quantity $*x_{ij}$ per unit of time of the product of the ith industry, including labor, where $i = 1 \cdots m$. Such inputs are purchasable and have prices attached to them; they should not be confused with their own properties.[2] A specification of the inputs can be stated also in terms of input *coefficients* as follows. To produce and sell the physical quantity $*X_j$ per unit of time of the product of the jth industry requires the input of a_{ij} physical units of product of the ith industry per unit of product of the jth industry.

Under Leontief assumptions, for a given product, a_{ij} is independent of the level of output $*X_j$. Precisely for that reason we are free to let a_{ij} represent quality and selling effort. Should the Leontief assumptions not be used, we would not know whether a change in a_{ij} reflects a change in the level of output, in the quality of the product, or in the selling effort. Leontief assumptions exclude the level of output. Thus a change in the input coefficient for labor always reflects a change in the workmanship of the product, and a change in the input coefficient for a certain material always reflects a change in the product property that depends upon that material, say purity, hardness, tensile strength, heat resistance, etc. Even for selling effort, in fact, such an approach comes very close to the businessman's mode of thinking. There

---

[2] Hollis B. Chenery, "Engineering Production Functions," *The Quarterly Journal of Economics*, Vol. LXIII, No. 4 (Nov., 1949), pp. 507–531; and his "Process and Production Functions from Engineering Data," *Studies in the Structure of the American Economy* (New York: Oxford, 1953), pp. 297–325, has emphasized the distinction between the inputs and their properties. The former have prices, the latter do not, The former are called "physical inputs" or "economic quantities," the latter "engineering variables."

is some evidence that businessmen try to maintain a constant proportion between advertising and sales,[3] thinking of an increase in the proportion as a more intensive, and a decrease as a less intensive, selling effort.

The second element needed for a complete description of the method of producing and distributing the product is the specification of the order of time of the inputs. Certainly it would do no good to use the following time order in the process—painting an automobile body by first applying the baked enamel, then two primer coats, and finally bonderizing. Timing, however, is frequently so obvious that no explicit reference to it is made, as is the case in the Leontief system.

2. THE MODEL

Nonprice parameters now being measurable, we can quantify the theory of nonprice competition to the same extent that we can, say, the theory of production. The notation follows.

Variables

c_j = the number of dollars' worth of cost incurred annually by a firm in industry j

p_j = the number of dollars' worth of profits earned annually by a firm in industry j

x_{ij} = the number of physical units of the product of industry i absorbed annually by a firm in industry j

X_j = the number of physical units of product produced annually by a firm in industry j

σ_j = the number of physical units of product sold annually by a firm in industry j

[3] For empirical evidence see the following articles by Roy W. Jastram, "Advertising Outlays under Oligopoly," *The Review of Economics and Statistics*, Vol. XXXI, No. 2 (May, 1949), pp. 106–109; "Advertising Ratios Planned by Large-Scale Advertisers," *The Journal of Marketing*, Vol. XIV, No. 1 (July, 1949), pp. 13–21; "The Development of Advertising Appropriation Policy," *The Journal of Business of the University of Chicago*, Vol. XXIII, No. 3 (July, 1950), pp. 154–166. See also *Cost Behavior and Price Policy* (New York: National Bureau of Economic Research, 1943), chap. IX.

Parameters

a_{ij} = the number of physical units of the product of industry i absorbed per physical unit of product of a firm in industry j, to be manipulated

π_i = the price of the input absorbed from industry i, a parameter not to be manipulated

π_j = the price of the output produced by a firm in industry j, a parameter to be manipulated

As always, there is a price to be paid for extending a model. In return for including quality and selling effort, we shall exclude all input constraints. In other words, any input may be purchased in unlimited quantities at its fixed price. Furthermore, we shall exclude the possibility of producing several qualities of output simultaneously. The chain of causation in our model should be stated as: Price, selling efforts, and quality of product are fixed by the firm; sales is a function of these; output is a function of sales; and input is a function of output. As before, the variables are ex ante variables and as usual will carry asterisks.

The firm in industry j is assumed to produce only one product and to absorb as inputs the products of industry i, where i stands for m industries, including labor but not industry j itself. The first fundamental equation needed for the analysis is the demand equation faced by the firm:

$$(1) \qquad *\sigma_j = *\sigma_j(\pi_j, a_{1j}, \cdots, a_{mj}) \qquad \text{Demand}$$

Demand here is seen to depend upon price and all the input coefficients. Directly, of course, the consumer's attitude is determined by his appraisal of the appearance and expected performance of the product, but such appraisal, in turn, is determined by the complete specification of the production and distribution process of the product as revealed by the list of input coefficients. Doing some violence to reality we shall assume that the demand equation (1) is continuous and differentiable.

The second fundamental equation in the analysis is the cost equation, also assumed to be continuous and differentiable:

$$(2) \qquad *c_j = \sum_{i=1}^{m} (\pi_i *x_{ij})$$

where

$$(3) \qquad *x_{ij} = a_{ij} *X_j \qquad \text{for} \qquad i = 1 \cdots m$$

Equation (2) is a definitional equation. When interpreted in the Leontief tradition, Equation (3) becomes a behavior equation. In this tradition, for a given product the input coefficient a_{ij} is not allowed to vary with the level of output. Only by using this assumption are we free to let a_{ij} represent quality and selling effort. Taking (2) and (3) together, we write cost as

$$(3a) \qquad *c_j = *X_j \sum_{i=1}^{m} (\pi_i a_{ij})$$

Ignoring inventory problems, we assume that annual output planned by the firm equals annual sales expected by the firm:

$$*X_j = *\sigma_j$$

Finally, we need the definitional equation stating that profits equal revenue minus cost:

$$(4) \qquad *p_j = \pi_j *\sigma_j - *c_j$$

3. QUALITY EQUILIBRIUM

Let us vary one input coefficient a_{ij} in isolation and take the partial derivative of profits $*p_j$ with respect to input coefficient a_{ij}:

$$\frac{\partial *p_j}{\partial a_{ij}} = \pi_j \frac{\partial *\sigma_j}{\partial a_{ij}} - \left[\pi_i *\sigma_j + \frac{\partial *\sigma_j}{\partial a_{ij}} \sum_{i=1}^{m} (\pi_i a_{ij}) \right]$$

Here, the a_{ij} appearing under the summation sign is the general a_{ij} where, as indicated, $i = 1 \cdots m$. The three a_{ij}'s, outside the summation sign represent the specific input coefficient now being varied in isolation.

Let η_{ij} be the elasticity of demand faced by the firm in industry j with respect to the input coefficient a_{ij}. Setting the above partial derivative equal to zero and rearranging, we get: [4]

$$(5) \qquad \eta_{ij} = \frac{\partial^*\sigma_j}{\partial a_{ij}} \frac{a_{ij}}{{}^*\sigma_j} = \frac{\pi_i a_{ij}}{\pi_j - \sum_{i=1}^{m}(\pi_i a_{ij})}$$

As a necessary condition for profit maximization, the input of the product of the ith industry into the product of the jth industry must be adjusted in such a way as to cause the expenditure for that input per unit of output of the jth industry divided by the profit per unit of output of the jth industry to equal the elasticity of demand faced by the firm of the jth industry with respect to the input coefficient a_{ij}. So far, the analysis sounds rather complicated, but paradoxically gets much simpler as it is extended.

That the partial derivative of profits ${}^*p_j$ with respect to the input coefficient a_{ij} be zero is one necessary condition for the maximization of profits. Another is that the second derivative of profits ${}^*p_j$ be negative:

$$\frac{\partial^2 {}^*p_j}{\partial a_{ij}^2} = \frac{\partial^2 {}^*\sigma_j}{\partial a_{ij}^2}\left[\pi_j - \sum_{i=1}^{m}(\pi_i a_{ij})\right] - 2\pi_i \frac{\partial^*\sigma_j}{\partial a_{ij}} < 0$$

Assume that over the relevant range the quality-quantity relationship can be illustrated by a curve similar to the one shown in Figure 41. As any input coefficient a_{ij} increases, quantity ${}^*\sigma_j$ responds less. Such an assumption is reasonable both for quality and for selling effort. Although consumers seem to appreciate an increase in horsepower of a passenger car from 150 to 200, they could

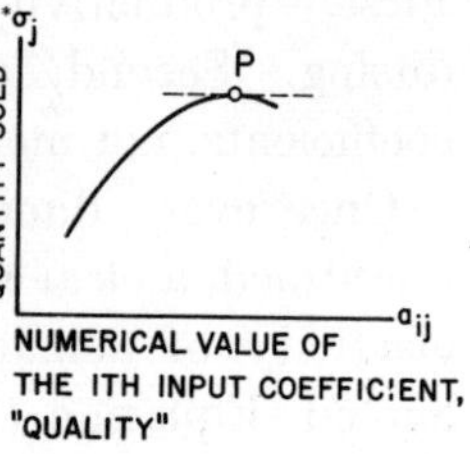

Figure 41

4 Cf. Rasmussen, *op. cit.*, p. 203.

not possibly use an increase from 500 to 550. Selling effort, no doubt, can also be increased *ad nauseam*. Consequently, the second derivative of $*\sigma_j$ with respect to a_{ij} is negative. The expression in brackets represents profit per unit of output which is positive. The entire first term, then, is negative. In the second term π_i is positive, and up to the point P, the first derivative of $*\sigma_j$ with respect to a_{ij} is positive. Consequently, in that range, the entire second derivative of profits $*p_j$ is negative.

If not one but all dimensions of quality and selling effort are manipulated, Equation (5) holds simultaneously for *any i*. Write it in the form:

$$(5a) \qquad \frac{\pi_i}{\dfrac{\partial *\sigma_j}{\partial a_{ij}}} = \frac{\pi_j - \sum\limits_{i=1}^{m} (\pi_i a_{ij})}{*\sigma_j}$$

holding for any i. Consequently, we can write

$$(5b) \qquad \frac{\pi_1}{\dfrac{\partial *\sigma_j}{\partial a_{1j}}} = \frac{\pi_2}{\dfrac{\partial *\sigma_j}{\partial a_{2j}}} = \cdots = \frac{\pi_m}{\dfrac{\partial *\sigma_j}{\partial a_{mj}}}$$

In Equation (5b) we see that as a necessary condition for maximization of profits, quality must continue to be improved and selling effort intensified in each of the m possible dimensions until the ratio between the price of an input and the marginal "productivity" of the corresponding input coefficient is the same for all m inputs. The similarity to the neoclassical theory of production and distribution is evident. But there are two differences. First, "productivity" is productivity in selling, not only in producing. Second, condition (5b) is stated in terms of input coefficients, not merely inputs.

Once every dimension of quality and selling effort has been quantified, a clear meaning can be gained of the concept "quality elasticity of demand" and the concept put to good use. As agreed, Equation (5) must hold for any i. Adding together all the m versions of the equation we get:

$$(6) \qquad H = \sum_{i=1}^{m} \eta_{ij} = \frac{\displaystyle\sum_{i=1}^{m} (\pi_i a_{ij})}{\pi_j - \displaystyle\sum_{i=1}^{m} (\pi_i a_{ij})}$$

The meaning of this aggregate elasticity H, the sum of all elasticities η_{ij}, can be clarified by the following hypothetical operation. Letting the first input coefficient a_{1j} rise by one-nth of its numerical value, watch the effect upon the quantity sold *σ_j.

Next, letting the second input coefficient a_{2j} rise by one-nth, watch the effect upon *σ_j. Extend the examination to all m input coefficients. If n is sufficiently large, say 1000, the order in which we are increasing the a's is immaterial. Consequently, the sum H of all the m elasticities is equal to the number of $n$ths by which *σ_j will rise when *at the same time* every a_{ij} is increased by one-nth. In this aggregative sense, the concept "quality elasticity of demand" has a clear quantitative meaning. Let us now rewrite (6):

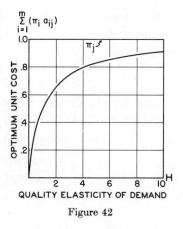

Figure 42

$$(6a) \qquad \sum_{i=1}^{m} (\pi_i a_{ij}) = \pi_j \frac{H}{1 + H}$$

that is, in equilibrium, unit cost should be carried, by means of quality improvement and intensification of selling effort, up to the point where it amounts to the fraction $H/(1 + H)$ of the price of the product. Equation (6a) employs unit cost relative to price, presumably in accordance with modes of thinking among businessmen, rather than marginalist terms, a circumstance that should not conceal the fact that the present analysis is a thoroughgoing marginalist one. H is a sum of partial derivatives in disguise; consequently, Equation (6a) is an equation of margins. It was, after all, derived from a summation of (5) which, in turn, was based upon profit maximization by partial derivation. Equation (6a) includes unit cost only because the Leontief assumptions equate unit and marginal costs. The relationship expressed by (6a) is shown graphically in Figure 42.

4. PRICE EQUILIBRIUM

Let us now vary price π_j in isolation and take the partial derivative of profit $*p_j$ with respect to the price π_j:

$$\frac{\partial *p_j}{\partial \pi_j} = \pi_j \frac{\partial *\sigma_j}{\partial \pi_j} + *\sigma_j - \frac{\partial *\sigma_j}{\partial \pi_j} \sum_{i=1}^{m} (\pi_i a_{ij}) = 0$$

Now let e be the familiar Marshallian price elasticity of demand faced by the firm in industry j. Setting the partial derivative above equal to zero and rearranging, we get:

$$(7) \qquad e = \frac{\partial *\sigma_j}{\partial \pi_j} \frac{\pi_j}{*\sigma_j} = - \frac{\pi_j}{\pi_j - \displaystyle\sum_{i=1}^{m} (\pi_i a_{ij})}$$

a result that can be expressed as: The price π_j of the product of the jth industry should be adjusted in such a way that price π_j divided by the profit per unit of output of the jth industry will equal the Marshallian price elasticity of demand with opposite sign.

That the partial derivative of profits $*p_j$ with respect to price π_j be zero is one necessary condition for profit maximization. Another is that the second derivative of $*p_j$ be negative:

$$\frac{\partial^2 *p_j}{\partial \pi_j{}^2} = \frac{\partial^2 *\sigma_j}{\partial \pi_j{}^2} \left[\pi_j - \sum_{i=1}^{m} (\pi_i a_{ij}) \right] + 2 \frac{\partial *\sigma_j}{\partial \pi_j} < 0$$

Within the relevant range, let it be assumed that the relationship between price and quantity sold can be described by a straight line with negative slope, as in Figure 43. In that very special case, the second derivative of $*\sigma_j$ with respect to π_j is zero. The expression within brackets represents profit per unit of output which is positive. The entire first term, then, is zero. In the second term, the derivative of $*\sigma_j$ with respect to π_j being negative, the entire second derivative of profits $*p_j$ is negative. If the price and quantity-sold relationship were not a straight line but rather a curve concave in respect to the origin, the second

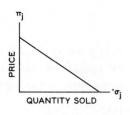

Figure 43

derivative of $*\sigma_j$ with respect to π_j would be negative, as would therefore both terms. If the relationship were a curve convex in respect to the origin, the first term would be positive, but if the convexity were moderate, the positive first term would be small enough to be outweighed by the negative last term.

Rewrite (7):

$$(7a) \quad \pi_j = \frac{e}{1 + e} \sum_{i=1}^{m} (\pi_i a_{ij})$$

As a necessary condition for profit maximization, price is marked up to the point where it amounts to $e/(1 + e)$ times the unit cost of the product, where e is the Marshallian price elasticity of demand for the product. Unlike (6a), (7a) is old and familiar.[5] Like (6a), (7a)

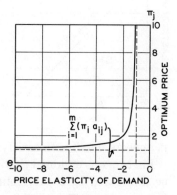

Figure 44

[5] Joan Robinson, *The Economics of Imperfect Competition* (London: Macmillan, 1933), on p. 54, says that monopoly optimum price is equal to marginal cost multiplied by $\epsilon/(\epsilon - 1)$. Since (1) her ϵ is the numerical value of Marshallian price elasticity, so that $\epsilon = -e$, and (2) under Leontief assumptions unit and marginal costs are equal, equation (7a) is identical with Joan Robinson's formulation. Equation (7a) is the microeconomic counterpart to the macroeconomic equation (24) in chapters 7 and 8. The λ there and the $e/(1 + e)$ here occupy similar positions.

employs terms of unit cost relative to price, terms better understood by the businessman, but is quite as marginalist as (6a). The relationship expressed by (7a) is shown in Figure 44.

5. FULL EQUILIBRIUM

If price and all dimensions of quality and selling effort are to be optimized, Equations (6a) and (7a) must be satisfied at the same time. Taking them together, we get:

$$(8) \qquad\qquad e + H = -1$$

a very simple result showing that in equilibrium, i.e., after everything has been fully adjusted, the sum of the price elasticity and

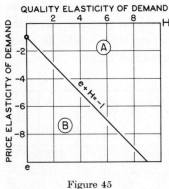

Figure 45

of the quality elasticity of demand (the latter defined in Section 3 above) should equal -1. The relationship expressed by Equation (8) is shown graphically in Figure 45.

Equation (8) is a condition requisite to full equilibrium, but is it always possible in the real world, even disregarding uncertainty, to satisfy it? Given the preceding, our not unreasonable assumptions, it appears possible to satisfy Equation (8).

First, it was assumed that the quality-quantity relationship can be illustrated by a curve similar to the one shown in Figure 41. Here, as any input coefficient a_{ij} increases, quantity $*\sigma_j$ becomes less responsive. This relationship holding for all input coefficients, at low numerical values of all a_{ij}'s the quality elasticity of demand H will be high, becoming progressively lower as the a_{ij}'s increase. Eventually H will turn negative.

Second, it was assumed that the relationship between price and quantity sold can be described approximately by a straight line with a negative slope (Figure 43). Here the Marshallian price elasticity of demand e at a high price π_j will be numerically greater than unity and will be progressively higher as price increases. At a low price π_j, e will be numerically less than unity and will numerically become progressively lower as price decreases.

If these assumptions can be accepted, there *is* a solution that will satisfy Equation (8). If the firm finds itself in the region A, where $e + H > -1$, it will be able to approach the line marked $e + H = -1$ in Figure 45 simply by raising both price and quality, still making sure that the system of Equations (5a) is satisfied. In Figures 46 and 47 the effects of simultaneous increases in price and quality are indicated. Figure 46 shows the usual price-

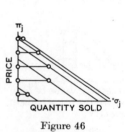

Figure 46

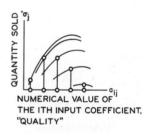

Figure 47

quantity relationship. Improving the quality of the product causes the price-quantity curve to shift upward. But since the quality elasticity of demand, H, has been assumed eventually to become progressively lower as a_{ij} rises, the demand curve must shift less as a_{ij} rises. Eventually, raising price and quality simultaneously must take us into an area in which the price elasticity of demand is numerically extremely high.

Figure 47 shows the corresponding phenomenon for quality. A rise in the price of the product causes the quality-quantity curve to shift downward. But since the price elasticity of demand e is assumed eventually to become numerically progressively higher as π_j rises, the demand curve in Figure 47 must shift more as π_j rises. Eventually, raising price and quality simultaneously must take us into an area in which the quality elasticity of demand is extremely low. But if the negative price elasticity e becomes numerically higher and higher, and if the positive quality elasticity H becomes lower and lower, a point must eventually be reached at which Equation (8) is satisfied.

Similarly, if the firm should find itself on the other side of the line marked $e + H = -1$, that is, in region B of Figure 45, where $e + H < -1$. The firm can approach the line by reducing price and quality, again making sure that the system of Equations (5a) is satisfied. Price elasticity will decrease numerically, and quality elasticity increase.

One cannot rule out on a priori grounds the possibility of several

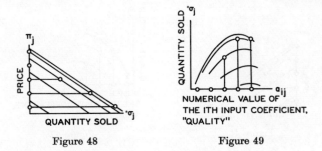

Figure 48   Figure 49

points existing at the same time that satisfy Equation (8). Suppose one such point is located upon the line shown in Fig. 45. Suppose, too, that quality is improved and price of the product reduced. Figure 48 shows the price-quantity relationship. A rise in the quality of the product will cause the price-quantity curve to shift upward. But since the quality elasticity of demand H is assumed eventually to become progressively lower as a_{ij} rises, the demand curve must shift less as a_{ij} rises. Eventually, therefore, reducing price but raising quality simultaneously will result in the price elasticity of demand being numerically quite low.

Figure 49 shows the corresponding phenomenon for quality. A reduction in the price of the product will cause the quality-quantity curve to shift upward. But since the price elasticity of demand e is assumed eventually to become numerically progressively lower as π_j falls, the demand curve must shift less as π_j falls. Eventually, reducing price but raising quality simultaneously will result in the quality elasticity of demand being also quite low, Equation (8) still being satisfied.

6. LIMITATIONS

The Leontief assumption that for a given product a_{ij} is independent of level of output represents the first limitation. It should be noted, however, that two restraints on the firm included in the model operate in a manner similar to that of the diminishing returns in the production function: first, the assumption that as price π_j is lowered, the numerical price elasticity will become progressively lower; and second, the assumption that as the input coefficient a_{ij} is increased, quantity sold $*\sigma_j$ will become less responsive.

Like the static Leontief model, our model is ill-equipped to cope with those inputs that consist of the services rendered by durable capital stock. In a treatment of product quality such input is likely to be quite important. Quality can be manipulated not only by varying workmanship or materials but also by varying the shape of things. If so, tools and dies will then have to be discarded and new ones installed. Such tools and dies introduce the problem of indivisibilities, and force us to abandon our assumption that the demand and cost functions are continuous and differentiable, in which case input constraints of the type studied in Chapter 16 become relevant.

Other obvious limitations are the static profit-maximization assumption and also the complete exclusion of rivals and of their behavior, expected and actual, limitations that are common to most treatments of nonprice competition. The decisive difference between the approach suggested here and elsewhere is that the adoption of the Leontief input-output coefficients as measures of product quality and selling effort enable us to state the theory of nonprice competition as quantitatively as we can the theory of production.   But now let us put the model to use and show how the neoclassical downward-sloping demand curve for inputs will reappear.

7. THE DEMAND FOR INPUT UNDER VARIABLE QUALITY OF OUTPUT

Write Equation (5a) as follows:

$$(5a) \qquad \pi_i = \frac{1}{a_{ij}} \, \eta_{ij} \left[\pi_j - \sum_{i=1}^{m} (\pi_i a_{ij}) \right]$$

that is, in equilibrium price π_i of the ith input must equal average productivity $1/a_{ij}$ of that input multiplied by the elasticity of demand faced by the firm in industry j with respect to the input coefficient a_{ij} multiplied by the profit per unit of output of the jth industry.   Or more briefly—price of input equals average productivity times demand elasticity times profit margin.

Assume an increase in the price of the ith input, π_i.   The left-hand side of (5a) as written above would rise.   If nothing happened to π_j, a_{ij}, and $*X_j$, the right-hand side would fall, for $\sum(\pi_i a_{ij})$ would rise.   Consequently, something *must* happen to them.   At constant price π_j of the product, a_{ij} would have to fall.   According to Figure 41, the elasticity η_{ij} is positive throughout the relevant range and will rise when a_{ij} falls.   Thus all the three factors of the product on the right-hand side of (5a) can be made to rise by reducing a_{ij}, an operation that would counteract the reduction of the third factor sufficiently to restore equilibrium.   The reduction of the third factor could, of course, also have been counteracted by raising π_j, the price of the product.

In summary, to satisfy condition (5a) after the price π_i of the ith input has risen, it is necessary either to reduce a_{ij}, raise π_j, or both.   In any case $*X_j$ would fall, and consequently, the product $a_{ij}*X_j = *x_{ij}$ would also fall.   Thus we have shown that a rise in the price π_i of the ith input is followed by a reduction of the total input $*x_{ij}$. In other words, there is a downward sloping demand curve for the ith input. This is true of any i.

8. CONCLUSION

Derivative (II) of Chapter 7 showed that if in a closed economy the price of *all* factors rises at a constant price of goods, the equilibrium gross private product, and with it employment, also rises. This proposition was a macroeconomic one, to which there were, we said, at least five important qualifications. We have now developed the fourth one of these. We have found that if the price of *one* factor, the ith input, rises at a constant price of goods, the total input $*x_{ij}$ within the firm is reduced.

The difference between the third and fourth qualifications is that the former, based upon the standard linear-programming approach, assumes the quality of the product to be constant, but the fourth is a theory of product quality adjustment.

18

Neoclassical Theory of Wages, Capital, and Output: All Capital Is Circulating

1. THE BÖHM-BAWERK MODEL

Although in the short run opportunities for substitution among inputs may be absent and the marginal productivity of any input may be zero, modern technology offers long-run opportunities of substitution between labor and capital. In Böhm-Bawerk's *Positive Theory of Capital*,[1] he presents an ingenious model in which labor productivity, the internal rate of return, the wage rate, and the period of production are determined by the stock of capital, the labor force, and the production function. With labor force a parameter and labor productivity determined, the model, like the Keynesian one, permits the determination of aggregate output. But unlike the Keynesian model it assumes full employment. Also unlike the Keynesian model it ignores effective demand. The consumers' goods industry buys man-hours from labor households and entrepreneurial ability from capitalist-entrepreneur households. Thanks to the capitalist, production may take time, and with the lapse of time labor inputs will ripen directly into finished

[1] Eugen von Böhm-Bawerk, *Positive Theorie des Kapitales* (Innsbruck: Wagner, 1888), translated by William Smart and published as *Positive Theory of Capital* (New York: Stechert, 1891), book VII, "The Rate in Market Transactions," and "The Market for Capital in its Full Development," pp. 381–424.

consumers' goods. Durable producers' goods are not included in the model. In return for labor and entrepreneurship the consumers' goods industry pays wages and profits. But exactly as in the open Leontief model, the wage and profit income of households does *not* affect the demand for consumers' goods, which are sold in a purely competitive market, for example the world market, a market that will absorb at a constant price *any* output that can be produced. A transactions table for the Böhm-Bawerk model is shown in Table 12.

TABLE 12. Planned Purchases of Factors

Purchasing from	Purchases Planned by		
	Consumers' Goods Industry	Entrepreneurial Households	Labor Households
Consumers' Goods Industry	—	—	—
Entrepreneurial Households	$*x_{ec}$	—	—
Labor Households	$*x_{lc}$	—	—

Böhm-Bawerk's theory of wages, profits, and output is a quantitative determination presented in the form of verbal reasoning and arithmetical examples. Very early, however, Wicksell restated it in rigorous form.[2] Wicksell's restatement may be summarized in a simple model employing the following notation:

[2] Knut Wicksell, *Über Wert, Kapital und Rente* (Jena: Gustav Fischer, 1893); reprint, *Series of Reprints of Scarce Tracts in Economic and Political Science, No. 15* (London: London School of Economics and Political Science, 1933); and published as *Value, Capital and Rent*, S. H. Frowein, trans. (London: Allen & Unwin, 1954).

Variables

i = the internal rate of return per annum in the consumers' goods industry

x_{ec} = the number of dollars' worth of profits earned annually by the capitalist-entrepreneurs who own the consumers' goods industry

x_{lc} = the number of man-hours absorbed annually from the labor households by the consumers' goods industry

X_c = the number of physical units of product produced annually by the consumers' goods industry

Parameters

θ = the period of production measured in years, to be manipulated

h_{lc} = hours worked per year per man

P = the labor force measured in number of men

π_c = the price of consumers' goods

π_l = the money wage rate

S_{lc} = the stock of capital measured in dollars at an instant of time

2. THE CAPITAL CONCEPT

Böhm-Bawerk saw the period of production as the parameter to be manipulated by the capitalist-entrepreneurs in order to maximize their internal rate of return. By the period of production he meant the period of time which elapses between the input of labor on the one hand, and the sale of the finished product on the other. Land he disregarded, considering only two factors of production, labor and capital. The lapse of time between input and output is made possible by capital, which must "advance" the wages of labor because wage earners cannot wait. Viewed from this angle, the input angle, capital is a wages fund. From a different angle, the output angle, capital is the stock of unfinished products building up during the period of production. Even though the two capital concepts apparently differ (a stock of finished products versus a stock of unfinished ones), no real inconsistency exists. Both describe the capitalistic process of production, one from the input angle, one from the output angle.

3. THE MODEL, MICROECONOMICS

Let a man work h_{lc} hours per year for θ years to finish his product, and let his wage rate be π_l dollars per hour. The combined wage earnings per man during the entire θ-year-long period of production is

$$(1) \qquad \frac{\pi_l{}^*x_{lc}\theta}{P} = \pi_l h_{lc}\theta$$

Let the man's wages be paid at the beginning of the year. At the beginning of the first year, then, the entrepreneur will have a capital stock of $\pi_l h_{lc}$ dollars per man, at the beginning of the second a capital stock of $2\pi_l h_{lc}$ dollars per man, and at the beginning of the last and θth year a capital stock of $\theta\pi_l h_{lc}$ dollars per man.

The expected internal rate of return being $*i$ per annum, profit earnings by entrepreneurs during the first year are $*i\pi_l h_{lc}$ dollars per man, during the second year $2*i\pi_l h_{lc}$ dollars per man, and during the last and θth year $\theta*i\pi_l h_{lc}$ dollars per man. The combined profit earnings per man during the entire θ-year-long period of production are

$$(2) \qquad \frac{*x_{ec}\theta}{P} = *i\pi_l h_{lc}\theta\,\frac{1+\theta}{2}$$

The third equation says that the value of output per man during the entire period of production is distributed between labor and capital

$$(3) \qquad \frac{\pi_c{}^*X_c\theta}{P} = \frac{\pi_l{}^*x_{lc}\theta}{P} + \frac{*x_{ec}\theta}{P}$$

Inserting (1) and (2) into (3), dividing by θ, and rearranging, we write:

$$(4) \qquad *i = 2 \, \frac{\dfrac{\pi_c * X_c}{P} - \pi_l h_{lc}}{\pi_l h_{lc}(1 + \theta)}$$

In the fifth equation the production function is stated as the value[3] of output per man per annum rising with increasing length of the period of production but by decreasing increments. These properties, shown graphically in Figure 50, should be implicit in the function:

$$(5) \qquad \frac{\pi_c * X_c}{P} = \frac{\pi_c * X_c}{P} (\theta)$$

The sixth equation states that at a given wage rate entre-

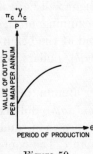

Figure 50

preneurs will manipulate the parameter under their control, the period of production θ, in a way that will maximize their internal rate of return. Why the rate, not the amount, of return?

In the short-run theory of the firm we are accustomed to the maximization of the amount of return. In such models the stock of capital invested is a constant. In our present model, however, the parameter under the control of the entrepreneurs is the period of production θ. By increasing θ, the entrepreneurs can always increase the *amount* of return per man per year $\pi_c * X_c/P - \pi_l h_{lc}$, for $\pi_c * X_c/P$ always rises with θ. At the given wage rate, however, the entrepreneurs

[3] The value of output may rise either because the physical quantity of output rises or because the quality of output improves. Wicksell emphasized the latter alternative when he assumed that "the price of the matured wine . . . is such that, when sold for consumption . . . , 3-year wine commands a wholesale price of 90s. per hl., 4-year wine 100s., and 5-year wine 110s." Knut Wicksell, *Lectures on Political Economy Volume One, General Theory* (London: Routledge and Kegan Paul, 1934), p. 174. The original Swedish edition was first published in 1901, and Wicksell's treatment of maturing wine may well be the first treatment of product quality as a variable in economic theory.

cannot increase θ without at the same time increasing the stock of capital per man. Capital should be increased only if the *rate* of return $*i$, as defined by Equation (4), is not reduced as a consequence. For should $*i$ fall, the entrepreneur could do better by investing the additional capital in the employment of a larger number of men at the original period of production θ, in which case $*i$ would not change. Accordingly, entrepreneurs seek to adjust the period of production θ in such a way as to maximize the rate, not the amount, of return:

$$(6) \qquad \frac{d*i}{d\theta} = 0$$

Carrying out the differentiation, using (6), then (4) and rearranging, we get:

$$(I) \qquad \frac{d\left(\dfrac{\pi_c * X_c}{P}\right)}{d\theta} = \frac{*i\pi_l h_{lc}}{2}$$

The implication of maximizing the rate of return at a given wage rate is, then, that the period of production will be such that the slope of the production function at that period of production will equal the rate of return per annum times the wage rate per annum divided by two. A very neat

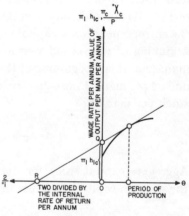

Figure 51

illustration of this solution is shown in Figure 51, introduced by Wicksell. Plotting the annual wage $\pi_l h_{lc}$ in the northern direction, we find the point Q. Through Q draw the tangent to the production function, reproduced from Figure 50. The slope of the tangent is the distance OQ (annual wage) divided by the distance OR. Given the necessity of satisfying equilibrium condition (I), the distance OR can represent nothing other than two divided by the expected internal rate of return per annum $2/*i$. The diagram in Figure 51 permits us to find in a very simple way the entrepreneurial response in terms of θ to any wage rate. For example, should the wage rate be higher, the period of production would be longer, and the internal rate of return per annum lower, for $2/*i$ would be higher.

4. MACROECONOMIC EQUILIBRIUM IN A STATIONARY ECONOMY

The Böhm-Bawerk—Wicksell theory was not merely a theory of the firm. By assuming aggregate capital stock and aggregate labor force to be parameters, Böhm-Bawerk and Wicksell could transform their theory of a stationary economy into macroeconomic terms. We have already seen that at the beginning of the first year the entrepreneur has a capital stock of $\pi_l h_{lc}$ dollars per man, at the beginning of the second year a capital stock of $2\pi_l h_{lc}$ dollars per man, and at the beginning of the θth year a capital stock of $\theta\pi_l h_{lc}$ dollars per man. Consequently, *on an average* he will have a capital stock per man of

$$\pi_l h_{lc} \frac{1 + \theta}{2}$$

Aggregate capital stock for the economy as a whole is equal to the average capital stock per man times number of men:

$$(7) \qquad S_{lc} = \pi_l h_{lc} \frac{1 + \theta}{2} P$$

where P is the aggregate labor force and S_{lc} the aggregate capital stock, both parameters.

From the point of view of the individual firm the wage rate is a parameter, but from the point of view of the economy as a whole a variable. Böhm-Bawerk and Wicksell determined its equilibrium level as follows. Assume for the moment the wage rate to be given. At the given wage rate and with the known production function (5), the entrepreneurs will adjust the period of production in a way to maximize the internal rate of return. From Equation (7) we can, knowing the available capital stock, find the number of men who can be employed at the given wage rate and the period of production as adjusted. If the number of men happens to be equal to the labor force actually available in the economy, we have been lucky enough to choose the equilibrium wage rate in the first instance.

If, however, the number of men who can be employed at the given capital stock is *less* than the available labor force, competition among laborers reduces the wage rate. At a lower wage rate a shorter period of production will become optimal, as illustrated in Figure 51. For two different reasons the same amount of capital stock can employ more men: the wage rate π_l is lower and the period of production θ shorter. Equation (7) shows that in either case the number employed increases. The wage rate continues to decline until there is full employment.

If finally the number of men who can be employed at the given capital stock is *larger* than the available labor force, competition among the capitalist-entrepreneurs raises the wage rate. At a higher wage rate a longer period of production will become optimal. For two different reasons capital stock can employ fewer men: the wage rate π_l is higher and the period of production θ longer. The wage rate will continue to rise until the capitalist-entrepreneurs do not wish to hire more than the available labor force. The Böhm-Bawerk—Wicksell theory thus illustrates the macroeconomic interdependence among the wage rate, the internal rate of return, and the period of production, their model being entirely independent of Böhm-Bawerk's much more familiar theory of saving, according to which (among other things) the economic near-sightedness of men in comparing present and future needs causes capital accumulation to be restricted. The Böhm-Bawerk—Wicksell macroeconomic interdependence model assumes capital stock to be a parameter.

5. THE EFFECT OF INCREASING CAPITAL ACCUMULATION

Capital stock being a parameter, we may examine the effect that increasing it will have upon the wage rate, the internal rate of return, and the period of production. It follows from (7) that at constant P, a higher S_{lc} must increase the wage rate π_l. Using Figure 51, we see that the higher wage rate will induce entrepreneurs to use a longer period of production θ and that the internal rate of return will fall.

Before 1914 there was some speculation about a zero rate of return in the coming millennium of prosperity. What if at extremely large values of θ the slope of the production function were to approach zero? At increasing capital stock $2/*i$ would then approach infinity, and the internal rate of return $*i$, would approach zero. Böhm-Bawerk himself was confident that this would never happen, but Wicksell refused to commit himself to any specific hypothesis about the limits of the slope of the production function at extremely large values of θ.

6. A CRITIQUE OF THE BÖHM-BAWERK MODEL

The importance of the Böhm-Bawerk model lies in its rigorous demonstration of the relationship between wages and capital. To a higher wage rate the capitalist-entrepreneur will respond by adopting a longer period of production, thus causing productivity of labor to rise. But the model is marred by the assumption of all capital being circulating capital. The favorite examples used by Böhm-Bawerk and Wicksell are maturing wine and growing forests. Ultimately, then, the empirical basis of neoclassical theory once again confines itself to the production functions of agriculture or forestry. Observation of slow biological growth must lead to a concept such as the Böhm-Bawerk period of production.

Once again it becomes desirable to restate the theory under the conditions of modern technology. In the following we shall make such an attempt. Making no use of the Böhm-Bawerk period of production and assuming all capital to consist of durable producers' goods, we shall treat the quality of such goods as a variable and shall express it in terms of three performance characteristics of durable producers' goods, all familiar to the businessman: the direct labor input-output coefficient, the reciprocal of the capital coefficient, and the durability or useful life. The three performance characteristics are optimized, and it is shown that a higher wage rate will raise the capital intensity of the production process.

19

A Modern Restatement of the Theory of Wages, Capital, and Output: All Capital Is Fixed

> Machinery and labour are in constant competition, and the former can frequently not be employed until labour rises.
>
> DAVID RICARDO, *The Principles of Political Economy and Taxation*

1. THE PROBLEM

It has frequently been observed that the capital-labor ratio ("capital intensity") is not the same in Britain and the United States, and the intuitive explanation usually offered is that the British wage rate does not put as high a premium on labor-saving designs as does the United States wage rate. Similar comparisons have been made between the economy of India and mature economies.[1]

From no simple theoretical model known to exist can such an

[1] Seymour Melman in his *Dynamic Factors in Industrial Productivity* (New York: Wiley, 1956) compared Britain and the United States. V. V. Bhatt in his "Capital Intensity of Industries, A Comparative Study of Certain Countries," *Bulletin of the Oxford University Institute of Statistics*, Vol. 18, No. 2 (May, 1956), pp. 179–194, compared India with The United Kingdom and Australia.

explanation readily be deduced. The Böhm-Bawerk model ignores the very type of producers' goods that are most important, the durable ones. The only dimension of capital quality optimized in the Böhm-Bawerk model is the average period of production,[2] which, unfortunately, is not a simple—perhaps not even a meaningful—concept when durable producers' goods are considered.[3]

2. THE MODEL

In the present chapter three sectors are considered, each producing a homogeneous product or service: the consumers' goods industry, the producers' goods industry, and the labor household sector. The subscripts used to designate the three sectors are c, p, and l, respectively. The consumers' goods industry has one output and two inputs, the former consisting of consumers' goods, the latter of labor services and the services rendered by durable producers' goods. The producers' goods industry has one output and one input, the former consisting of producers' goods, the latter of labor service. The notation follows:

[2] J. R. Hicks, *Value and Capital* (Oxford: Clarendon Press, 1939), chaps. XV–XVII, pp. 191–226. This alternative was criticized by (1) William Fellner and Howard S. Ellis, "Hicks and the Time-period Controversy," *The Journal of Political Economy*, Vol. XLVIII, No. 4 (Aug., 1940), pp. 563–578, and (2) Paul A. Samuelson, *Foundations of Economic Analysis* (Cambridge, Mass.: Harvard University Press, 1948), p. 188. For recent reformulations of the concept see: J. D. Sargan, "The Period of Production," *Econometrica*, Vol. 23, No. 2 (April, 1955), pp. 151–165; and also Conrad A. Blyth, "The Theory of Capital and its Time Measure," *Econometrica*, Vol. 24, No. 4 (Oct., 1956), pp. 467–479, with following comment by Sargan.

[3] But Gustaf Åkerman, *Realkapital und Kapitalzins* (Stockholm: Central-tryckeriet, 1923) devoted himself to the case in which durable producers' goods and free uninvested labor coöperate. The Åkerman model was summarized in rigorous form and further extended by Knut Wicksell in his long review article "Real-kapital och kapitalränta," *Ekonomisk Tidskrift*, Vol. 25, Nos. 5–6 (1923), pp. 145–180, since translated into English as the second appendix to his *Lectures, Volume One* (London: Routledge and Kegan Paul, 1934), pp. 258–299. In his example Wicksell used axes, but the only dimension of the ax optimized was its useful life. By introducing two additional dimensions, optimized simultaneously with the useful life, the present chapter is believed to go beyond the Wicksellian analysis.

Variables

a_{lp} = number of man-hours of labor required to produce one physical unit of producers' goods

ι = the internal rate of return per annum with continuous compounding

π_p = the price of producers' goods

Parameters

a_{lc} = number of man-hours of direct labor per annum required to coöperate with one physical unit of producers' goods, to be manipulated

$1/b_{pc}$ = number of physical units of consumers' goods produced per annum per physical unit of producers' goods, to be manipulated

L = useful life of one unit of producers' goods, to be manipulated

π_c = the price of consumers' goods

π_l = the money wage rate

3. THE THREE PERFORMANCE CHARACTERISTICS OF DURABLE PRODUCERS' GOODS

The quality of durable producers' goods is expressed in terms of the following three performance characteristics. First, the direct labor input coefficient a_{lc}, defined as the number of man-hours of direct labor required per annum to coöperate with one physical unit of producers' goods. Second, the productivity of producers' goods $1/b_{pc}$ defined as the output of consumers' goods per annum per physical unit of producers' goods. The ratio $1/b_{pc}$ is an output-capital ratio and is, of course, the reciprocal of the familiar Leontief capital coefficient b_{pc}. Third, the useful life of one physical unit of producers' goods L.

4. THE INPUT-OUTPUT COEFFICIENT IN THE PRODUCERS' GOODS INDUSTRY

The producers' goods industry having one output and one input, is characterized by the input-output coefficient $*a_{lp}$, defined as the number of man-hours of labor required to produce one physical unit of producers' goods. We shall call this coefficient $*a_{lp}$ the indirect labor coefficient.

5. THE INTERNAL RATE OF RETURN

Calling the wage rate π_l and the price of new producers' goods $*\pi_p$, and assuming the price of new producers' goods to equal their unit cost of production, we have

(1) $$*\pi_p = \pi_l *a_{lp}$$

From the point of view of a firm in the consumers' goods industry Equation (1) represents the indirect labor cost per unit of producers' goods. The direct labor cost per annum per unit of producers' goods is obtained by multiplying a_{lc} by the wage rate π_l, obtaining $\pi_l a_{lc}$. If the price of consumers' goods is π_c, revenue per annum per unit of producers' goods is then π_c/b_{pc}. Revenue minus direct labor cost per annum per unit of producers' goods is

$$\frac{\pi_c}{b_{pc}} - \pi_l a_{lc}$$

The present worth of revenue minus direct labor cost per small fraction dt of a year located t years away in the future is

$$\frac{\left(\dfrac{\pi_c}{b_{pc}} - \pi_l a_{lc}\right)dt}{(1 + i)^t}$$

where i is the rate of interest per annum, later to be defined more specifically. Let

$$1 + i = e^{*_l}$$

where e is the base of the natural system of logarithms, and where $*\iota$ is the rate of interest per annum with continuous compounding that corresponds to the rate of interest i per annum with interest compounded once a year.[4]   The sum total of the present worth of revenue minus direct labor cost for the entire useful life L is

$$\int_0^L \left(\frac{\pi_c}{b_{pc}} - \pi_l a_{lc}\right) e^{-*\iota t} \, dt$$

Carrying out the integration,[5] we get:

$$\left(\frac{\pi_c}{b_{pc}} - \pi_l a_{lc}\right) \frac{1 - e^{-*\iota L}}{*\iota}$$

We must now define more specifically the rate of interest i or $*\iota$ as that rate which makes the sum total of the present worth of revenue minus direct labor cost during the entire useful life of the unit of producers' goods equal to the price $*\pi_p$ of that unit:

$$(2) \qquad *\pi_p = \left(\frac{\pi_c}{b_{pc}} - \pi_l a_{lc}\right) \frac{1 - e^{-*\iota L}}{*\iota}$$

So defined, the rate of interest is the internal rate of return,[6] the Keynesian "marginal efficiency of capital," or the Wicksellian "natural rate" of interest.[7]

6. THE THREE PERFORMANCE CHARACTERISTICS MANIPULATED

Let us now examine the possible relationship between the performance characteristics a_{lc}, $1/b_{pc}$, and L on the one hand, and the

[4] See for example R. G. D. Allen, *Mathematical Analysis for Economists* (London: Macmillan, 1938), p. 232; or Knut Wicksell, *Lectures Volume One, op. cit.*, pp. 178 and 275.

[5] Allen, *op. cit.*, pp. 393–396.

[6] Cf. Armen A. Alchian, "The Rate of Interest, Fisher's Rate of Return over Costs and Keynes' Internal Rate of Return," *The American Economic Review*, Vol. XLV, No. 5 (Dec., 1955), pp. 938–943; and also Romney Robinson's comment with the same title, also in the *Review*, Vol. XLVI, No. 5 (Dec., 1956), pp. 972–973.

[7] J. M. Keynes, *General Theory* (London: Macmillan, 1936), p. 135; Knut Wicksell, *Geldzins und Güterpreise* (Jena: Gustav Fischer, 1898), translated by R. F. Kahn as *Interest and Prices* (London: Macmillan, 1936), p. 102.

indirect labor coefficient $*a_{lp}$ on the other. Realistically, the direct labor coefficient can be reduced, the productivity of producers' goods increased, and their durability increased, thereby raising the indirect labor coefficient.[8] Consequently, we can write

$$(3) \qquad *a_{lp} = *a_{lp}\left(a_{lc}, \frac{1}{b_{pc}}, L\right)$$

a function assumed to be continuous and differentiable and whose properties can perhaps be described in terms of elasticities. Let the elasticity of the indirect labor coefficient $*a_{lp}$ be η_{lc} with respect to the direct labor coefficient a_{lc}; call it η_{pc} with respect to productivity $1/b_{pc}$, and call it η_L with respect to the useful life L. What are the signs of these elasticities? Plausibly, $*a_{lp}$ will rise if (1) direct labor is to be saved, reducing a_{lc}, (2) the productivity of producers' goods is to be increased, raising $1/b_{pc}$, or (3) the longevity of producers' goods is to be increased, raising L. Thus η_{lc} is negative, η_{pc} and η_L are positive.

Next, what are the directions of change in the three elasticities? First, in η_{lc}. Let us start out with a relatively high value of the direct labor coefficient a_{lc} coupled with a relatively low value of the indirect labor coefficient $*a_{lp}$. As we start reducing a_{lc}, we may find it at first rather easy—a one percent reduction in a_{lc} giving rise initially to a *less*-than-one percent increase in $*a_{lp}$. But further reduction of a_{lc} will no doubt eventuate in a one percent reduction of a_{lc} giving rise to *more* than a one percent increase in $*a_{lp}$, Figure 52. The difference is seen clearly when direct labor saved is no longer purely manual labor but is also decision-making labor, as in the case of automation. We submit that for constant b_{pc} and L but a declining a_{lc} and a rising $*a_{lp}$, the elasticity η_{lc} is

[8] The sum total of all such eligible choices existing at a given moment defines "the technological horizon," cf. Joseph A. Schumpeter, *History of Economic Analysis* (New York: Oxford, 1954), p. 1027. The present chapter assumes the technological horizon to be constant and consequently deals with *induced* changes of the performance characteristics of producers' goods. In chap. 23 we shall relax the assumption of a constant technological horizon, thereby paving the way for an examination of *autonomous* changes in the performance characteristics.

numerically rising. The only empirical evidence known by the present writer confirms this hypothesis: Chenery's [9] isoquant diagram in his Figure 4, with capital (the same as our $*a_{lp}$) on one axis, and all current inputs including labor (the same as our a_{lc}) on the other. Beyond a relatively narrow range, when going west in his diagram the isoquants turn vertical, and when going east they turn horizontal, indicating elasticities ranging all the way from minus infinity to zero, respectively.

Second, the elasticity η_{pc}. Let us start with relatively low values of productivity $1/b_{pc}$ and of the indirect labor coefficient $*a_{lp}$. As we start increasing $1/b_{pc}$ we may find it at first rather easy: $*a_{lp}$ will rise less than in proportion to $1/b_{pc}$. But further

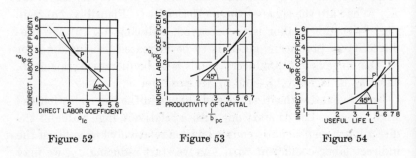

Figure 52   Figure 53   Figure 54

increase of $1/b_{pc}$ will cause a one percent increase in $1/b_{pc}$ to require an increase of *more* than one percent in $*a_{lp}$, as illustrated in Figure 53. For example, if an engine were to be scaled up beyond a certain maximum size, displacements may become too large relative to surfaces and surfaces too large relative to lengths (double length, surfaces will rise to four times their original value and displacements will rise to eight times their original value). Rather than increasing the size of the engine we would increase the number of them. We submit that for constant a_{lc} and L but rising $1/b_{pc}$ and rising $*a_{lp}$, the elasticity η_{pc} eventually rises. Again, the only available empirical evidence confirms this hy-

[9] Hollis B. Chenery, "Engineering Production Functions," *The Quarterly Journal of Economics*, Vol. LXIII, No. 4 (Nov., 1949), pp. 507–531.

pothesis: Chenery's [10] productivity-of-capital diagram in his Figure 5 with capital (the same as our $*a_{lp}$) plotted on one axis, and capacity (the same as our productivity $1/b_{pc}$) on the other.

Third η_L. Frequently, durability can be increased by increasing the capacity of a producers' good but operating it somewhat below capacity. For example, if operated at the same power output, a large-displacement internal-combustion engine will last longer than will a small-displacement internal-combustion engine. Reasoning analogously to the earlier argument for η_{pc}, we find that for a rising L and a rising $*a_{lp}$, the elasticity η_L will rise, cf. Figure 54.

7. MAXIMIZATION OF THE INTERNAL RATE OF RETURN

In order to determine the optimum values of the three performance characteristics we need to refer to the theory of the firm. As usual, the capitalist-entrepreneurs manipulate the parameters under their control (the three performance characteristics a_{lc}, $1/b_{pc}$, and L) in such a way as to maximize the internal rate of return, just defined. Such manipulation gives the three equations:

$$(4) \qquad \frac{\partial *\iota}{\partial a_{lc}} = 0$$

$$(5) \qquad \frac{\partial *\iota}{\partial \left(\dfrac{1}{b_{pc}}\right)} = 0$$

$$(6) \qquad \frac{\partial *\iota}{\partial L} = 0$$

Inserting (1) into (2), taking the first derivatives of (2) with respect to the three performance characteristics a_{lc}, $1/b_{pc}$, and L,

[10] Chenery, *op. cit.*, p. 526. Also, "The Advantages of Very Big Tankers," *The Economist*, Feb. 2, 1957, p. 399. On parallels in the realm of zoology see the charming essay by J. B. S. Haldane, "On Being the Right Size," *Possible Worlds* (New York: Harper, 1928).

using (4) through (6), and using (2) again, we get the following three equations that describe optimization of a_{lc}, $1/b_{pc}$, and L:

(I)
$$\eta_{lc} = \frac{\partial {}^*a_{lp}}{\partial a_{lc}} \frac{a_{lc}}{{}^*a_{lp}} = -\frac{\pi_l a_{lc} b_{pc}}{\pi_c - \pi_l a_{lc} b_{pc}}$$

(II)
$$\eta_{pc} = \frac{\partial {}^*a_{lp}}{\partial \left(\dfrac{1}{b_{pc}}\right)} \frac{\dfrac{1}{b_{pc}}}{{}^*a_{lp}} = \frac{\pi_c}{\pi_c - \pi_l a_{lc} b_{pc}}$$

(III)
$$\eta_L = \frac{\partial {}^*a_{lp}}{\partial L} \frac{L}{{}^*a_{lp}} = L \frac{{}^*\iota}{e^{{}^*\iota L} - 1}$$

Equation (I) indicates the extent to which the firm should increase indirect labor in order to save direct labor. Extension should continue until the elasticity of the indirect labor coefficient ${}^*a_{lp}$ with respect to the direct labor coefficient a_{lc} is equal to minus the ratio between the direct labor cost per unit of output on the one hand and the price minus direct labor cost per unit of output on the other. From (I) it follows that if in equilibrium the price π_c of output happens to be equal to twice the direct labor cost per unit of output $\pi_l a_{lc} b_{pc}$, the elasticity η_{lc} equals minus one, in which case the point P in Figure 52 is seen to be the equilibrium point. If price is higher than that, we find ourselves to the right of P; if price is lower than that, we find ourselves to the left of P.

Equation (II) tells us to what extent the firm should increase indirect labor in order to increase the productivity of producers' goods. Such extension should continue until the elasticity of the indirect labor coefficient ${}^*a_{lp}$ with respect to productivity $1/b_{pc}$ is equal to the ratio between the price of output on the one hand and the price minus direct labor cost per unit of output on the other. From (II) it follows that in equilibrium, the elasticity η_{pc} is always in excess of one. Consequently, we always find ourselves to the right of point P in Fig. 53.

Equation (III) defines the extent to which the firm should increase indirect labor in order to lengthen the useful life of producers' goods. Lengthening should continue until the elasticity of the indirect labor coefficient $*a_{lp}$ with respect to the useful life L is equal to the useful life L times the factor

$$\frac{*\iota}{e^{*\iota L} - 1}$$

where $*\iota$ is the internal rate of return at its maximum. From (III) and a consultation of any compound-interest table it follows that in equilibrium the elasticity η_L is always smaller than one. Consequently, we must always find ourselves to the left of the point P in Figure 54.

That the partial derivatives of the internal rate of return with respect to the performance characteristics a_{lc}, $1/b_{pc}$, and L be zero is a necessary condition for maximization of that rate. Another necessary condition is negativity of the three second derivatives:

$$\text{(IV)} \qquad \frac{\partial^{2}*\iota}{\partial a_{lc}{}^{2}} = \frac{\dfrac{\partial^{2}*a_{lp}}{\partial a_{lc}{}^{2}}}{m}$$

$$\text{(V)} \qquad \frac{\partial^{2}*\iota}{\partial\left(\dfrac{1}{b_{pc}}\right)^{2}} = \frac{\dfrac{\partial^{2}*a_{lp}}{\partial\left(\dfrac{1}{b_{pc}}\right)^{2}}}{m}$$

$$\text{(VI)} \qquad \frac{\partial^{2}*\iota}{\partial L^{2}} = \frac{\dfrac{\partial^{2}*a_{lp}}{\partial L^{2}} + \left(\dfrac{\pi_{c}}{\pi_{l}b_{pc}} - a_{lc}\right)*\iota e^{-*\iota L}}{m}$$

where, after the second differentiation, the first derivative has been set equal to zero, and where the common denominator m equals

$$\text{(VII)} \qquad m = \left(\frac{\pi_{c}}{\pi_{l}b_{pc}} - a_{lc}\right)\frac{*\iota L e^{-*\iota L} - (1 - e^{-*\iota L})}{*\iota^{2}}$$

Under our assumptions about the curvature of the three functions shown in Figures 52 to 54, all three numerators are positive.

The parenthesis in (VI) and (VII) is positive as long as revenue minus direct labor cost per annum is positive.   The quotient in the common denominator m, however, is negative, as revealed by any compound-interest table.   Consequently, all three second derivatives of the internal rate of return are negative.[11]

8. THE EFFECT OF A RISING WAGE RATE UPON THE PERFORMANCE CHARACTERISTICS

It is now possible to draw some conclusions about the effects of a rising wage rate upon the three performance characteristics of producers' goods, the direct labor coefficient a_{lc}, the productivity $1/b_{pc}$, and the useful life L.

From (I) it is unequivocal that for constant π_c, a_{lc}, and b_{pc}, an increase in the wage rate π_l will reduce the right-hand side of (I). Since the right-hand side is negative, it must rise numerically. According to our assumptions, the elasticity η_{lc} is numerically rising for falling a_{lc}. Consequently, for the left-hand side to "catch up," a_{lc} must fall. This fall will at the same time slow down the numerical rise of the right-hand side—once again the partial equilibrium condition (I) is satisfied.

From (II) we see unequivocally that for constant π_c, a_{lc}, and b_{pc}, an increase in the wage rate π_l will raise the right-hand side of (II).   According to our assumptions, the elasticity η_{pc} is rising for rising $1/b_{pc}$.   Consequently, for the left-hand side to "catch up," $1/b_{pc}$ must rise.   At the same time, this rise will slow down the rise of the right-hand side, and yet again the partial equilibrium condition (II) is satisfied.

[11] The reader may be disturbed by the maximization of the internal rate of return rather than that of present net worth under a constant external rate of interest.   Let capitalists, then, be distinguished from entrepreneurs, and let the latter borrow from the former at the constant external rate of interest*ι. Because of this constancy, equations (4) through (6) still hold.   Let entrepreneurs maximize present net worth, which equals the right-hand side minus the left-hand side of equation (2).   Take the derivative of this difference with respect to the three variables, set it equal to zero, and get our conditions (I) through (III). The two approaches, then, give exactly the same result.

Finally, let us study the effect of a rising wage rate π_l upon L. Equation (2) defined the internal rate of return $*\iota$ as that rate which makes the sum total of the present worth of revenue minus direct labor cost throughout the entire future life of the unit of producers' goods equal to the price $*\pi_p$ of that good. According to Equation (1) that price was equal to π_l*a_{lp}. From (1) and (2) we conclude that for constant π_c, a_{lc}, $*a_{lp}$, b_{pc}, and L, the internal rate of return must fall with rising π_l, for revenue minus direct labor cost is lower, and the price of one unit of producers' goods is higher. Only if discounted at a lower rate of return will the sum of smaller future amounts add up to a larger present amount! With this in mind, let us look at (III). Any compound-interest table will show that

$$\frac{*\iota}{e^{*\iota L} - 1}$$

is rising with falling rate $*\iota$. *Ceteris paribus* then, the right-hand side of (III) must rise. To be true, adjustment of L will go some of the way toward restoration of the original internal rate of return. But it will never go all the way; after adjustment of L we shall still have a lower $*\iota$ than before the wage increase. *Ceteris paribus*, the right-hand side of (III) is rising with falling L. If therefore the adjustment of L left us with a *lower* L than before the wage increase, then for two reasons the right-hand side of (III) should have risen. Furthermore, since η_L has been assumed to be falling for falling L, the left-hand side should have fallen, and satisfaction of (III) would have been impossible. Instead, the adjustment of L must have left us with a *higher* L than before the wage increase. *Ceteris paribus*, this reduces the right-hand side of (III) and raises the left-hand side, again permitting satisfaction of (III).

In summary, then, a rising wage rate will induce entrepreneurs to make producers' goods more (1) *labor-saving* by causing them to reduce a_{lc}, (2) *productive* by causing them to increase $1/b_{pc}$, and (3) *durable* by causing them to increase L.

9. THE EFFECT OF A RISING WAGE RATE UPON CAPITAL INTENSITY

By capital intensity is meant capital stock per man-hour per annum. Capital stock may be measured in terms of either money or wage units. Avoiding trivialities, we shall choose the latter. A unit of producers' goods is priced at $*\pi_p$ which, according to Equation (1), represents $*a_{lp}$ wage units. A unit of producers' goods requires a_{lc} man-hours per annum of direct labor to co-operate with it. A unit of producers' goods requires $*a_{lp}$ man-hours of indirect labor to produce it. If useful life is L years, in stationary equilibrium $*a_{lp}/L$ man-hours per annum per unit of producers' goods must be devoted to the replacement of retired units. The sum total of direct and indirect man-hours per annum per unit of producers' goods is, $a_{lc} + *a_{lp}/L$. Consequently, capital intensity is

$$\frac{*a_{lp}}{a_{lc} + \dfrac{*a_{lp}}{L}} = \frac{1}{\dfrac{a_{lc}}{*a_{lp}} + \dfrac{1}{L}}$$

Ceteris paribus, a reduction in a_{lc}, necessitating an increase of $*a_{lp}$, will increase capital intensity. Raising $1/b_{pc}$, again necessitating an increase in $*a_{lp}$, will do the same. Finally, raising L, necessitating an increase in $*a_{lp}$, will do the same. In summary, the rising wage rate, inducing entrepreneurs to make capital goods more labor-saving, more productive, and more durable, in three ways causes a rise in capital intensity.

10. MACROECONOMIC EQUILIBRIUM IN A STATIONARY ECONOMY

The findings may now be combined with the Böhm-Bawerk—Wicksell assumptions for the stationary economy as a whole of a given capital stock and of a given labor force. In our restatement "capital intensity" simply takes the place formerly occupied by Böhm-Bawerk's "period of production." Equation (7) in Chapter 18 is replaced by a new equation stating that aggregate available capital stock is equal to capital intensity multiplied by the number of man-hours per annum that can be employed at that intensity.

Our argument follows. Assume for the moment that the wage rate is given. At the given wage rate entrepreneurs will adjust their capital intensity in a way to maximize the internal rate of return. Given that capital intensity and also the available capital stock, we can find the number of man-hours per annum the economy is able to employ. If that number happens to be equal to the actually available labor force in terms of man-hours per annum, we have luckily chosen the equilibrium wage rate at the beginning.

If, on the other hand, the number of man-hours per annum that can be employed in accordance with the available capital stock and the given capital intensity should be *smaller* than the available labor force, competition among laborers must reduce the wage rate. Or, in modern language, labor unions may accept wage reductions. At a lower wage rate a lower capital intensity will be more profitable, hence the given amount of capital can now employ more man-hours per annum.

If, finally, the number of man-hours per annum that can be employed in accordance with the given stock of capital and the given capital intensity is *larger* than the available labor force, competition among the entrepreneurs will increase the wage rate. Or, unions will successfully press for higher wages. At a higher wage rate, a higher capital intensity will be most profitable, hence less employment will result.

11. CONCLUSION

Derivative (II) of Chapter 7 shows that if in a closed economy the price of all factors rises at a constant price of goods, the equilibrium gross private product, and with it employment, also rises.   We have now developed the last of the five important qualifications of this proposition.   At a higher wage rate, a higher capital intensity will be most profitable, and less employment will result.[12]

---

[12] The first four qualifications were developed in chaps. 7, 11, 16, and 17, respectively.

CONCLUSIONS

Part III is devoted to a further study of the demand for inputs. Established neoclassical doctrine treats inputs as substitutable and the physical marginal productivity of any input as positive but diminishing. Chapter 14 developed the implication that, within the individual firm, substitution will be carried to the point where, for any input, the price and the marginal-value productivity are equal. Chapter 15 showed that under pure competition and absence of economies of scale, and under equality between price and marginal-value productivity, the distributive shares will exactly exhaust the value of national output and, further, that if competition is not pure, a residual share of profits will exist.

Neoclassical doctrine relies heavily on the assumption of a positive but diminishing physical marginal productivity of inputs, a reliance from which liberation would be desirable. Such liberation is undertaken in Chapter 16 by applying modern linear programming. The substitution studied in Chapter 16 is that among a finite number of processes, all producing the same product quality. The neoclassical result—raising the price of an input may reduce the demand for it—is salvaged. In Chapter 17 the substitution among alternative product qualities is examined. Here, an increase in the price of an input will induce manufacturers to adopt a product quality embodying less of that input.

The last two chapters of Part III are devoted to the complications arising from the employment of roundabout methods of production. First, the straight Böhm-Bawerk theory is developed, according to which higher wage rates encourage the use of more circulating capital. Second, the assumption of all capital to be circulating is abandoned, and the concept of capital intensity introduced. It is shown that at a given stock of capital and at a higher wage rate, a higher capital intensity would be most profitable, employment being less as a result.

PART IV

Dynamization of the Keynesian Model

We that are young
Shall never see so much
Nor live so long.
SHAKESPEARE

The first three parts of the present volume are devoted to the determination of stationary equilibrium levels, whether of output or of inputs. Except in Chapter 18, no explicit reference has thus far been made to time. Indeed, since all variables implicitly referred to the same point or period of time, no need arose to date them explicitly. Part IV of the present volume, devoted to the modification of the Keynesian model in a new direction, dynamization, will attempt to determine paths over time, whether of output or of inputs. Consequently, all variables will have to be dated.

Chapter 20 reproduces the Harrod-Domar theory of growth in a form in which its Keynesian roots are clearly visible. The remainder of Part IV is devoted to modifications and extensions of this theory. The assumption of one over-all proportionate equilibrium rate of growth is attacked in Chapter 21, where different, but constant, rates of growth of output, labor force, hours, and productivity are determined. In Chapter 22 the assumption that the proportionate equilibrium rate of growth is a constant is tested. Chapter 23 utilizes the model previously developed in Chapter 19 to permit an examination of the effects of specific types of technological progress upon the proportionate equilibrium rate of growth. Chapter 24 relaxes the Harrod-Domar assumption of a closed economy and provides an examination of the interaction of two economies whose growth potentials are inherently very different.

By stability of an equilibrium is usually meant capacity of the equilibrium to restore itself after having been disturbed. It was Harrod's contention that the growth equilibrium was always unstable. Chapters 25 and 26 are devoted to a stability test of our growth equilibrium, and matters are found to be far less simple than Harrod believed them to be.

20

A Proportionate Equilibrium Rate of Growth

1. THE ARITHMETIC OF LONG-RUN GROWTH

The simple Keynesian model assumed net investment to be autonomous, as we saw in Chapter 3. Several possible motives may cause businessmen to wish to add to their capital stock, but the most important must be the growth of output over time. The simple Keynesian model is merely a determination of the level of the net national product for some particular period. To allow for growth the model must be modified, that is, dynamized. As we did in the simple Keynesian model, let us ignore government. In a purely private economy a delicate dynamic balance exists between output and demand, a balance based upon two fundamental historical parameters. The first parameter is the propensity to consume. For the United States an empirical value of the average propensity to consume must be around nine-tenths. The second parameter is the ratio between capital stock and annual net national product. This ratio is called the capital

---

NOTE: Chaps. 20 and 25 have been slightly expanded from the author's "Stability and Growth," *The Economic Journal*, Vol. LXV, No. 260 (Dec., 1955).

coefficient, and for the United States its empirical value must be around three. In other words, it takes around three dollars' worth of capital stock to produce one dollar's worth of annual net national product.

Using these two fundamental constants, we may set out the problem of long-run growth in simple arithmetic as follows. Let the net national product of year t be 100. How large would the net national product of year $t + 1$ have to be if the delicate dynamic balance between output and demand is to be preserved? It would have to be 103.45, no more, no less. If the net national product in year $t + 1$ is 103.45 then consumption demand, or nine-tenths of 103.45, is 93.10. Furthermore, if the net national product rises from 100 in year t to 103.45 in year $t + 1$, capital stock, always three times net national product, must rise from 300 to 310.35, the net increase in capital stock being 10.35. In other words, the net demand for producers' goods in year $t + 1$ would be 10.35. If the demand for consumers' goods in year $t + 1$ is 93.10, and the net demand for producers' goods in year $t + 1$ is 10.35, the aggregate net demand in year $t + 1$ is 103.45. Since demand and output are equal, inventory will neither accumulate nor be depleted; hence there is equilibrium in our economy. The first growth model based upon the propensity to consume and the capital coefficient was built by Cassel, later models by Harrod and Domar.[1]

---

[1] In Section 7 of Gustav Cassel, *Theoretische Sozialökonomie* (Leipzig: A. Deichertsche Verlagsbuchhandlung, Fifth Ed., 1932), translated by S. L. Barron as *The Theory of Social Economy* (New York: Harcourt Brace, 1932), p. 61, we find a growth equation which, except for notation, is identical with Harrod's equation $GC = s$. See R. F. Harrod, *Towards A Dynamic Economics* (London: Macmillan, 1948), p. 77. Harrod's G = Cassel's $p/100$, Harrod's C = Cassel's C/I, and Harrod's s = Cassel's $1/s$. Estimating the propensity to save to be one-fifth, the capital-income ratio to be slightly below 7, Cassel estimated the rate of growth to be 3 percent per annum. See also Evsey D. Domar, "Capital Expansion, Rate of Growth, and Employment," *Econometrica*, Vol. 14, No. 2 (April, 1946), pp. 137–147, and "Expansion and Employment," *The American Economic Review*, Vol. XXXVII, No. 1 (March, 1947), pp. 34–55.

2. THE ALGEBRA OF LONG-RUN GROWTH

Let us sketch more rigorously a simple version of the theory of growth. Our model has five variables

C = real consumption demand
g = the proportionate rate of growth[2] of net real national output
I = net real investment demand
S = real capital stock
Y = net real national output

In any growth model variables must be dated, and we shall use the parenthetical expression (t) to indicate that a flow variable refers to the period t and that a stock variable refers to the *end* of period t. To determine our five variables we have five equations, the easiest being the definitional ones, of which we have two.

The first definitional equation defines the rate of growth of net real national output:

$$(1) \qquad Y(t) = (1 + g)Y(t - 1)$$

The second definitional equation defines net real investment. Current net real investment, of course, is the net increase of real capital stock over the current period:

$$(2) \qquad I(t) = S(t) - S(t - 1)$$

Next, let us turn to the two behavior equations, one governing consumption demand, the other investment demand. In the

---

[2] The term "rate of growth" is used in two different meanings by economists. First, it may mean the time rate of growth of a variable Y, i.e. $g = \Delta Y/\Delta t$. Second, it may mean the *proportionate* time rate of growth of a variable Y, i.e.

$$g = \frac{\Delta Y}{Y} \Big/ \Delta t$$

In its former sense the term was used by William J. Baumol, *Economic Dynamics* (New York: Macmillan, 1951), particularly p. 43; in its second sense it was used by Domar and Harrod, see Evsey D. Domar, "Expansion and Employment," *op. cit.*, pp. 34–55, and R. F. Harrod, *op. cit.*, particularly on p. 80 n. The present book will follow Harrod and Domar.

former current consumption demand is a function of current net real national output:

(3a) $$C(t) = A(t) + aY(t)$$

where A and a are parameters. $A(t)$ is the autonomous term of the consumption function. It is reasonable to assume that $A(t)$ rises at the same proportionate rate of growth as does equilibrium net real national output:

(3b) $$A(t) = (1 + g)A(t - 1)$$

In the consumption function the parameter a is the marginal propensity to consume. The entire function is shown in Figure 55.

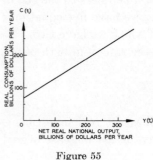

Figure 55

Our second behavior equation is that of investment demand. Being cautious, let us start at the sector level, assuming as many sectors as products, each sector producing only one product. No sector produces the plant and equipment inputs used by itself; all such inputs must be purchased from other sectors. Let the physical output of sector j be Y_j. Let sector j use the product of sector i as capital stock, and let S_{ij} be the physical capital stock of goods produced by sector i and held by sector j. Let I_{ij} be the net increase in physical capital stock of goods produced by sector i and demanded by sector j. Let b_{ij} be the capital coefficient of sector j with respect to sector i. Assume sector j to try continuously to establish a physical capital stock at the end of the current period which will be in direct proportion to current physical output. Then, $S_{ij}(t) = b_{ij}Y_j(t)$, and $S_{ij}(t - 1) = b_{ij}Y_j(t - 1)$. Deducting the latter equation from the former, we get

(4a) $$I_{ij}(t) = b_{ij}[Y_j(t) - Y_j(t - 1)]$$

which determines current physical net investment demand by

sector j from sector i as a function of the change of sector j's current physical output.

Now let us proceed to the aggregation. Multiply all physical outputs and all physical capital stocks by their respective money values. Add all outputs thus multiplied on the one hand, and add all capital stock thus multiplied on the other; divide the total capital stock by total output to obtain the aggregate capital coefficient. If all intersector physical capital coefficients remain constant, if all the money values remain constant, and if the relative importance of sectors remains constant, the aggregate capital coefficient also remains constant. If so we can draw Figure 56, showing the aggregate function $S(t) = bY(t)$. We also

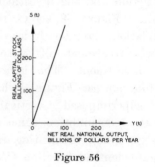

Figure 56   Figure 57

have $S(t - 1) = bY(t - 1)$; deduct the latter from the former to obtain the aggregate investment demand function:

$$(4b) \qquad I(t) = b[Y(t) - Y(t - 1)]$$

which determines current aggregate net real investment demand as a function of the change of current net real national output. Thus current aggregate net real investment demand is in direct proportion to the excess of *current* net real national output over and above *last* period's net real national output. For the current period the investment demand function is, graphically, a straight line whose slope is the capital coefficient b, rising from the point of the output axis that indicates *last* period's net real national output, as shown in Figure 57.

Having now completed the definitional and behavior equations, let us define the equilibrium condition. For the system to be in equilibrium there must be no unintentional accumulation or depletion of inventory. This necessity requires that aggregate demand, which is equal to the sum of consumption demand and investment demand, be exactly equal to current net national output:

(5) $$Y(t) = C(t) + I(t)$$

3. SOLUTION

To solve graphically for current equilibrium output we need only consolidate the consumption function and the investment

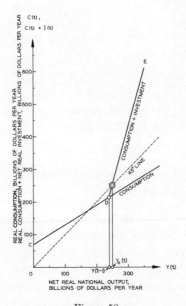

Figure 58

function. Figure 58 shows the consolidation, familiar from the textbook treatment of autonomous investment. The investment function (see Figure 57) has been superimposed vertically upon the consumption function (see Figure 55), illustrating the aggregate demand function CDE (see Figure 58). In the usual manner intersect aggregate demand CDE in Figure 58 by a 45° line through zero to express equilibrium condition (5), and get the equilibrium current output $Y_0(t)$.

The solution can be stated much more succinctly, of course, in algebraic terms. By inserting (3a) and (4b) into (5) and by using the preceding period's net real national output and also the autonomous term $A(t)$ of the consumption function as parameters, we solve the system for current equilibrium net real national output.   We get the following first-order difference equation:

$$(I) \qquad Y(t) = \frac{A(t) - bY(t - 1)}{1 - a - b}$$

By this difference equation current equilibrium output in terms of past equilibrium output is determined, thus allowing the path of equilibrium output to be traced in time.   Rather than solving for the equilibrium path, we may wish to solve for the equilibrium rate of growth *per se*.   If so it will be convenient to begin by dividing Equation (3b) by Equation (1), denoting the result y:

$$(3c) \qquad \frac{A(t)}{Y(t)} = \frac{A(t - 1)}{Y(t - 1)} = \cdots = y$$

where y is a new parameter that expresses the ratio between the autonomous terms of the consumption function on the one hand, and of the equilibrium net real national output on the other.   It appears from Equation (3c) that the value of y remains constant in time.   Solving the system for the equilibrium rate of growth, we get

$$(II) \qquad g = \frac{1 - a - y}{a + b + y - 1}$$

Here we see the equilibrium rate of growth as determined by the parameters of the consumption and investment functions. Familiar conclusions about the respectability of thriftiness in a growth model can be drawn.   *Ceteris paribus*, should the value of y, the ratio between the autonomous term of the consumption function and the equilibrium net real national output, be reduced, the value of g, the proportionate equilibrium rate of growth, would rise.   *Ceteris paribus*, should the value of a, the marginal propensity to consume, be reduced, the same thing would happen. Finally, the economy would also have a higher equilibrium rate of growth if, *ceteris paribus*, should the value of b, the capital coefficient, be reduced.

The meaning of (II) may be summed up in the following words: A system passing through successive stages of equilibrium will grow steadily at the proportionate rate of growth determined by Equation (II). For, if business firms plan output to rise by this growth rate, adjust their investment plans accordingly, and carry out their output and investment plans, aggregate demand will exactly exhaust net national output, and no unintentional accumulation or depletion of inventory will occur. From this the businessman will conclude that his growth plans were right, and he will see no reason to revise his idea of a growth rate as determined by (II).

21

Growth Rates of Output, Labor Force, Hours, and Productivity

1. THE PROBLEM

Current theoretical growth models of the Harrod-Domar type have determined "the" growth rate, by which is usually meant the proportionate rate of growth of net or gross national product. But the rates of growth of labor force, hours, and productivity are ignored in such models, very much in the Keynesian tradition. The static Keynesian model makes no distinction between goods and factors and between the level of output (of goods) and the level of employment (of factors). In dynamizing the Keynesian model, growth models of the Harrod-Domar type consequently make no distinction between the time path of output and the time path of employment.

The purposes of the present chapter are to examine more closely the relationships between the four growth rates of output, labor force, hours, and output per man-hour, and in particular[1] to find

[1] Galenson and Leibenstein submit that the appropriate economic goal of development should be "the maximization of *per capita* output . . . either over time, or at some time in the future." Walter Galenson and Harvey Leibenstein,

---

NOTE: The present chapter is a slight revision of the author's "Growth Rates of Output, Labor Force, Hours, and Productivity," *The Review of Economics and Statistics*, Vol. XXXIX, No. 4 (Nov., 1957).

the determinants of the proportionate rate of growth of output per man-hour. For this purpose a slight disaggregation of the Harrod-Domar model becomes necessary. If only two sectors are desired, the most obvious division in the economy is that between firms and households. We shall therefore consider a closed economy, ignoring government. For disaggregation purposes the best notation is probably the Leontief notation.[2]

Variables

a_{hf}	= number of man-hours required per unit of product
g	= proportionate rate of growth of net national output
γ	= proportionate rate of growth of net national output per man-hour
h_{hf}	= number of hours worked per year per worker
P	= labor force
π_h/π_f	= the ratio between the price of factors and the price of goods
S_{ij}	= physical capital stock of goods, produced by sector i, held by sector j
X_j	= time rate of physical output of goods produced by sector j
x_{ij}	= time rate of physical purchase from sector i by sector j
σ_{ij}	= time rate of physical sale by sector i to sector j

Parameters

a_{fh}	= propensity to consume expected real personal income
b_{ff}	= number of machine-hours per unit of product
G	= proportionate rate of growth of labor force
Γ	= proportionate rate of change of number of hours worked per year per worker
h_{ff}	= number of machine-hours of operation per year per machine

"Investment Criteria, Productivity, and Economic Development," *Quarterly Journal of Economics*, Vol. LXIX, No. 3 (Aug., 1955), p. 345 and *passim*. If leisure has economic value, one might alternatively maximize output *per man-hour* rather than output per capita. Without trying to determine the economic value of leisure, in the present chapter we assume the former maximization to be the more interesting one.

[2] Wassily Leontief, "Static and Dynamic Theory," *Studies in the Structure of the American Economy* (New York: Oxford, 1953), pp. 53–90.

s = ratio of business undistributed profits to money value of output. Due to the homogeneity of input-output function (4), a particularly simple relationship exists between s and the mark-up coefficient λ used in chapters 7, 8, and 11, $s = 1 - 1/\lambda$ or $\lambda = 1/(1 - s)$.

As in Chapter 7, the subscript f refers to firms, the subscript h to households. Three transactions, shown in Table 13, are considered. First, firms plan to purchase goods from other firms

TABLE 13. Planned Purchases of Goods and Factors: Three Transactions

Purchasing from	Purchases Planned by	
	Firms	Households
Firms	$*x_{ff}$	$*x_{fh}$
Households	$*x_{hf}$	—

$*x_{ff}$; second, households plan to purchase goods from firms $*x_{fh}$; and third, firms plan to purchase factors from households $*x_{hf}$.

Asterisks indicate ex ante values, absence of an asterisk ex post values; t is the time coördinate, and period t is the period ending at time t. We are now ready to set up the behavior equations of the model.

2. THE MODEL, NET INVESTMENT

The first transaction to be considered is net investment $*x_{ff}$. By definition planned net investment equals planned net change in capital stock:

$$(1) \qquad *x_{ff}(t) = *S_{ff}(t) - S_{ff}(t - 1)$$

which defines ex ante net investment. Removal of asterisks gives the definition of ex post net investment in Equation (2), not written. As the relationship between planned capital stock and planned output we have

$$(3) \qquad *S_{ff}(t) = \frac{b_{ff}}{h_{ff}} *X_f(t)$$

where b_{ff} is the number of machine-hours per unit of product, and h_{ff} number of machine-hours of operation per year per machine. Obviously $h_{ff} \leqq 8760$. Both are parameters.

3. THE MODEL, PURCHASE OF FACTORS FROM HOUSEHOLDS

Factors coöperating with producers' goods include labor and entrepreneurship purchased by firms from households. Let both factors be measured in man-hours. Planned purchase of factors by firms as measured in man-hours per year $*x_{hf}$ is assumed to be in direct proportion to planned output:

$$(4) \qquad *x_{hf}(t) = a_{hf}(t)*X_f(t)$$

where $a_{hf}(t)$ is number of man-hours per unit of product at time (t). Unlike b_{ff}, machine-hours per unit of product, which is a parameter, a_{hf}, man-hours per unit of product, varies in time. In fact, we have already committed ourselves to a specific hypothesis about its variation in time. By taking (3) and (4) together, we get

$$\frac{1}{a_{hf}(t)} = \frac{h_{ff}*S_{ff}(t)}{b_{ff}*x_{hf}(t)}$$

If $a_{hf}(t)$ is man-hours per unit of product at time (t), then $1/a_{hf}(t)$ is output per man-hour or simply labor productivity at time (t). Now if h_{ff}/b_{ff} is constant over time, the equation says that labor productivity at time (t) is in direct proportion to capital intensity at time (t), defined as capital stock per man-hour per year in year (t). The only justification for this hypothesis is empirical: whatever the causal relationship, such proportionality has existed, at least approximately, in our own past.[3]

4. HOURS AND LABOR FORCE

Let the number of hours worked per year per worker be $h_{hf}(t)$ and total labor force $P(t)$. Planned purchase of factors by firms $*x_{hf}(t)$ must be given by

$$(5) \qquad *x_{hf}(t) = h_{hf}(t)P(t)$$

5. RATES OF CHANGE OF HOURS AND LABOR FORCE

Let Γ be the proportionate rate of change in the number of hours worked per year per worker. Let G be the proportionate rate of change in the total labor force; Γ and G are parameters. We now have the two definitional equations:

$$(6) \qquad h_{hf}(t + 1) = (1 + \Gamma)h_{hf}(t)$$

$$(7) \qquad P(t + 1) = (1 + G)P(t)$$

[3] From the decade 1869–78 until 1929–38 the United States net national product per man-hour in 1929 prices increased slightly less than threefold; from 1879 to 1939 the United States reproducible capital stock per man-hour, in 1929 prices, increased practically threefold. Cf. tables 9 and 11 of Simon Kuznets, "Long-Term Changes in the National Income of the United States of America Since 1870," *Income and Wealth of the United States* (Cambridge, England: Bowes & Bowes, 1952), pp. 71 and 78. Seymour Melman, in his *Dynamic Factors in Industrial Productivity* (New York: Wiley, 1956), tests the hypothesis that installed horsepower per production worker (Bureau of the Census data 1899–1939) and output per production worker man-hour (Fabricant data for the same period) vary in direct proportion to each other. Melman finds that horsepower per production worker rose at an average annual compound rate of increase of 2.8 percent and that output per production worker man-hour rose at 3.1 percent. Melman is quite satisfied with this result, but he would have been even more satisfied had he replaced horsepower per worker by horsepower per man-hour. Kuznets' data suggest that man-hours per year per worker have declined at an average annual compound rate of 0.4 percent. If this rate of decline holds for the period examined by Melman, horsepower *per man-hour* would have risen by 3.2 percent per annum or practically by the same rate as did output per man-hour.

6. CONSUMPTION

Good evidence exists to indicate that in the long run consumption is in proportion to expected real personal income. The parameter a_{fh} being the marginal and average propensity to consume real personal income, and π_f and π_h being the prices of goods and factors, respectively, we have

$$(8) \qquad *x_{fh}(t) = a_{fh} \frac{*\sigma_{hf}(t)\pi_h(t)}{\pi_f(t)}$$

7. WAGE AND PRICE POLICY

In the simplest possible case, price and wage policy is assumed to keep business net money saving equal to a constant (call it s) times the money value of net output. Business net money saving is the difference between the money value of net output $\pi_f(t)*X_f(t)$ on the one hand, and the money value of factor purchases including dividends $\pi_h(t)*x_{hf}(t)$ on the other.   Hence,

$$(9) \qquad \pi_f(t)*X_f(t) - \pi_h(t)*x_{hf}(t) = s\pi_f(t)*X_f(t)$$

Using (4) we rewrite (9):

$$(9a) \qquad \frac{\pi_h(t)}{\pi_f(t)} = (1 - s) \frac{1}{a_{hf}(t)}$$

In the form of (9a), (9) is very easy to interpret: simply, the real wage rate is in direct proportion to labor productivity.

8. PLANNED NET NATIONAL OUTPUT

Ignoring planned inventory changes, we assume that planned net national product equals expected sale of all goods:

$$(10) \qquad *X_f(t) = *\sigma_{ff}(t) + *\sigma_{fh}(t)$$

9. ALL PLANS ARE CARRIED OUT

In a buyer's market a unit of time can be chosen such that plans made at the beginning of that period are not changed until the beginning of the next period. First, *purchase* plans are carried out:

(11) through (13) $\qquad *x_{ij}(t) = x_{ij}(t)$

where ij refers to ff, hf, and fh, respectively. Second, *production* plans are carried out:

(14) $\qquad\qquad *X_f(t) = X_f(t)$

10. WHAT IS PURCHASED IS SOLD

A buyer's realized purchase equals the seller's realized sale to that buyer:

(15) through (17) $\qquad x_{ij}(t) = \sigma_{ij}(t)$

where ij refers to ff, hf, and fh, respectively.

11. EQUILIBRIUM CONDITIONS

If equilibrium is to prevail, the activity of the economy must be self-justifying in the sense that any sector's expected sales must materialize:

(18) through (20) $\qquad *\sigma_{ij}(t) = \sigma_{ij}(t)$

where ij refers to ff, hf, and fh, respectively.

12. RATES OF GROWTH OF OUTPUT AND OUTPUT PER MAN-HOUR

The proportionate rate of growth G of the labor force is assumed to be a parameter, according to Equation (7). We shall now assume that the proportionate rates of growth g and γ of net national output and of net national output per man-hour are unknowns. But whatever their values, we shall assume those values to remain constant in time, thus obtaining the two definitional equations:

(21) $$*X_f(t + 1) = (1 + g)*X_f(t)$$

(22) $$\frac{1}{a_{hf}(t + 1)} = (1 + \gamma)\frac{1}{a_{hf}(t)}$$

13. SOLUTION

The system now includes the 22 variables: number of man-hours required per unit of product a_{hf}, the rate of growth of net national output g, the rate of growth of productivity γ, hours h_{hf}, labor force P, the factor-goods price ratio π_h/π_f, one planned and one realized capital stock $*S_{ff}$ and S_{ff} respectively, one planned and one realized output $*X_f$ and X_f respectively, three planned and three realized purchases $*x_{ij}$ and x_{ij} respectively, three expected and three realized sales $*\sigma_{ij}$ and σ_{ij} respectively. Solving for the two unknown growth rates, let us begin [4] with the Harrod-Domar rate of growth of net national output g:

(I) $$g = \frac{1}{1 - \left[1 - a_{fh}(1 - s)\right]\dfrac{h_{ff}}{b_{ff}}} - 1$$

Next,[5] let us find the rate of growth of productivity:

(II) $$\gamma = \frac{1}{(1 + G)(1 + \Gamma)\left\{1 - \left[1 - a_{fh}(1 - s)\right]\dfrac{h_{ff}}{b_{ff}}\right\}} - 1$$

---

[4] Use equations (2) and (11) through (20) to see that the x's and the σ's, with and without asterisks, are equal. Then use equations (10), (1), (8), (3), (4), (9), and (21) in that order.

[5] Use equations (22), (4), (5), (6), (7), and (21) in that order to get

$$\gamma = \frac{1 + g}{(1 + G)(1 + \Gamma)} - 1$$

Insert (I) into the equation just obtained and get (II).

14. THE SIX MULTIPLIERS

Keynes used the term multiplier for the ratio between incremental output and incremental autonomous investment. His multiplier concept can be generalized into a derivative of any variable with respect to any parameter. The variable we have been solving for is the rate of growth of productivity γ. Solution (II) being established, it is easy to explore the role played by the individual parameters included: a_{fh}, b_{ff}, G, Γ, h_{ff}, and s. We need only take the derivatives of (II) with respect to any of the six parameters to find the six multipliers. To save space we shall use the abbreviation m for the entire denominator of the first right-hand term of (II). The six multipliers are

$$(\text{III}) \qquad \frac{\partial \gamma}{\partial a_{fh}} = - \frac{(1 + G)(1 + \Gamma)(1 - s)\dfrac{h_{ff}}{b_{ff}}}{m^2}$$

$$(\text{IV}) \qquad \frac{\partial \gamma}{\partial b_{ff}} = - \frac{(1 + G)(1 + \Gamma)[1 - a_{fh}(1 - s)]\dfrac{h_{ff}}{b_{ff}^2}}{m^2}$$

$$(\text{V}) \qquad \frac{\partial \gamma}{\partial G} = - \frac{(1 + \Gamma)\left\{1 - [1 - a_{fh}(1 - s)]\dfrac{h_{ff}}{b_{ff}}\right\}}{m^2}$$

$$(\text{VI}) \qquad \frac{\partial \gamma}{\partial \Gamma} = - \frac{(1 + G)\left\{1 - [1 - a_{fh}(1 - s)]\dfrac{h_{ff}}{b_{ff}}\right\}}{m^2}$$

$$(\text{VII}) \qquad \frac{\partial \gamma}{\partial h_{ff}} = + \frac{(1 + G)(1 + \Gamma)[1 - a_{fh}(1 - s)]\dfrac{1}{b_{ff}}}{m^2}$$

$$(\text{VIII}) \qquad \frac{\partial \gamma}{\partial s} = + \frac{a_{fh}(1 + G)(1 + \Gamma)\dfrac{h_{ff}}{b_{ff}}}{m^2}$$

From close inspection we see that if

$$a_{fh} > 0 \qquad\qquad G > -1$$
$$\frac{b_{ff}}{h_{ff}} > 1 - a_{fh}(1 - s) > 0 \qquad \Gamma > -1$$
$$\qquad\qquad\qquad\qquad\qquad h_{ff} > 0$$
$$b_{ff} > 0 \qquad\qquad 1 > s$$

then the right-hand side of

(III)	is negative	(VI)	is negative
(IV)	is negative	(VII)	is positive
(V)	is negative	(VIII)	is positive

Before translating our six multipliers (III) through (VIII) into words, let us see whether the seven inequalities are empirically plausible. The first inequality certainly is, for household propensity to consume real personal income must surely be positive. On the left-hand side of the second inequality is the ratio b_{ff}/h_{ff}, according to Equation (3) nothing but the capital coefficient. Kuznets[6] has found that the ratio between the dollar value of fixed capital stock (structures and durable equipment) and the dollar value of annual net national product has shown no significant increase during the last two to three decades, but that during the decades 1874–83 through 1924–33 the ratio rose fairly steadily from 2.2 to 3.1. Grosse,[7] however, convincingly suggested that undepreciated accounting data afford a better explanation of investment behavior than do depreciated accounting data, the type used by Kuznets. One way of recognizing undepreciated data is to use a capital coefficient somewhat larger than Kuznets' figure, say 3.7.

In the middle of the second inequality is the expression $1 - a_{fh}(1 - s)$. According to Equations (4), (8), and (9), $a_{fh}(1 - s)$ is the ratio of consumption to net national output. For the United States in the last eight decades, the empirical value of this ratio is around 0.88, and consequently $1 - a_{fh}(1 - s)$

---

[6] Simon Kuznets, *op. cit.*, p. 127.
[7] Robert N. Grosse, "The Structure of Capital," in *Studies in the Structure of the American Economy*, table 3, p. 209.

will be around 0.12. On an annual basis, then, the second inequality is comfortably satisfied.[8]

The remaining five inequalities are also easily satisfied. First, b_{ff} is the number of machine-hours per unit of product and is, of course, positive. G is the proportionate rate of growth of the labor force; for the last eight decades, the United States labor force has been growing at a rate around 0.019 per annum, as shown in Table 14; G is seen to be easily in excess of -1. Γ is the proportionate rate of change of man-hours per year per worker;

TABLE 14.   Kuznets' Data for Period 1869–78 to 1944–53

	Proportionate Rate of Growth per Annum	
*$X_f(t)$, Net National Product	0.035	(g)
$P(t)$, Labor Force	0.019	(G)
*$x_{hf}(t)$, Total Number of Man-Hours per Year	0.015	
*$X_f(t)/P(t)$, Product per Worker	0.015	
*$X_f(t)/$*$x_{hf}(t)$, Product per Man-Hour	0.019	(γ)
$h_{hf}(t)$, Man-Hours per Year per Worker	-0.004	(Γ)

SOURCE: Kuznets' revised estimates extended to 1953, reproduced by Moses Abramovitz, "Resource and Output Trends in the United States Since 1870," *The American Economic Review, Papers and Proceedings*, XLVI (May, 1956), p. 8.

for the same period, Γ has been around -0.004 per annum and also is easily in excess of -1. Now h_{ff} is the number of machine-hours of operation per year per machine and may, of course, be anywhere between zero and 8760. Finally, s is the ratio of business undistributed profits to the money value of output. For

---

[8] But is it also satisfied on the basis of a longer unit of time? Chap. 25 makes the point that the value of the capital coefficient is in roughly inverse proportion to the length of the time unit. Consequently, would not the capital coefficient approach zero for an infinitely long time unit? Footnote 2 in chap. 25 explains that it would not because of our habit of letting a stock variable refer to the *end* of the period. If the capital coefficient based on an n-year time unit is called b_n, the formula in the footnote shows that for n approaching infinity, b_n will approach (one minus the community's propensity to consume). For any time unit shorter than infinity it is seen that our inequality will, in fact, be satisfied.

the last eight decades in the United States, a plausible value of s is 0.02 or 0.03.   All inequalities are easily satisfied.

Now to translate the six multipliers into words.   The equilibrium rate of growth γ of productivity will rise (1) if due to increased thriftiness, the household propensity a_{fh} to consume real personal income falls; (2) if due to technological progress, the number b_{ff} of machine hours required per unit of product falls; (3) if due to certain sociological factors, the proportionate rate of growth G of the labor force falls; (4) if due to an acceleration of the demand for leisure, the proportionate rate of change Γ of the number of hours worked per year per worker falls (for instance from -0.004 to -0.005 per annum); (5) if due to better utilization of capital stock, the number h_{ff} of machine-hours per year per machine increases; or (6) if due to more far-sighted business planning, the ratio s between undistributed profits and the money value of output rises.

15. GRAPHICAL ILLUSTRATION

Since in most of the six multipliers the numerator and the denominator have different dimensions, the numerical value of those multipliers is dependent upon the choice of units of measurement.   In such cases time-honored elasticity is a better tool.   To afford study of the elasticities we have plotted in Figures 59 through 64 the rate of growth of productivity against each of the six parameters on double-logarithmic paper, elasticity appearing simply as the steepness of the curve.   Choosing the six empirically plausible values of our parameters shown in Table 15, and keeping the last five values constant, we varied slightly the value of a_{fh} and watched the effect upon γ: the result appears in Figure 59.   Next we have kept all parameters constant except b_{ff} which we have varied, see Figure 60, and so on.   The general impression gained from Figures 59 through 64 can be summarized as follows.

The numerically highest of all six elasticities is that of γ with respect to a_{fh}, the propensity to consume.   In view of the fact that

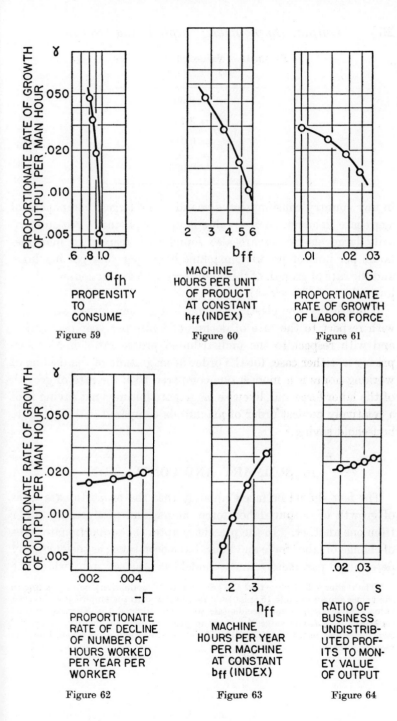

Figure 59

Figure 60

Figure 61

Figure 62

Figure 63

Figure 64

TABLE 15.   Values of Parameters
Used for Graphs

$$a_{fh} = 0.90$$
$$\frac{b_{ff}}{h_{ff}} = 3.7$$
$$G = 0.019$$
$$\Gamma = -0.004$$
$$s = 0.025$$

in any country consumption demand is the largest component of aggregate demand, such a value is not surprising.   But numerically large elasticities are also found with respect to machine-hours per unit of product, machine-hours per year per machine, and the rate of growth of the labor force, at least for comparatively low values of this growth rate.

Numerically low elasticities, much less than unity, are found with respect to the rate of decline of hours per year per worker and with respect to the undistributed profits ratio, hardly surprising in either case, for the order of magnitude of the decline of working-hours is a modest one compared with the rate of growth of the labor force and, likewise, aggregate business net saving is of a relatively modest order of magnitude compared with aggregate household saving.[9]

16. SUMMARY AND CONCLUSION

The fact should be faced squarely that the proportionate rates of growth of output, labor force, hours, and productivity differ from one another.   In the present chapter the proportionate rates of change of labor force and hours have been taken as sociologically determined parameters, and a model has been set up by which the

[9] The reader will observe that the growth rate of productivity corresponding to the values shown in table 15 is 0.019, a rate identical to the empirically observed value.   This result is not accidental; we have adjusted the Kuznets' capital coefficient to 3.7, the value necessary to produce such an identity.   Kuznets' own figure was based upon depreciated capital stock, and some upward adjustment is in order.

remaining two growth rates can be determined.   The model is an equilibrium model requiring that everybody's expectations come true.   In this sense our growth rates are both variants of the Harrodian "warranted" rate of growth.

Particular attention has been paid to the rate of growth of output per man-hour; the reasons for such emphasis are first, the importance of this growth rate in overseas development policy and second, the traditional neglect of it by theory of the Harrod-Domar type.   The rate of growth of output per man-hour is determined in Equation (II); furthermore, the direction and the force of the parameters affecting it have been examined, partly by the multiplier approach, partly by the elasticity approach.

As for the directions of the six parameters, the rate of growth of output per man-hour will rise, if (1) the household propensity to consume falls, (2) the number of machine-hours required per unit of product falls, (3) the rate of growth of the labor force falls, (4) the rate of change of the number of hours worked per year per worker falls, (5) the number of machine-hours per year per machine increases, and (6) the business propensity to withhold profits rises.

As for the relative forces of the six parameters, Figures 59 through 64 indicate that the force of the six determining parameters varies considerably from one parameter to another, the one most powerful seeming to be the propensity of households to consume, the two least powerful the rate of change in hours and the business propensity to withhold profits.

All six parameters seem important.   But it should be recalled that in reaching our conclusion we manipulated slightly such empirically plausible values of the six parameters as could be gathered from the American past.   It would be highly interesting to insert, say, Indian data into our model.

22

Constancy of the Proportionate Equilibrium Rate of Growth: Result or Assumption?

1. SETTING OF THE PROBLEM

In their path-breaking analyses of long-run dynamics, Harrod and Domar assumed equilibrium national income to grow at a constant proportionate equilibrium rate of growth.

The purpose of the present chapter is to set up, for a closed economy, a growth model in which the constancy of the proportionate equilibrium rate of growth is not an assumption but something to be tested. Also the conventional net approach is replaced by the gross-national-product approach, thus permitting the inclusion of an explicit replacement function in the model. The replacement function is usually ignored in growth models of the Harrod-Domar type, quite legitimately as long as the proportionate rate of growth is assumed to be a constant over time, for in that case the ratio between gross and net investment will be

NOTE: The first 16 sections of the present chapter represent a slight revision of the author's "Constancy of the Proportionate Equilibrium Rate of Growth: Result or Assumption?" *Review of Economic Studies*, Vol. XXIV, No. 2 (Feb., 1957).

constant over time, and the former can thus be said to be represented by the latter. But the replacement function cannot legitimately be ignored if a constant proportionate rate of growth is no longer assumed. The replacement function used here is based upon the concept of a constant useful life of producers' goods. If the useful life is L, current retirement is equal to gross investment L units of time ago. Once the replacement function of this type is admitted, the order of the difference equations governing the time-path of the system becomes rather high. But, fortunately, to the modern high-speed digital computer such high orders are no serious obstacle.

As usual we shall use Leontief notation.

Variables

R_{ij} = time rate of physical retirement of goods produced by sector i, held by sector j

S_{ij} = physical capital stock of goods produced by sector i, held by sector j

X_j = time rate of physical output of goods produced by sector j

x_{ij} = time rate of physical purchase of product of sector i by sector j

σ_{ij} = time rate of physical sale of product of sector i to sector j

Parameters

a_{fh} = the propensity to consume out of expected real personal income

a_{hf} = planned purchase of factors by firms per unit of planned output

b_{ff} = planned stock of producers' goods held by firms per unit of planned output

L = the useful life of one unit of producers' goods

π_f = the price of goods charged by firms

π_h = the price of factors charged by households

2. GROSS INVESTMENT

Let the subscript f refer to firms, the subscript h to households. The first transaction to be considered is gross investment $*x_{ff}$. By definition, planned net investment is equal to planned purchase of producers' goods minus planned retirement of producers' goods:

$$(1) \qquad *S_{ff}(t) - S_{ff}(t-1) = *x_{ff}(t) - *R_{ff}(t)$$

Equation (1) defines ex ante investment. Removal of the asterisks provides Equation (2), not written, the definition of ex post investment. Now assume that at any particular time a fixed capital coefficient b_{ff} exists:

$$(3) \qquad *S_{ff}(t) = b_{ff}*X_f(t)$$

Finally, let the useful life of one unit of producers' goods be L units of time. Therefore, planned retirement of producers' goods for period t is equal to the realized purchase of producers' goods L years earlier:

$$(4) \qquad *R_{ff}(t) = x_{ff}(t-L)$$

3. PURCHASE OF FACTORS

Factors coöperating with producers' goods include labor and entrepreneurship purchased by firms from households. Planned purchase of factors by firms $*x_{hf}$ is assumed to be in direct proportion to planned output:

$$(5) \qquad *x_{hf}(t) = a_{hf}*X_f(t)$$

where a_{hf} is a parameter indicating purchase of factors per unit of planned output.

4. CONSUMPTION

Planned purchases of consumers' goods by households are assumed to be in direct proportion to expected real personal income:

$$(6) \qquad *x_{fh}(t) = a_{fh} \frac{*\sigma_{hf}(t)\pi_h}{\pi_f}$$

where a_{fh} is the propensity to consume expected real personal income, π_f the price of goods charged by firms, and π_h the price of factors charged by households.

5. PLANNED GROSS NATIONAL OUTPUT

Ignoring planned inventory changes, we assume that planned gross national product equals expected sale of all goods:

$$(7) \qquad *X_f(t) = *\sigma_{ff}(t) + *\sigma_{fh}(t)$$

6. ALL PLANS ARE CARRIED OUT

In a buyers' market a unit of time can be chosen such that plans made at the beginning of that period are not changed until the beginning of the next period. First, *purchase* plans are carried out:

$$(8) \text{ through } (10) \qquad *x_{ij}(t) = x_{ij}(t)$$

where ij refers to ff, hf, and fh, respectively. Second, *retirement* plans are carried out:

$$(11) \qquad *R_{ff}(t) = R_{ff}(t)$$

and third, *production* plans are carried out:

$$(12) \qquad *X_f(t) = X_f(t)$$

7. WHAT IS PURCHASED IS SOLD

A buyer's realized purchase equals the seller's realized sale to that buyer:

(13) through (15) $x_{ij}(t) = \sigma_{ij}(t)$

where ij refers to ff, hf, and fh, respectively.

8. EQUILIBRIUM CONDITIONS

If equilibrium is to prevail, the activity of the economy must be self-justifying in the sense that any sector's expected sales must materialize:

(16) through (18) $*\sigma_{ij}(t) = \sigma_{ij}(t)$

where ij refers to ff, hf, and fh, respectively.

9. SOLUTION

The system of equations includes 18 variables: one planned and one realized retirement $*R_{ij}$ and R_{ij}; one planned and one realized capital stock $*S_{ij}$ and S_{ij}; one planned and one realized output $*X_j$ and X_j; three planned and three realized purchases $*x_{ij}$ and x_{ij}; three expected and three realized sales $*\sigma_{ij}$ and σ_{ij}. Solving for gross national output, we get

(I) $n_1 X_f(t) + n_2 X_f(t-1) - (n_1 + n_2) X_f(t-L) = 0$

where:

$$n_1 = 1 - b_{ff} - a_{fh} a_{hf} \frac{\pi_h}{\pi_f}$$

$$n_2 = b_{ff}$$

10. INTERPRETATION OF THE PARAMETERS OF THE SOLUTION

The interpretation of (I) is comparatively easy. First, let us try to find the economic meaning of $(n_1 + n_2)$. Here we have the expression $a_{fh}a_{hf}\pi_h/\pi_f$. According to the factor purchase function, Equation (5) in Section 3, a_{hf} is physical number of factors purchased by firms per unit of planned output. Multiply by π_h and get the money value of factors purchased by firms per unit of output. Or, which is the same thing, household money income per unit of output. Divide by π_f and get household real income per unit of output. Finally multiply by a_{fh}, the propensity to consume out of expected real personal income. This will give us household purchase of consumers' goods per unit of output. In the United States for the last eight decades, gross capital formation has accounted for about one-fifth of the gross national product, and the flow of goods to consumers for about four-fifths.[1] Thus $a_{fh}a_{hf}\pi_h/\pi_f = 0.80$, and $(n_1 + n_2) = 1 - a_{fh}a_{hf}\pi_h/\pi_f = 0.20$. Essentially, then, the coefficient of $X_f(t - L)$ is the community's gross propensity to save.

Second, let us examine the coefficient n_2 of $X_f(t - 1)$, which is b_{ff} or the capital coefficient. In Chapter 21 we were constructing a net national product model and cited Kuznets' result that the capital-net national product ratio was 3.1.[2] Hence the capital-gross national product ratio (needed for the gross national product model in the present chapter) would be 2.8. We also cited Grosse[3] to the effect that undepreciated accounting data are a better approximation of the explanation of investment behavior than are depreciated accounting data, such as those used by Kuznets. Finally, Schiff[4] has called attention to the fact that in some cases after some time it will be economical for the owner of a durable producers' good to remove it from the service line in

[1] Simon Kuznets, "Long-Term Changes in the National Income of the United States of America since 1870," *Income and Wealth of the United States* (Cambridge, England: Bowes & Bowes, 1952), p. 156.

[2] Kuznets, *op. cit.*, p. 127.

[3] Robert N. Grosse, "The Structure of Capital," *Studies in the Structure of the American Economy*, W. Leontief (ed.) (New York: Oxford, 1953), Table 3, p. 209.

[4] Eric Schiff, "A Note on Depreciation, Replacement, and Growth," *The Review of Economics and Statistics*, Vol. XXXVI, No. 1 (Feb., 1954), pp. 47–56.

which it was first employed, relegating it to services quantitatively or qualitatively less exacting, a device that points a way out of our dilemma. As a rough approximation to reality let physical capital stock include *only* producers' goods younger than, say, half their full lifetime. At half-age they would have to be removed from first-line service and replaced by brand-new producers' goods. Full lifetime has been estimated at around 30 years. Consequently, half-age or the average useful life of physical capital stock as we have now defined it would be only about 15 years. Physical capital stock thus defined and taken at its *undepreciated* value would have the same current dollar value as a physically twice as large capital stock, with a useful life twice as long, but *depreciated* according to the straight-line principle. With this interpretation we can use the Kuznets figure 2.8; let us set the average useful life of physical capital stock at 16 years.

For empirically plausible values of our parameters we use average ex post data, although marginal ex ante data would seem to be relevant. But from the long-run constancy or almost constancy of the propensity to consume as well as of the capital coefficient, it follows that long-run average and marginal values differ little. Furthermore, ex ante and ex post are less likely to differ in the long run than in the short run.

Finally, for technical reasons we shall use a two-year period for a time unit. This choice has certain consequences for the numerical values of our n's. The coefficient $(n_1 + n_2) = 0.20$ remains the same, for the propensity to save is a flow-flow ratio, and the ratio between two flows remains the same regardless of the time unit used. But the capital coefficient n_2 is a stock-flow ratio whose value is roughly in inverse proportion to the length of the time unit used. Thus, the capital coefficient if on an annual basis is 2.8, but merely 1.4 on a two-year time-unit basis. Finally, the useful life L of producers' goods, if 16 years, is merely eight two-year time units.

11. NUMERICAL SOLUTION

It is well known [5] that the solution

$$(19) \qquad X_f(t) = r^t$$

satisfies our difference Equation (I) for any r for which:

$$(Ia) \qquad n_1 r^L + n_2 r^{L-1} - (n_1 + n_2) = 0$$

Equation (Ia) is the characteristic equation of difference equation (I). According to assumption, $n_1 = -1.20$, $n_2 = +1.4$, and $L = 8$, the characteristic equation is of the eighth degree. It is also well known that if $r_1 \cdots r_8$ are the eight roots of the characteristic equation (Ia) and if none of them is a multiple root,

$$(II) \qquad X_f(t) = a_1 r_1{}^t + \cdots + a_8 r_8{}^t$$

will be a solution to our difference equation (I) where the a's are eight arbitrary constants chosen to fit the initial conditions. The eight roots, found on the University of Illinois high-speed electronic digital computer are

$r_1 = +1.0400927$ $r_5 = -0.2090617 + 0.6970307\,i$

$r_2 = +1.0000000$ $r_6 = -0.2090617 - 0.6970307\,i$

$r_3 = +0.4187178 + 0.6521725\,i$ $r_7 = -0.6463691 + 0.2932309\,i$

$r_4 = +0.4187178 - 0.6521725\,i$ $r_8 = -0.6463691 - 0.2932309\,i$

The positive real root equal to unity is easily discovered by a quick glance at (Ia). In addition, one positive real root is larger than unity, $r_1 = 1.0400927$. All remaining six roots are complex, and their moduli each less than unity. In the following argument we shall call the largest root r_d the dominant root; in (II) let $r_1 = r_d$.

[5] William J. Baumol, *Economic Dynamics* (New York: Macmillan, 1951), pp. 163–165.

12. A GOOD APPROXIMATION TO $X_f(t)$

From (II) it follows that since $r_1 = r_d$, $r_2 = 1$, and $r_3 \cdots r_8$ are each numerically smaller than unity

$$(\mathrm{III}) \qquad X_f(t) \sim \bar{X}_f(t) = a_1 r_d{}^t + a_2 \qquad \text{as} \qquad t \to \infty$$

meaning that $X_f(t)$ is asymptotic to $\bar{X}_f(t)$ as t tends toward infinity, for when $r_3 \cdots r_8$ are each numerically smaller than unity, the sum of the last six terms of (II) will vanish irrespective of the values of the arbitrary constants $a_3 \cdots a_8$.

13. HOW SOON WILL $\bar{X}_f(t)$ BECOME A GOOD APPROXIMATION TO $X_f(t)$?

Practically it is of great importance to know how *soon* (III) becomes a good approximation to (II). The sum of the last six terms of (II) is ever decreasing with rising t, and the sum of the first two terms of (II) is ever rising with rising t. Consequently, it would seem advisable to ask for which value of t the relative deviation of $X_f(t)$ from $\bar{X}_f(t)$ is smaller than a certain arbitrarily small constant. More specifically, for which value of t is:

$$(\mathrm{IV}) \qquad \frac{X_f(t) - \bar{X}_f(t)}{\bar{X}_f(t)} < \epsilon$$

where ϵ is an arbitrarily small constant? Taking (II) and (III) together we can rewrite (IV)

$$(\mathrm{IVa}) \qquad \frac{a_3 r_3{}^t + \cdots + a_8 r_8{}^t}{a_1 r_d{}^t + a_2} < \epsilon$$

Clearly the answer to our question depends upon the values of the arbitrary constants $a_1 \cdots a_8$; their values, in turn, depend upon the initial conditions, which are real, but the six roots $r_3 \cdots r_8$ are complex. Let the roots be:

$$
\begin{aligned}
r_3 &= \alpha_3 + \beta_3 i & \qquad r_6 &= \alpha_5 - \beta_5 i \\
r_4 &= \alpha_3 - \beta_3 i & \qquad r_7 &= \alpha_7 + \beta_7 i \\
r_5 &= \alpha_5 + \beta_5 i & \qquad r_8 &= \alpha_7 - \beta_7 i
\end{aligned}
$$

According to Baumol,[6] the complete solution (II) may be written

(IIa) $\quad X_f(t) = a_1 r_1^t + a_2 + D_3^t[e_3 \cos (tR_3) + f_3 \sin (tR_3)]$
$$+ D_5^t[e_5 \cos (tR_5) + f_5 \sin (tR_5)]$$
$$+ D_7^t[e_7 \cos (tR_7) + f_7 \sin (tR_7)]$$

where

$$D_3 = \sqrt{\alpha_3^2 + \beta_3^2}, \quad D_5 = \sqrt{\alpha_5^2 + \beta_5^2}, \quad D_7 = \sqrt{\alpha_7^2 + \beta_7^2}$$

$$\cos R_3 = \frac{\alpha_3}{D_3}, \qquad \cos R_5 = \frac{\alpha_5}{D_5}, \qquad \cos R_7 = \frac{\alpha_7}{D_7}$$

$$\sin R_3 = \frac{\beta_3}{D_3}, \qquad \sin R_5 = \frac{\beta_5}{D_5}, \qquad \sin R_7 = \frac{\beta_7}{D_7}$$

and the e's and the f's are real constants to be determined to accord with the initial conditions.

Which initial conditions should be specified? In order to compare widely different cases five alternative sets of initial conditions are reproduced in Table 16. The first set, indicated by A,

TABLE 16. Five Alternative Sets of Initial Conditions Selected

$X_f(t)$	A	B	C	D	E
$X_f(0)$	1.0000	1.0000	1.0000	1.0000	1.0000
$X_f(1)$	1.0300	1.0500	1.0500	1.0000	1.0400
$X_f(2)$	1.0609	1.1025	1.0609	1.0000	1.0820
$X_f(3)$	1.0927	1.1576	1.1576	1.0000	1.1260
$X_f(4)$	1.1255	1.2155	1.1255	1.0000	1.1710
$X_f(5)$	1.1593	1.2763	1.2763	1.0000	1.2170
$X_f(6)$	1.1941	1.3401	1.1941	1.0000	1.2660
$X_f(7)$	1.2299	1.4071	1.4071	1.0000	1.3170

is based upon the starting point unity and a proportionate rate of growth of 3 percent per unit of time. The second set, indicated by B, is based upon the same starting point but on a 5 percent growth rate. C is characterized by the same starting point but

[6] Baumol, *op. cit.*, Proposition Eleven, p. 190.

by alternation between the 3 percent and the 5 percent growth path. D is a completely stationary path, and E is a path with the starting point unity and a proportionate rate of growth of $g = r_d - 1$, where r_d is the dominant root of (Ia).

For each of these five sets of initial conditions, A through E, the eight values of $X_f(t)$ for $t = 0$ through 7 provide eight corresponding versions of (IIa). For the known values of the eight roots $r_1 \cdots r_8$ of (Ia), the eight versions constitute a system of eight equations in eight unknowns, the unknowns being the arbitrary constants a_1, a_2, e_3, f_3, e_5, f_5, e_7, and f_7. The computer solved this system and gave us five alternative sets of arbitrary constants reproduced in Table 17. Together with the eight roots $r_1 \cdots r_8$ these constants can now be inserted into (IIa). (IIa)

TABLE 17. Five Alternative Sets of Arbitrary Constants Determined in Accordance with Initial Conditions

Constant	A	B	C	D	E
a_1	$+0.7193$	$+1.2960$	$+1.4854$	0.0000	$+1.0000$
a_2	$+0.2831$	-0.3006	-0.5781	$+1.0000$	0.0000
e_3	$+0.0001$	$+0.0027$	-0.1141	0.0000	0.0000
f_3	-0.0021	$+0.0030$	$+0.1039$	0.0000	0.0000
e_5	-0.0016	$+0.0002$	-0.0548	0.0000	0.0000
f_5	-0.0011	$+0.0009$	$+0.1988$	0.0000	0.0000
e_7	-0.0009	$+0.0017$	$+0.2617$	0.0000	0.0000
f_7	0.0000	$+0.0009$	$+0.2811$	0.0000	0.0000

and (III) can then be inserted into (IV), and five sets of values of (IV), the relative deviation of $X_f(t)$ from its own limit $\bar{X}_f(t)$, can be found, one for each of the five models A through E. The first three of these have been reproduced in Table 18.

The general impression gained from Table 18 is that the limit $\bar{X}_f(t)$ is indeed a good approximation to $X_f(t)$. For example, in case C at time 10, $X_f(t)$ deviates only about two-tenths of one percent from $\bar{X}_f(t)$, but the deviation becomes progressively

TABLE 18.   Relative Deviation of $X_f(t)$ from Its Own Limit $\bar{X}_f(t)$
as a Function of Time

t	$\dfrac{X_f(t) - \bar{X}_f(t)}{\bar{X}_f(t)}$		
	A	B	C
10	+ 0.00003031	− 0.00018684	+ 0.00211688
20	− 0.00000673	+ 0.00000833	− 0.00012775
30	+ 0.00000035	− 0.00000030	− 0.00001477
40	− 0.00000002	0.00000000	+ 0.00000082
50	0.00000000	0.00000000	− 0.00000006
100	0.00000000	0.00000000	0.00000000

smaller as t rises, and the relative deviation at any given time in
cases A and B is even smaller than the relative deviation in C at
the same time.

The relative deviation of $X_f(t)$ from $\bar{X}_f(t)$ in the last two models
D and E is not shown in the table.   In the case of D, $X_f(t)$ is
stationary during the first eight periods, causing all arbitrary
constants except a_2 to equal zero (see Table 17, column D).   The
economy will continuously maintain identity between $X_f(t)$ and
$\bar{X}_f(t)$, both being equal to a_2 and the relative deviation remaining
zero.

In the case of E, $X_f(t)$ grows at the proportionate rate $g =
r_d - 1$, causing all arbitrary constants except a_1 to equal zero
(see Table 17, column E).   Here, too, the economy will continuously maintain identity between $X_f(t)$ and $\bar{X}_f(t)$, both being
equal to $a_1 r_d{}^t$ and the relative deviation remaining zero.

14. A ROUGH APPROXIMATION TO $X_f(t)$

The growth pattern of $\bar{X}_f(t)$, described in (III), is not characterized by *constancy* of the proportionate rate of growth.   On
the contrary, (III) consists of two terms, the first of which grows

at the constant proportionate rate of growth $g = r_d - 1$, or roughly 4 percent per two-year period or 2 percent per annum, but the last term is simply a constant. Their sum will have a variable proportionate rate of growth, but lack of constancy in the proportionate rate of growth of (III) is not necessarily very serious. Of the two terms the first is explosive, the latter constant. Consequently, the former will eventually swamp the latter. For purely practical purposes, then, the expression:

$$\text{(V)} \qquad \overline{\overline{X}}_f(t) = a_1 r_d{}^t$$

may sometimes be used as an approximation to (III). But it should be clearly understood that (V) is not the limit of (III) for the difference between them will remain equal to a_2, no matter how much time elapses. Also, it should be pointed out that if the coefficient a_2 is large and the coefficient a_1 is small, "eventually" should be taken *sub specie aeternitatis*.

15. HOW SOON WILL $\overline{\overline{X}}_f(t)$ BECOME A GOOD APPROXIMATION TO $X_f(t)$?

It is here important again to know how *soon* (V) becomes a good approximation to (II). More specifically, for which value of t is

$$\text{(VI)} \qquad \frac{X_f(t) - \overline{\overline{X}}_f(t)}{\overline{\overline{X}}_f(t)} < \epsilon$$

where ϵ is an arbitrarily small constant? Taking (II) and (V) together, we rewrite (VI)

$$\text{(VIa)} \qquad \frac{a_2 + a_3 r_3{}^t + \cdots + a_8 r_8{}^t}{a_1 r_d{}^t} < \epsilon$$

Into (VIa) can be inserted magnitudes identical to those used in (IVa). The only difference between (IVa) and (VIa) is that in (IVa) the magnitude a_2 appears in the denominator, but in (VIa) in the numerator. The relative deviation of $X_f(t)$ from $\overline{\overline{X}}_f(t)$ is found for the five cases A through E, results for the three cases

TABLE 19. Relative Deviation of $X_f(t)$ from Rough Approximation $\overline{\overline{X}}_f(t)$ as a Function of Time

t	$\dfrac{X_f(t) - \overline{\overline{X}}_f(t)}{\overline{\overline{X}}_f(t)}$		
	A	B	C
10	+0.2654	−0.1566	−0.2609
20	+0.1792	−0.1055	−0.1772
30	+0.1208	−0.0712	−0.1195
40	+0.0815	−0.0480	−0.0806
50	+0.0549	−0.0323	−0.0543
100	+0.0077	−0.0045	−0.0076

A through C being tabulated in Table 19. The general impression to be gained from Table 19 is that in the three cases considered, $\overline{\overline{X}}_f(t)$ is a far poorer approximation to $X_f(t)$ than is $\overline{X}_f(t)$. At time 10, for example, in cases A and C the relative deviations are still around 26 percent, and more than 50 time units from zero are required to reduce the relative deviation to less than five percent. While in case B the relative deviation is somewhat smaller, it is still uncomfortably large.

In the case of D, not shown in the table, since all the arbitrary constants except a_2 are zero, $X_f(t)$ will be equal to a_2, and $\overline{\overline{X}}_f(t)$ to zero, the relative deviation (VI) becoming undefined. In the case of E (also not shown in the table) since all the arbitrary constants except a_1 are zero, $X_f(t)$ and $\overline{\overline{X}}_f(t)$ will remain identical, both being equal to $a_1 r_d{}^t$, and in this case, the relative deviation will remain equal to zero.

16. CONCLUSION

In the short run—depending upon the initial conditions—the rough approximation $\overline{\overline{X}}_f(t)$, characterized by a constant proportionate rate of growth, may or may not be a good approximation to $X_f(t)$. In the long run, since the dominant root r_d will eventually swamp any other root, $\bar{\bar{X}}_f(t)$ is bound to be a good approximation irrespective of the initial conditions. As the examples show, however, the long run may sometimes be very long indeed.

17. APPLICATION OF THE SOLUTION

Let us accept, then, the approximation $\bar{\bar{X}}_f(t)$ growing, as we saw, at the constant proportionate rate of growth $g = r_d - 1$, and let us examine the effects upon g of manipulation of parameters. Starting from the not implausible case that the community's propensity to save is 0.20, the capital coefficient on a two-year basis 1.4, and useful life 8, we get $g = 0.040$, a not entirely implausible result.[7]   Next, we find the effects of isolated

TABLE 20. Empirical Percentage Rates of Growth of National Product per Decade in Constant Prices for 19 Countries During First Half of Twentieth Century

Union of South Africa	49.7	Netherlands	24.6
Canada	41.4	Switzerland	24.4
Japan	37.9	Italy	22.2
Sweden	37.8	Germany	19.9
United States	33.8	United Kingdom	17.2
Norway	33.5	Hungary	15.5
Russia and the U.S.S.R.	33.1	Spain	14.9
New Zealand	32.7	Ireland and Eire	14.6
Denmark	30.6	France	11.1
Australia	28.4		

SOURCE: Table 1 in Simon Kuznets, "Quantitative Aspects of the Economic Growth of Nations," *Economic Development and Cultural Change*, Vol. V, No. 1 (October, 1956), p. 10.

[7] This result would correspond to a 2 percent rate of growth per annum, or a 21.9 percent rate of growth per decade. For purposes of comparison, table 20 cites some national growth rates published by Simon Kuznets. Our numerical result, 21.9 percent per decade, is roughly twice as high as the lowest of the 19 growth rates, i.e., that of France. And it is roughly half as high as the highest of the 19 growth rates, i.e., those of Canada and the Union of South Africa. Our result is roughly two-thirds of the figure for the United States, i.e., 33.8. Realizing

variations of these three parameters in turn, results being presented in Figures 65 through 67, plotted as usual on double-logarithmic paper in order to show elasticity more clearly. It appears that the proportionate equilibrium rate of growth has a

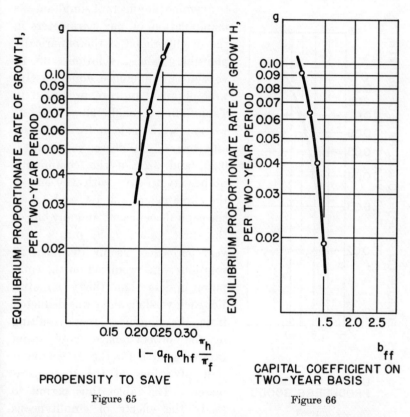

Figure 65

Figure 66

very high elasticity indeed with respect to any of the three parameters: the growth rate will (1) rise sharply if the propensity to

---

the difficulty involved in measuring even Kuznets' depreciated capital stock, and realizing the arbitrariness with which we have adjusted his capital coefficients, we should expect no close correspondence. As we shall see in table 22, a slight reduction of the value we have used for the capital coefficient is all that is needed to produce complete correspondence.

save increases, (2) decline sharply if the capital coefficient increases, or (3) rise sharply if the useful life of producers' goods is lengthened.[8]

But what if changes of parameters are not isolated? In order to examine the effects of simultaneous manipulation of our parameters in the neighborhood of the empirically plausible values, solutions of 27 versions of difference equation (Ia) were obtained and are presented in Tables 21 through 23. The 27 versions were made up by combining any one of the three values 0.18, 0.20, and 0.22 of the community propensity to save with any one of the three values 1.3, 1.4, and 1.5 of the capital coefficient and any one of the three values 7, 8, and 9 two-year periods of useful life. The 27 solutions were produced on the computer in less than thirty minutes. For each version, unity was deducted from the dominant root, resulting in the proportionate equilibrium rate of growth for the 27 combinations of values of the three parameters. The tables thus permit to study the effects of simultaneous variations in parameters. In 6 out of the 27 versions of (Ia), the largest root was positive, real, and

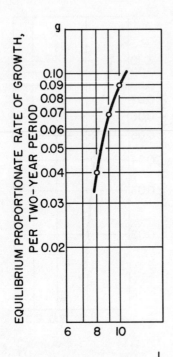

USEFUL LIFE OF
PRODUCERS' GOODS

Figure 67

---

[8] The low degree of correspondence between our figure 21.9 and the Kuznets' figure 33.8 percent per decade could easily have been raised by slight variations of the parameters, as indicated. For example, a slight reduction of the capital coefficient from 1.4 to 1.3 would have brought the two figures into line, in which case the rate of growth per two-year time unit would have been 0.064, corresponding to a 36.7 percent per decade growth rate.

TABLE 21. Equilibrium Growth Rates for
$L = 7$ Based upon a Two-Year Time Unit

b_{ff}	$1 - a_{fh}a_{hf}\dfrac{\pi_h}{\pi_f}$		
	0.18	0.20	0.22
1.3	0.000	0.025	0.061
1.4	0.000	0.000	0.033
1.5	0.000	0.000	0.009

TABLE 22. Equilibrium Growth Rates for
$L = 8$ Based upon a Two-Year Time Unit

b_{ff}	$1 - a_{fh}a_{hf}\dfrac{\pi_h}{\pi_f}$		
	0.18	0.20	0.22
1.3	0.030	0.064	0.097
1.4	0.008	0.040	0.071
1.5	0.000	0.019	0.048

TABLE 23. Equilibrium Growth Rates for
$L = 9$ Based upon a Two-Year Time Unit

b_{ff}	$1 - a_{fh}a_{hf}\dfrac{\pi_h}{\pi_f}$		
	0.18	0.20	0.22
1.3	0.059	0.092	0.123
1.4	0.038	0.069	0.099
1.5	0.020	0.049	0.077

equal to unity. The economic significance is that in these versions the capital coefficient is too high, the community propensity to save too low, or the useful life of producers' goods too short to allow the economy to have any growth potential whatsoever. In the remaining 21 cases the largest root was positive, real, and in excess of unity, values indicating the economy to be growing.

18. SOME PARAMETERS NOT INDEPENDENT

Studying simultaneous variations in parameters becomes necessary when it is suspected that the parameters may not, after all, be mutually independent. Lack of independence between the community's gross propensity to save and the useful life of producers' goods may well be suspected. May not longer useful life induce reduced depreciation allowances? If so, either more dividends are distributed per unit of output, in which case the value of a_{hf} rises; or, the price π_f of goods will be lowered at unchanged price of factors π_h. In either case $1 - a_{fh}a_{hf}\pi_h/\pi_f$ will decrease, the community's gross propensity to save being smaller. The positive effect upon the growth rate of a longer useful life could possibly be offset by the negative effect upon the growth rate of a community's lower gross propensity to save. In Chapter 23 we shall see that for empirically plausible values of parameters the positive effect is likely to swamp the negative effect. Needless to say, not until we have committed ourselves to a specific behavior hypothesis about the relationship between useful life and the internal rate of return, and to another specific behavior hypothesis about the relationship between the internal rate of return and dividends, can we determine the effect of a longer useful life of producers' goods upon the community's gross propensity to save. Such hypotheses are bound to complicate the model quite considerably; they will be developed in Chapter 23.

23

Growth and Technological Progress

1. THE MODEL

Chapter 22 posed the problem whether the positive effect upon the growth rate of a longer useful life of producers' goods would or would not be offset by the negative effect upon the growth rate of the accompanying reduction of the community's gross propensity to save. That problem is part of the broader problem of the effect of technological progress upon growth, now to be studied.

In Chapter 19 we studied induced changes of the performance parameters a_{lc}, $1/b_{pc}$, and L. In an aggregative dynamic model let us now study the effects of autonomous changes in those performance parameters upon the rate of growth. The notation is

Variables

g = the equilibrium proportionate rate of growth which will eventually materialize

ι = the internal rate of return per annum with continuous compounding

π_p = the price of producers' goods

R_{ij} = time rate of physical retirement of goods produced by sector i, held by sector j

S_{ij} = physical capital stock of goods produced by sector i, held by sector j

X_j = time rate of physical output of goods produced by sector j

x_{ij} = time rate of physical purchase of product of sector i by sector j

σ_{ij} = time rate of physical sale of product of sector i to sector j

Parameters

a_{ce} = marginal propensity to consume of capitalist-entrepreneurs

a_{cl} = marginal propensity to consume of labor

a_{ec} = dividend dollars distributed per profits dollar made by firms

a_{lc} = number of man-hours of direct labor per annum required to coöperate with one physical unit of producers' goods

a_{lp} = number of man-hours of labor required to produce one physical unit of producers' goods

$1/b_{pc}$ = number of physical units of consumers' goods produced per annum per physical unit of producers' goods

L = useful life of one unit of producers' goods

π_c = the price of consumers' goods

π_l = the money wage rate

Only four sectors will be considered: a consumers' goods industry, a producers' goods industry, a labor household sector, and a capitalist-entrepreneur household sector. The subscripts used

TABLE 24. Planned Purchases of Goods and Factors

Purchasing from	Purchases Planned by			
	Consumers' Goods Industry	Producers' Goods Industry	Entrepreneurial Households	Labor Households
Consumers' Goods Industry	—	—	$*x_{ce}$	$*x_{cl}$
Producers' Goods Industry	$*x_{pc}$	—	—	—
Entrepreneurial Households	$*x_{ec}$	—	—	—
Labor Households	$*x_{lc}$	$*x_{lp}$	—	—

to designate the four sectors are c, p, l, and e, respectively. Table 24 shows the six transactions to be considered.

2. CAPITAL STOCK, INVESTMENT, RETIREMENT, AND LABOR INPUTS

The first transaction is gross investment $*x_{pc}$. By definition, planned net investment is equal to planned purchase of producers' goods minus planned retirement of producers' goods:

(1) $$*S_{pc}(t) - S_{pc}(t-1) = *x_{pc}(t) - *R_{pc}(t)$$

Asterisks as usual indicate ex ante values, absence of an asterisk ex post values. The time coördinate is t, and period t is the period ending at time t. Equation (1) defines ex ante investment. When the asterisks are removed from (1) a definition of ex post investment appears as Equation (2), not to be written.

The consumers' goods industry has one output and two inputs, the output consisting of consumers' goods, the inputs of labor services and of services rendered by durable producers' goods. The quality of those producers' goods is expressed in terms of the three now familiar performance characteristics, analyzed in Chapter 19. First the direct labor input coefficient a_{lc}, defined as the number of man-hours of direct labor required per annum to coöperate with one physical unit of producers' goods:

(3) $$*x_{lc}(t) = a_{lc}*S_{pc}(t)$$

The second performance characteristic is the productivity $1/b_{pc}$ of producers' goods defined as the output of consumers' goods per annum per physical unit of producers' goods. The ratio $1/b_{pc}$ is an output-capital ratio and is the reciprocal of the familiar Leontief capital coefficient b_{pc}:

(4) $$*S_{pc}(t) = b_{pc}*X_c(t)$$

The third performance characteristic is the useful life L of one physical unit of producers' goods. Planned retirement of producers' goods for period t is equal to the realized purchase of producers' goods L years earlier:

$$(5) \qquad\qquad *R_{pc}(t) = x_{pc}(t - L)$$

The producers' goods industry has one output and one input, and is characterized by the input-output coefficient a_{lp}, defined as the number of man-hours of labor required to produce one physical unit of producers' goods, and referred to as the indirect labor coefficient:

$$(6) \qquad\qquad *x_{lp}(t) = a_{lp}*X_p(t)$$

3. THE INTERNAL RATE OF RETURN

Call the wage rate π_l and the price of new producers' goods $*\pi_p$. Assume the price of new producers' goods to equal their unit cost of production:

$$(7) \qquad\qquad *\pi_p = \pi_l a_{lp}$$

From the point of view of a firm in the consumers' goods industry Equation (7) represents the indirect labor cost per unit of producers' goods. The direct labor cost per annum per unit of producers' goods is a_{lc} times the wage rate π_l, or $\pi_l a_{lc}$. The price of consumers' goods being π_c, revenue per annum per unit of producers' goods is π_c/b_{pc}. Revenue minus direct labor cost per annum per unit of producers' goods is

$$\frac{\pi_c}{b_{pc}} - \pi_l a_{lc}$$

The internal rate of return $*\iota$ is that rate which makes the sum total of the present worth of revenue minus direct labor cost during the entire useful life of the unit of producers' goods equal to the price $*\pi_p$ of that unit. As shown in Chapter 19, Section 5, the algebraic definition is

$$(8) \qquad\qquad *\pi_p = \left(\frac{\pi_c}{b_{pc}} - \pi_l a_{lc}\right) \frac{1 - e^{-*\iota L}}{*\iota}$$

4. EARNINGS AND DIVIDENDS

From the definition of the internal rate of return given in Equation (8) it follows that for every unit of producers' goods held by the consumers' goods industry the profit earnings of the latter are $*\iota*\pi_p$ per annum. Multiply by the number of units of producers' goods in existence and get the aggregate profit earnings per annum. Let the dividend-to-earnings ratio be a_{ec}, which is less than unity. The aggregate of dividend payments to the capitalist-entrepreneur households is

$$(9) \qquad *x_{ec}(t) = a_{ec}*\iota*\pi_p*S_{pc}(t)$$

5. CONSUMPTION

Planned real purchases of consumption goods are assumed to be in proportion to expected real income, which, of course, equals the *money* value of sales of entrepreneurship and labor by households to business divided by the price of consumers' goods. Then:

$$(10) \qquad *x_{ce}(t) = a_{ce}\frac{*\sigma_{ec}(t)}{\pi_c}$$

$$(11) \qquad *x_{cl}(t) = a_{cl}\pi_l\frac{*\sigma_{lc}(t) + *\sigma_{lp}(t)}{\pi_c}$$

where a_{ce} and a_{cl} are the propensities to consume of capitalist-entrepreneur and of labor households, respectively.[1]

---

[1] Purchase (and sale) of entrepreneurship is unique among our transactions by its money dimension. All other transactions in the model are measured in physical units. This difference accounts for the fact that in equation (10) expected sales of factor is not multiplied by any price of factor, whereas in equation (11) expected sales of factor is multiplied by π_l.

6. PLANNED OUTPUT

Ignoring planned inventory changes, we assume that planned output of producers' goods and consumers' goods equal their respective expected sales:

(12) $$*X_p(t) = *\sigma_{pc}(t)$$

(13) $$*X_c(t) = *\sigma_{ce}(t) + *\sigma_{cl}(t)$$

7. PLANS ARE CARRIED OUT

In a buyers' market a unit of time can be chosen such that plans made at the beginning of that period are not changed until the beginning of the next period. First, *purchase* plans are carried out:

(14) through (19) $$*x_{ij}(t) = x_{ij}(t)$$

where ij refers to ce, cl, ec, lc, lp, and pc, respectively. Second, *retirement* plans are carried out:

(20) $$*R_{pc}(t) = R_{pc}(t)$$

and third, *production* plans are carried out:

(21) $$*X_p(t) = X_p(t)$$

(22) $$*X_c(t) = X_c(t)$$

8. WHAT IS PURCHASED IS SOLD

A buyer's realized purchase equals the seller's realized sale to that buyer:

(23) through (28) $$x_{ij}(t) = \sigma_{ij}(t)$$

where ij has the same meaning as in Section 7.

9. EQUILIBRIUM CONDITIONS

If equilibrium is to prevail, the activity of the economy must be self-justifying in the sense that any sector's expected sales must equal its realized sales, a condition holding for each of our six transactions:

(29) through (34) $\qquad *\sigma_{ij}(t) = \sigma_{ij}(t)$

where ij has the same meaning as in Section 7.

10. SOLUTION

The system of equations includes 34 variables: one planned and one realized retirement $*R_{ij}$ and R_{ij}; one planned and one realized capital stock $*S_{ij}$ and S_{ij}; two planned and two realized outputs $*X_j$ and X_j; six planned and six realized purchases $*x_{ij}$ and x_{ij}; six expected and six realized sales $*\sigma_{ij}$ and σ_{ij}; the internal rate of return $*\iota$; and the price of producers' goods $*\pi_p$. Upon solving for the national output of consumers' goods (see the Appendix to this chapter), we get the following linear homogeneous difference equation:

(I) $\qquad n_1 X_c(t) + n_2 X_c(t - 1) - (n_1 + n_2)X_c(t - L) = 0$

where

$$n_1 = \frac{1 - \dfrac{\pi_l}{\pi_c} b_{pc}(a_{ce}a_{ec}*\iota a_{lp} + a_{cl}a_{lc})}{\dfrac{\pi_l}{\pi_c} a_{cl}a_{lp}b_{pc}} - 1$$

$$n_2 = 1$$

The coefficient n_1 contains, except for one variable (the internal rate of return $*\iota$) nothing but parameters. If taken together, Equations (7) and (8) define the internal rate of return $*\iota$ in terms of the parameters a_{lc}, a_{lp}, b_{pc}, L, π_c, and π_l.

11. A SIMPLIFICATION

The formidable array of parameters in the coefficient n_1 can be greatly simplified if specific assumptions are made with respect to the two propensities to consume a_{ce} and a_{cl}. Thinking of the entrepreneurs' propensity to consume a_{ce} as being much smaller than one, and of labor's propensity to consume a_{cl} as equal to one,[2] using Equations (7) and (8), one could simplify as follows:

$$(\mathrm{II}) \qquad \frac{1 - \dfrac{\pi_l}{\pi_c} b_{pc}(a_{ce}a_{ec}*_{\iota}a_{lp} + a_{cl}a_{lc})}{\dfrac{\pi_l}{\pi_c} a_{cl}a_{lp}b_{pc}} = \frac{*_{\iota}}{1 - e^{-*_{\iota}L}} - a_{ce}a_{ec}*_{\iota}$$

12. THE EFFECT OF TECHNOLOGICAL PROGRESS UPON THE EXPRESSION (II)

What happens to the right-hand side of (II), representing its new simplified form, under the impact of technological progress? Technological progress can be thought of as follows. At constant values of the other three parameters, either the parameter a_{lc}, the direct labor input coefficient, is reduced; the parameter $1/b_{pc}$, the productivity of producers' goods, is increased; the parameter L, the useful life of producers' goods, is lengthened; or the indirect labor input coefficient a_{lp} is reduced.

A reduction of a_{lc}, an increase of $1/b_{pc}$, or an increase of L will tend to raise the right-hand side of (8), and at constant left-hand side of (8), the equality can be preserved only if $*_{\iota}$ rises. Only if discounted at a higher internal rate of return will the sum of larger future amounts add up to a constant present amount!

---

[2] Cf. Simon Kuznets, "Economic Growth and Income Inequality," *The American Economic Review*, Vol. XLV, No. 1 (March, 1955), p. 7, according to which only the upper-income groups save and the total savings of groups below the top decile of income are near zero. Milton Friedman in his *A Theory of the Consumption Function* (Princeton, Princeton University Press, 1957) finds permanent consumption to be a much lower fraction of permanent income in urban entrepreneurial families than in urban wage-earner families.

A reduction of a_{lp} will tend to reduce the left-hand side of (8), and at constant right-hand side of (8), the equality can be preserved only if $*_\iota$ rises. Only if discounted at a higher internal rate of return will the sum of constant future amounts add up to a smaller present amount!

Thus technological progress manifesting itself in any of the four ways indicated, or combinations of them, will raise the internal rate of return. If so, what happens to the right-hand side of (II)? The latter consists of two terms, and any compound-interest table will reveal that both are rising with rising $*_\iota$. Whether the difference between them will fall or rise, depends upon their relative weight, the constant $a_{ce}a_{ec}$. To find the critical value of $a_{ce}a_{ec}$ which marks the boundary between falling and rising (II), we set the derivative of the right-hand side of (II) with respect to $*_\iota$ equal to zero and get

$$\frac{1 - e^{-*_\iota L}(1 + *_\iota L)}{(1 - e^{-*_\iota L})^2} = a_{ce}a_{ec}$$

In Table 25, we have mapped this function, and we can see that the critical value rises with a rising L as well as with rising $*_\iota$.

TABLE 25. Partial Map of $\dfrac{1 - e^{-*_\iota L}(1 + *_\iota L)}{(1 - e^{-*_\iota L})^2}$

		L	
$*_\iota$	7	8	9
0.15	0.670	0.691	0.713
0.20	0.719	0.746	0.771
0.25	0.766	0.795	0.822

Selected entries in the table read as follows: for $L = 8$ and $*_\iota = 0.20$ the critical value of $a_{ce}a_{ec}$ is 0.746. For values of $a_{ce}a_{ec}$ higher than that, (II) is falling slowly for slightly rising $*_\iota$ but falling rapidly for slightly rising L. For values of $a_{ce}a_{ec}$ lower than 0.746, (II) is rising slowly for slightly rising $*\iota$ and—as before—falling rapidly for slightly rising L.

13. THE EFFECT UPON GROWTH

Having now determined what happens to the right-hand side of (II), we ask: What does this imply for the proportionate equilibrium rate of growth? Two different cases should be distinguished.

First, assume that technological progress affects a_{lc}, $1/b_{pc}$, or a_{lp} but not L. This case is quite simple to deal with. Since there can be no doubt that in the real world $a_{ce}a_{ec}$ will fall short of the critical values indicated in Table 25,[2] any technological progress that increases $*\iota$ without affecting L will also raise (II). For example, let $a_{ce}a_{ec} = 0.538$. At unchanged $L = 8$, let $*\iota$ pass through the values 0.150, 0.200, and 0.300. Our expression (II), which is nothing but the coefficient $(n_1 + n_2)$ in our original difference equation (I), will then pass through the values 0.1340, 0.1429, and 0.1685, respectively. The coefficient n_2 being equal to one, the coefficient n_1 will pass through the values -0.8660, -0.8571, and -0.8315, respectively. But in that case, the largest root r_d of the characteristic equation corresponding to Equation (I) will pass through the values 1.020, 1.040, and 1.096, respectively, cf. Table 26 and Figure 68. Finally, then, the equilibrium proportionate rate of growth $g = r_d - 1$ must pass through the values 0.020, 0.040, and 0.096, respectively. In this case, then, technological progress will accelerate growth.

Second assume that technological progress does affect L. This

---

[2] It would be hard to imagine a_{ce}, the propensity to consume dividend income, being higher than, say 4/5. It would be hard to imagine a_{ec}, the propensity to distribute earnings as dividends, being higher than, say 3/4. Consequently, it would be hard to imagine their product $a_{ce}a_{ec}$ being higher than 0.6. For empirically plausible values of $*\iota$ and L, this is well below the critical values shown in table 25. The reader is warned that the present chapter follows chap. 22 in using a time unit equaling two years. On a one-year basis the values of L would be twice those shown in table 25, and the values of $*\iota$ would be roughly one-half of those shown in that table.

TABLE 26. Largest Root r_d of Characteristic
Equation $n_1r^L + n_2r^{L-1} - (n_1 + n_2) = 0$

$*_\iota$	L	$a_{ce}a_{ec}$	r_d
0.150	8	0.538	1.020
0.200	8	0.538	1.040
0.300	8	0.538	1.096

case is less simple. Technological progress by reducing vibration, friction, or corrosion may increase L, while simultaneously

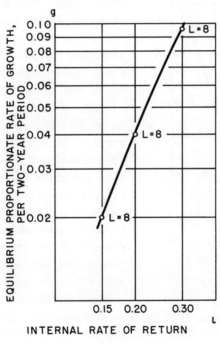

Figure 68

accelerating obsolescence and shortening L. Discussion will deal with lengthening L, but results can easily be reversed if L is thought of as being shortened by technological progress. To facilitate the discussion, let us assume that the other three parameters a_{lc}, $1/b_{pc}$, and a_{lp} are not affected by technological progress. From their constancy, from the assumed constancy of π_c and of π_l, and from Equations (7) and (8), it follows that $*\iota/(1 - e^{-*\iota L})$ must remain constant. Accordingly, increases in

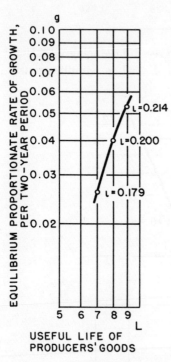

USEFUL LIFE OF
PRODUCERS' GOODS

Figure 69

L must be accompanied by such increases in $*\iota$ as to ensure such constancy. What are the changes ensuring such constancy like? Any compound-interest table will reveal that for relatively low values of L and $*\iota$, lengthening L will make $*\iota$ rise in more than proportion to the lengthening L. For relatively high values of L and $*\iota$, $*\iota$ will rise in less than proportion. Where, in such a table, do we find the values of the real world? On a two-year basis, we have considered $L = 8$ an empirically acceptable value. Still on a two-year basis, an internal rate of return $*\iota = 0.20$ seems to be of a plausible order of magnitude, corresponding to approximately 10 percent per annum. If these two values are concurrent, $*\iota/(1 - e^{-*\iota L})$ will assume the value 0.2505. In

order to maintain that value as L passes through the values 7, 8, and 9, $*\iota$ must correspondingly pass through the values 0.179, 0.200, and 0.214. Still the coefficient $(n_1 + n_2)$ in our original difference equation (I), (II) will successively pass through the values 0.1542, 0.1429, and 0.1354. The coefficient n_2 being equal to one, the coefficient n_1 correspondingly passes through the

TABLE 27. Largest Root r_d of Characteristic
Equation $n_1 r^L + n_2 r^{L-1} - (n_1 + n_2) = 0$

$*_\iota$	L	$a_{ce} a_{ec}$	r_d
0.179	7	0.538	1.026
0.200	8	0.538	1.040
0.214	9	0.538	1.053

values -0.8458, -0.8571, and -0.8646. Now, the largest root r_d of the characteristic equation corresponding to Equation (I) will correspondingly pass through the values 1.026, 1.040, and 1.053 (see Table 27 and Figure 69). Finally, the equilibrium proportionate rate of growth $g = r_d - 1$ must correspondingly pass through the values 0.026, 0.040, and 0.053. A lengthening of L causes the equilibrium rate of growth to increase. The present example is probably characteristic of what happens within bounds empirically plausible. But for values of L and $*_\iota$ substantially lower than those used in the example, and for values of $a_{ce} a_{ec}$ substantially higher, lengthening of L would reduce g.

14. A QUALIFICATION

Our entire discussion of technological progress has been based upon the assumption that the price of goods π_c as well as the wage rate π_l remained constant. Obviously competitive reductions in π_c and/or increases in π_l, insisted upon by labor unions, are possible. The limiting case is that in which such adjustments happen to restore exactly the internal rate of return prevailing before the technological progress occurred. Let us study this limiting case. As long as the useful life L is unaffected by technological progress, matters are again very simple—L and $*_\iota$ both being unaffected, (II) also unaffected, and in consequence $n_1 + n_2$ unaffected. All roots of the characteristic equation are unaffected, and the proportionate rate of growth is similarly unaffected.

But what if L is affected? For example, at unchanged $*\iota = 0.200$, let L successively pass through the values 7, 8, and 9. Expression (II), as usual the coefficient $(n_1 + n_2)$ in original difference equation (I), will correspondingly pass through the values 0.1579, 0.1429, and 0.1320. The coefficient n_2 being equal to one, coefficient n_1 will pass through the values -0.8421, -0.8571, and -0.8680, respectively. But in this case, the largest root r_d of the characteristic equation corresponding to Equation (I) will pass through the values 1.035, 1.040, and 1.046, respectively (see Table 28 and Figure 70). Finally, the equilibrium proportionate rate of growth $g = r_d - 1$ must pass through the values 0.035, 0.040, and 0.046, respectively. It is seen therefore, that technological change which lengthens L increases the proportionate rate of growth, but only slightly.

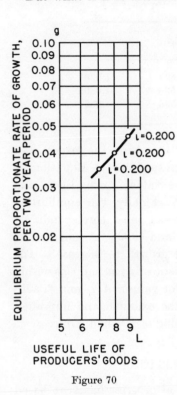

Figure 70

TABLE 28. Largest Root r_d of Characteristic
Equation $n_1 r^L + n_2 r^{L-1} - (n_1 + n_2) = 0$

$*\iota$	L	$a_{ce}a_{ec}$	r_d
0.200	7	0.538	1.035
0.200	8	0.538	1.040
0.200	9	0.538	1.046

If price reductions and/or wage increases are carried beyond the limiting case in a way as to actually reduce $*\iota$, conclusions drawn in the present chapter simply need be reversed.

15. TWO ALTERNATIVE KINDS OF TECHNOLOGICAL PROGRESS

Not all technological progress is of the kind studied in the previous sections, that is, the kind where less input is required per unit of output of a given product. The input less of which is required may be direct or indirect labor, or it may be physical capital stock. This kind of technological progress may be called process innovation.

An alternative type of technological progress might be called product innovation: Here, the product itself is changed. Product innovation is frequently designed to accelerate obsolescence of durable consumers' goods, automobiles affording an excellent example. But in doing so, product innovation also accelerates obsolescence of the durable producers' goods used to produce the consumers' goods. Hence, as we have seen, the proportionate rate of growth tends to decline. Furthermore, product innovation may increase the required input of selling effort per unit sold of the product. But input of selling effort is nothing but the input of direct or indirect labor. Again, then, the proportionate rate of growth would tend to fall.

In Chapter 9 we found that rapid obsolescence of durable producers' goods and high selling-effort requirements per unit of output would raise effective demand and thus have beneficial effects in an underemployed economy. In the present chapter we have found those same two things to reduce the proportionate rate of growth. The parallel to an increased propensity to consume is perfect: the latter, like product innovation, will raise the level of output but reduce the rate of growth of output. This contrast between short-run effects and long-run effects, or—the same thing—between what happens to the level of output and what happens to the time path of output, should always be borne in mind.

APPENDIX: THE MECHANICS OF FINDING THE SOLUTION (I)

From Equations (2) and (14) through (34) it follows that all asterisks are removable and that x and σ are interchangeable, an opportunity of which the present Appendix takes advantage. Insert (10) and (11 into (13) and get:

$$X_c(t) = a_{ce}\frac{x_{ec}(t)}{\pi_c} + a_{cl}\pi_l\frac{x_{lc}(t) + x_{lp}(t)}{\pi_c}$$

Using (9), (7), (3), (6), and (4), we get

$$(35) \qquad X_p(t) = \frac{1 - \dfrac{\pi_l}{\pi_c}b_{pc}(a_{ce}a_{ec}{}^*\iota a_{lp} + a_{cl}a_{lc})}{\dfrac{\pi_l}{\pi_c}a_{cl}a_{lp}}X_c(t)$$

Next use (1), (4), (5), and (12) to get:

$$(36) \qquad X_c(t) - X_c(t-1) - \frac{X_p(t)}{b_{pc}} + \frac{X_p(t-L)}{b_{pc}} = 0$$

Insert (35) into (36) and get (I).

24

The Foreign-Trade Accelerator and
the International Transmission
of Growth

1. THE PROBLEM

In Keynesian models of international trade, international demand is either assumed to be consumption demand exclusively,[1] or, if investment demand is at all considered, investment is assumed to be autonomous. The more recent Harrod-Domar theory of growth and its paraphernalia of capital coefficients and accelerators have as yet scarcely penetrated the theory of international trade.[2]

[1] As we did in chaps. 4, 10, and 11 of this book.

[2] One exception is Harry G. Johnson, "Equilibrium Growth in an International Economy," *The Canadian Journal of Economics and Political Science*, Vol. XIX, No. 4 (November, 1953), pp. 478–500. The accelerator was used in an international trade model by Herbert Giersch, "Akzelerationsprinzip und Importneigung," *Weltwirtschaftliches Archiv*, Band 70, Heft 2 (1953), pp. 241–283, translated as "The Acceleration Principle and the Propensity to Import," *International Economic Papers*, No. 4 (1954), pp. 197–229. A most useful framework is the dynamic Leontief input-output model; see Wassily Leontief, "Static and Dynamic Theory," *Studies in the Structure of the American Economy* (New York: Oxford, 1953), pp. 53–90. Unlike the Leontief model the present chapter uses the gross-national-product approach, thus making room for a specific

NOTE: The first 16 sections of the present chapter represent a slight revision of the author's "The Foreign Trade Accelerator and the International Transmission of Growth," *Econometrica*, Vol. 24, No. 3 (July, 1956).

Two recent ambitious works in the econometrics of international trade [3] have by-passed the Harrod-Domar contribution completely. But considerable interest, theoretical as well as practical, is attached to the interaction of different national growth potentialities.

Our problem is this. If two economies when isolated have different inherent growth potentials, what will be their growth patterns under alternative degrees of international trade? The present chapter proposes to study such interaction after disaggregating the growth model and after relaxing the conventional and convenient assumption of a constant (in time as well as in space) proportionate equilibrium rate of growth.

2. A SUMMARY OF THE MODEL

We shall set up a two-country dynamic equilibrium model in which effective demand in each country is the sum of the three items of demand for domestically produced goods: (1) domestic consumption demand, which is in direct proportion to the domestic gross national product; (2) domestic demand for producers' goods, composed of a growth term and a replacement term, the former being in direct proportion to the amount of growth of the domestic gross national product, and the latter being equal to domestic demand for producers' goods L years ago, where L is the useful life of producers' goods; and (3) export demand for producers' goods,[4] also composed of two terms: the former being in direct proportion to the amount of growth of the foreign gross national product and the latter being equal to foreign demand for pro-

replacement function. Another difference is that while the dynamic Leontief model is an open one in the sense that all consumption is autonomous, the present chapter makes all consumption induced.

[3] J. J. Polak, *An International Economic System* (Chicago: University of Chicago Press, 1953) and Hans Neisser and Franco Modigliani, *National Incomes and International Trade* (Urbana: University of Illinois Press, 1953).

[4] Reversing the assumption used in chaps. 4, 10, and 11, we are now ignoring international trade in consumers' goods.

ducers' goods domestically produced L years ago. The notation is:

Variables

R_{ij} = time rate of physical retirement of goods produced by sector i, held by sector j

S_{ij} = physical capital stock of goods produced by sector i, held by sector j

X_j = time rate of physical output of goods produced by sector j

x_{ij} = time rate of physical purchase of product of sector i by sector j

σ_{ij} = time rate of physical sale of product of sector i to sector j

Parameters

a_{fh} = the domestic propensity to consume domestically produced goods out of expected real personal domestic income

a_{FH} = the foreign propensity to consume foreign-produced goods out of expected real personal foreign income

a_{hf} = the physical number of domestic factors purchased by domestic firms per unit of domestic output

a_{HF} = the physical number of foreign factors purchased by foreign firms per unit of foreign output

b_{ff} = the planned stock of domestically produced producers' goods held by domestic firms per unit of domestic planned output

b_{Ff} = the planned stock of foreign-produced producers' goods held by domestic firms per unit of domestic planned output

b_{FF} = the planned stock of foreign-produced producers' goods held by foreign firms per unit of foreign planned output

b_{fF} = the planned stock of domestically produced producers' goods held by foreign firms per unit of foreign planned output

L = the useful life of one unit of producers' goods

π_f = the price of domestic goods charged by domestic firms

π_h = the price of domestic factors charged by domestic households

π_F = the price of foreign goods charged by foreign firms

π_H = the price of foreign factors charged by foreign households

We shall consider the eight transactions shown in Table 29, where subscripts f, h, F, and H refer respectively to domestic firms, domestic households, foreign firms, and foreign households.

TABLE 29.   Planned Purchases of Goods and Factors

Purchasing from	Purchases Planned by			
	Domestic Firms	Domestic Households	Foreign Firms	Foreign Households
Domestic Firms	$*x_{ff}$	$*x_{fh}$	$*x_{fF}$	—
Domestic Households	$*x_{hf}$	—	—	—
Foreign Firms	$*x_{Ff}$	—	$*x_{FF}$	$*x_{FH}$
Foreign Households	—	—	$*x_{HF}$	

Asterisks refer to ex ante values and, as usual, the absence of an asterisk to ex post values. The time coordinate is t, and period t is the period ending at time t.

3. PURCHASES OF PRODUCERS' GOODS

We begin with a familiar definition. A sector's planned net investment in input is equal to the capital stock of input planned to be held at the end of the period minus the capital stock of that input actually held at the end of the preceding period, or $*S_{ij}(t) - S_{ij}(t-1)$.

Assuming that a sector never sells its inputs, we can express a sector's planned net investment in inputs as its planned purchases of inputs minus planned retirement of inputs, or $*x_{ij}(t) - *R_{ij}(t)$. For either of the two firm sectors with respect to either of the two categories of producers' goods we can write

$$(1) \qquad *S_{ff}(t) - S_{ff}(t-1) = *x_{ff}(t) - *R_{ff}(t)$$

$$(2) \qquad *S_{Ff}(t) - S_{Ff}(t-1) = *x_{Ff}(t) - *R_{Ff}(t)$$

$$(3) \qquad *S_{FF}(t) - S_{FF}(t-1) = *x_{FF}(t) - *R_{FF}(t)$$

$$(4) \qquad *S_{fF}(t) - S_{fF}(t-1) = *x_{fF}(t) - *R_{fF}(t)$$

Equations (1) through (4) define ex ante net investment. Asterisks removed, we have the definitions of ex post net investment, in Equations (5) through (8), not written.

In order to determine the capital stock of any input that an industrial sector will hold, we shall assume that at any particular time a fixed capital coefficient, b_{ij} exists between (1) the planned stock of producers' goods produced by sector i and held by sector j, $*S_{ij}(t)$, on the one hand, and (2) the output planned by sector j, $*X_j(t)$, on the other hand. This assumption holds for either sector with respect to either category of producers' goods:

$$(9) \qquad *S_{ff}(t) = b_{ff}*X_f(t)$$

$$(10) \qquad *S_{Ff}(t) = b_{Ff}*X_f(t)$$

$$(11) \qquad *S_{FF}(t) = b_{FF}*X_F(t)$$

$$(12) \qquad *S_{fF}(t) = b_{fF}*X_F(t)$$

Finally, let the useful life of one unit of a producers' good be L units of time for all four categories of producers' goods. Planned retirement of producers' goods for period t, $*R_{ij}(t)$, will, then, be equal to the realized purchases of producers' goods L years ago, $x_{ij}(t - L)$. That is,

$$(13) \qquad *R_{ff}(t) = x_{ff}(t - L)$$

$$(14) \qquad *R_{Ff}(t) = x_{Ff}(t - L)$$

$$(15) \qquad *R_{FF}(t) = x_{FF}(t - L)$$

$$(16) \qquad *R_{fF}(t) = x_{fF}(t - L)$$

By inserting (9) through (16) into (1) through (4), we can express the current planned purchase of a producers' good $*x_{ij}(t)$ as a linear function of current planned output $*X_j(t)$, of past realized capital stock $S_{ij}(t - 1)$, and of the past realized purchase $x_{ij}(t - L)$.

4. PURCHASES OF OTHER FACTORS

Factors coöperating with durable producers' goods include labor and entrepreneurship, and such factors are purchased by firms from households in their own country. Consequently, there are two such purchase equations. First, planned purchases of domestic factors by domestic firms are assumed to be in direct proportion to planned domestic output:

$$(17) \qquad *x_{hf}(t) = a_{hf}*X_f(t)$$

Second, planned purchases of foreign factors by foreign firms are assumed to be in direct proportion to planned foreign output:

$$(18) \qquad *x_{HF}(t) = a_{HF}*X_F(t)$$

5. PURCHASES OF CONSUMERS' GOODS

For consumers' goods, not traded internationally, there are two demand equations. First, planned purchases of domestically produced consumers' goods by domestic households are assumed to be in direct proportion to expected real personal domestic income:

$$(19) \qquad *x_{fh}(t) = a_{fh} \frac{*\sigma_{hf}(t)\pi_h}{\pi_f}$$

Second, planned purchases of foreign-produced consumers' goods by foreign households are assumed to be in direct proportion to expected real personal foreign income:

$$(20) \qquad *x_{FH}(t) = a_{FH} \frac{*\sigma_{HF}(t)\pi_H}{\pi_F}$$

6. PLANNED GROSS NATIONAL OUTPUTS

Ignoring planned inventory changes, we shall assume that planned gross national product equals expected sales of nationally produced goods. Thus domestic planned gross national product equals the sum of expected sales to (1) domestic firms, (2) foreign firms, and (3) domestic households:

(21) $$*X_f(t) = *\sigma_{ff}(t) + *\sigma_{fF}(t) + *\sigma_{fh}(t)$$

Likewise, foreign planned gross national product equals the sum of expected sales to (1) foreign firms, (2) domestic firms, and (3) foreign households:

(22) $$*X_F(t) = *\sigma_{FF}(t) + *\sigma_{Ff}(t) + *\sigma_{FH}(t)$$

7. PLANS ARE CARRIED OUT

In a buyers' market a unit of time can be chosen such that plans made at the beginning of a given period are not changed until the beginning of the next period. First, we assume that *purchase* plans are carried out,

(23) through (30) $$*x_{ij}(t) = x_{ij}(t)$$

where ij represents $ff, Ff, FF, fF, hf, HF, fh,$ and FH, respectively.

Secondly, we assume that, for each of the four types of capital stock, *retirement* plans are carried out,

(31) through (34) $$*R_{ij}(t) = R_{ij}(t)$$

where ij represents $ff, Ff, FF,$ and fF, respectively.

Thirdly, for both countries we assume that *production* plans materialize,

(35) through (36) $$*X_j(t) = X_j(t)$$

where j represents f and F, respectively.

8. WHAT IS PURCHASED IS SOLD

Any buyer's realized purchases from a seller constitute the latter's realized sales to the former. This is true for all our eight transactions so

(37) through (44) $$x_{ij}(t) = \sigma_{ij}(t)$$

where ij has the same meaning as in Equations (23) through (30).

9. EQUILIBRIUM CONDITIONS

If equilibrium is to prevail, the activity of the two economies must be self-justifying in the sense that any sector's expected sales must equal realized sales, or

(45) through (52) $*\sigma_{ij}(t) = \sigma_{ij}(t)$

where ij has the same meaning as in Equations (23) through (30).

10. SOLUTION

The system of 52 equations includes 52 unknowns, i.e., four planned and four realized retirements $*R_{ij}$ and R_{ij}, four planned and four realized capital stocks $*S_{ij}$ and S_{ij}, two planned and two realized outputs $*X_j$ and X_j, eight planned and eight realized purchases $*x_{ij}$ and x_{ij}, and eight expected and eight realized sales $*\sigma_{ij}$ and σ_{ij}. Solving for the two national outputs $X_f(t)$ and $X_F(t)$ we obtain the following system of two simultaneous linear homogeneous difference equations:

(I) $n_1 X_f(t) + n_2 X_f(t-1) - (n_1 + n_2) X_f(t-L)$
$$- n_3 X_F(t) + n_3 X_F(t-L) = 0$$

(II) $n_4 X_f(t) - n_4 X_f(t-1) - n_5 X_F(t) - n_6 X_F(t-1)$
$$+ (n_5 + n_6) X_F(t-L) = 0$$

where

$$n_1 = 1 - b_{ff} - \frac{a_{fh}a_{hf}\pi_h}{\pi_f} \qquad n_4 = b_{Ff}$$

$$n_2 = b_{ff} \qquad\qquad n_5 = 1 - b_{FF} - \frac{a_{FH}a_{HF}\pi_H}{\pi_F}$$

$$n_3 = b_{fF} \qquad\qquad n_6 = b_{FF}$$

As the first step in solving this system we shall write the equations in matrix-operator form:[5]

[5] We are following the method outlined in William J. Baumol, *Solution of Simultaneous Linear Difference Equation Systems* (mimeographed), published January, 1954, in New York: Project for Advanced Training in Social Research at Columbia University. See also section 6 of chap. 12 of D. W. Bushaw and R. W. Clower, *Introduction to Mathematical Economics* (Homewood, Ill.: Irwin, 1957).

$$\begin{bmatrix} n_1E^L + n_2E^{L-1} - (n_1 + n_2) & -n_3E^L + n_3E^{L-1} \\ n_4E^L - n_4E^{L-1} & -n_5E^L - n_6E^{L-1} + (n_5 + n_6) \end{bmatrix}$$
$$\times \begin{bmatrix} X_f(t) \\ X_F(t) \end{bmatrix} = \begin{bmatrix} 0 \\ 0 \end{bmatrix}$$

where by definition the operator E is such that $EX(t) = X(t + 1)$ for every $X(t)$. On the left-hand side we have, first, a two-by-two square matrix, and second, a two-element column vector $\mathbf{X}(t)$. On the right-hand side we have a two-element column vector whose elements are both zero. To solve a dynamic system such as this, we first equate to zero the determinant of the two-by-two square matrix after replacing E everywhere by r, getting the following equation for r:

$$\begin{aligned} (\text{III}) \quad & + r^{2L}(n_3n_4 - n_1n_5) - r^{2L-1}(n_1n_6 + n_2n_5 + 2n_3n_4) \\ & + r^{2L-2}(n_3n_4 - n_2n_6) + r^L[n_1(n_5 + n_6) + n_5(n_1 + n_2)] \\ & + r^{L-1}[n_2(n_5 + n_6) + n_6(n_1 + n_2)] - (n_1 + n_2)(n_5 + n_6) \\ & = 0 \end{aligned}$$

As in Chapter 22, we shall adopt the value 8 for L. Consequently, Equation (III) is an equation of the sixteenth degree. Let its sixteen roots be $r_1 \cdots r_{16}$. It is now known [6] that if no root is multiple, then

$$X(t) = \sum_{j=1}^{16} a_j r_j{}^t P_i(r_j)$$

will be a solution to the system of difference Equations (I) and (II), where a_j represents arbitrary constants, and $P_i(r_j)$ any column of the two-by-two matrix $P(r_j)$ obtained as the adjoint of the original square matrix after substitution of r for E. (The reader is reminded that the adjoint of a matrix $\mathbf{A}$ is the transposed of the matrix of the cofactors of $\mathbf{A}$.) In our particular case $P(r_j)$ is then

$$\begin{bmatrix} -n_5r^L - n_6r^{L-1} + (n_5 + n_6) & +n_3r^L - n_3r^{L-1} \\ -n_4r^L + n_4r^{L-1} & n_1r^L + n_2r^{L-1} - (n_1 + n_2) \end{bmatrix}$$

[6] Baumol, *op. cit.*, p. 9.

Call the first-column first-row element $P_{11}(r_j)$; call the first-column second-row element $P_{21}(r_j)$. In a slightly less compact form the solution to the system of difference equations (I) and (II) can then be written

$$\begin{bmatrix} X_f(t) \\ X_F(t) \end{bmatrix} = a_1 r_1{}^t \begin{bmatrix} P_{11}(r_1) \\ P_{21}(r_1) \end{bmatrix} + \cdots + a_{16} r_{16}{}^t \begin{bmatrix} P_{11}(r_{16}) \\ P_{21}(r_{16}) \end{bmatrix}$$

Equations (I) and (II) require L initial conditions for variable $X_F(t)$ and L initial conditions for variable $X_f(t)$, or in total $2L$ initial conditions in order to permit determination of the time paths of these variables. It can be shown that the solution to system (I) and (II), as written above, has the same number of arbitrary constants a_j as of initial conditions. Since $L = 8$, the number is 16. In any term of the sum above, the elements $P_{11}(r_j)$ and $P_{21}(r_j)$ are to be multiplied by the *same* a_j, from which it follows that if the elements $P_{11}(r_j)$ and $P_{21}(r_j)$, corresponding to the root of largest absolute value, have the same signs, then the two national outputs will eventually have the same signs. But if the elements corresponding to the root of largest absolute value have opposite signs, national outputs will eventually have opposite signs, one being negative of course. With this fact in mind we can find and use the roots of the determinantal Equation (III). But first we must see if an economic meaning, and perhaps even an empirically plausible order of magnitude, can be attached to the coefficients, the n's, used in (III).

11. ECONOMIC MEANING OF THE n's

Let us begin with n_1. The parameter a_{hf} is the physical quantity of domestic factors purchased by domestic firms per unit of domestic output. Upon multiplying by π_h we obtain the money value of domestic factors purchased by domestic firms per unit of domestic output, or in other words, domestic household money income per unit of domestic output. Upon dividing by π_f we obtain domestic household real income per unit of domestic output. Finally, multiplying by a_{fh}, the propensity to consume domestically produced goods out of expected real personal domestic income, we obtain the amount of domestic household purchases of consumers' goods generated per unit of domestic output. For this magnitude, 0.80 is not an entirely implausible approximation, and consequently we shall set $1 - a_{fh}a_{hf}\pi_h/\pi_f$ equal to 0.20.

Similarly, in n_5 the magnitude $a_{FH}a_{HF}\pi_H/\pi_F$ is the amount of foreign household purchases of consumers' goods generated per unit of foreign output. Since we know that the propensity to consume differs drastically among nations, and since we are interested in the ultimate implications of such differences, we shall set this magnitude equal to 0.75. Consequently, $1 - a_{FH}a_{HF}\pi_H/\pi_F$ equals 0.25.

Finally, we have the four capital coefficients n_2, n_3, n_4, and n_6. The overall domestic capital coefficient is $b_{ff} + b_{Ff} = n_2 + n_4$. The overall foreign capital coefficient is $b_{FF} + b_{fF} = n_3 + n_6$. No known evidence indicates that over-all capital coefficients differ significantly from economy to economy (see Appendix I of this chapter). Accordingly, for a general impression of the order of magnitude we refer to the empirical value of the United States overall capital coefficient, the ratio between dollar capital stock, whether of domestic or foreign origin, and dollar gross national product. As in Chapter 22, we shall use the value 2.8 on an annual basis for the capital coefficient. Great computational advantages may be gained, however, by lengthening the time unit somewhat. Since the equilibrium path of a growth model is unaffected by the length of the time unit chosen, we can without damage lengthen the time unit to, say two years,[7] thus causing the values of all capital coefficients to be halved. The over-all domestic and foreign capital coefficients will then be 1.4.

The six alternative pairs of values of b_{ff} and b_{Ff} to be considered are

| b_{ff}: | 0.2 | 0.4 | 0.6 | 0.8 | 1.0 | 1.2 |
| b_{Ff}: | 1.2 | 1.0 | 0.8 | 0.6 | 0.4 | 0.2 |

[7] As we did in chap. 22.

The same six pairs will be considered for b_{FF} and b_{fF}, the over-all capital coefficient being 1.4 at home as well as abroad. Any of the six pairs of the domestic side may be combined with any of the six pairs on the foreign side, giving a total of 36 different sets of values of n's to consider.

As in Chapter 22, we shall set the useful life of domestic and foreign producers' goods on an annual basis, L equal to 16. Obviously, on a two-year basis the useful life will then be $L = 8$.

12. THE WICKED ROOTS

In some of the 36 cases the root of largest absolute value will give opposite signs to the two elements of any column of the corresponding adjoint. A root doing this will be called "wicked" because of the absurd consequences ensuing. The 15 cases in which wicked roots appear have been listed in Table 30. All

TABLE 30. Largest Roots r_D Producing National Outputs of Opposite Signs in the Two Countries

Domestic, Low-saving Economy b_{ff}		0.2	0.4	0.6	0.8	1.0	1.2
b_{Ff}		1.2	1.0	0.8	0.6	0.4	0.2
Foreign, High-saving Economy							
b_{FF}	b_{fF}	(1)	(2)	(3)	(4)	(5)	(6)
0.2	1.2	(1)	—				
0.4	1.0	(2)		—				-4.773
0.6	0.8	(3)			—		-5.930	2.508
0.8	0.6	(4)				-7.855	2.364	1.641
1.0	0.4	(5)			-11.697	2.231	1.585	1.373
1.2	0.2	(6)		-23.207	2.108	1.527	1.328	1.230

NOTE. All 15 roots are real. If preceded by no sign they are positive. The 36 possible elements of this table are referred to by first mentioning the row, then the column. Thus the value of the element (5, 4) is 2.231.

roots are located in the southeastern half of the table, which is characterized by comparatively less intensive international trade. Some roots are positive, some are negative. If the wicked root is positive, then when raised to the tth power it will remain positive for any t. This means that one country will eventually have positive output all the time, the other will eventually have negative output all the time. If on the other hand the wicked root is negative, when raised to the tth power it will become positive when t is an even number, but it will become negative when t is an odd number. Thus the roles will alternate, each country having positive output every other period and negative output the rest of the time, but eventually the outputs of the two countries will always have opposite signs within the same year.

Let us now follow our mathematics boldly and, with all restrictions removed, examine the absurd situation that

$$X_f(t) = a_D r_D{}^t P_{11}(r_D)$$
$$X_F(t) = a_D r_D{}^t P_{21}(r_D)$$

where r_D is the wicked root and where, consequently, $P_{11}(r_D)$ and $P_{21}(r_D)$ have opposite signs, say, positive for the former, negative for the latter. Let a_D be positive, causing national output to be positive at home, negative abroad.

Let us first examine gross investment and import in the domestic economy. From the fact that $*X_f(t)$ is positive and larger than $*X_f(t-1)$ it follows, using Equations (1), (2), (9), and (10), that $*x_{ff}(t) - *R_{ff}(t)$ and $*x_{Ff}(t) - *R_{Ff}(t)$ are both positive. Since retirement of positive capital stock is positive, $*x_{ff}(t)$ and $*x_{Ff}(t)$ must both be positive.

Next consider gross investment and import in the foreign economy. From the fact that $*X_F(t)$ is negative and numerically larger than $*X_F(t-1)$ it follows, using Equations (3), (4), (11), and (12), that $*x_{FF}(t) - *R_{FF}(t)$ and $*x_{fF}(t) - *R_{fF}(t)$ are both negative. Since retirement of negative capital stock (sic!) is negative, $*x_{FF}(t)$ and $*x_{fF}(t)$ must both be negative.

Let us examine consumption at home. From Equation (19)

combined with (27), (41), (49), and (17) it follows that for a positive $*X_f(t)$, $*x_{fh}(t)$ is also positive.

Consumption abroad is negative. From Equation (20) combined with (28), (42), (50), and (18) it follows that if $*X_F(t)$ is negative $*x_{FH}(t)$ is also negative.

We are now equipped to examine the composition of domestic and foreign output. Domestic output is determined by Equation (21). The first term of the sum is $*x_{ff}(t)$, which we have found to be positive. The second term is $*x_{fF}(t)$, which we have found to be negative. The third term is $*x_{fh}(t)$, which we have found to be positive. We can now understand why the domestic economy can grow at such a tremendously high rate. For illustration consider case (5, 5) in Table 30. Here, the wicked root is equal to $+1.585$, which means that the economy will grow at the proportionate rate of growth 58.5 percent per unit of time. Since the coefficient b_{ff} is equal to 1.0, *net* investment of domestically produced producers' goods, $*x_{ff}(t) - *R_{ff}(t)$, will be equal to 58.5 percent of the last period's national output, or in other words, equal to 36.9 percent of the current period's national output! To this 36.9 percent we add consumption, always 80 percent of the current period's national output, and we get 116.9 percent of current national output, which figure does not even include replacement. What makes all this possible, of course, is the fact that the export term $*x_{fF}(t)$ is *negative*.

The other side of the coin is the foreign economy. Here, output is determined by Equation (22). We have found $*x_{FF}(t)$ and $*x_{FH}(t)$ to be negative and $*x_{Ff}(t)$ positive. Numerically, the sum of $*x_{FF}(t)$ and $*x_{FH}(t)$ exceeds output $*X_F(t)$, a circumstance made possible by the fact that export $*x_{Ff}(t)$ is *positive*.

Whether the wicked roots, in the 15 cases where they exist, will have a chance to come into play and produce the absurd results just described depends upon the coefficients a_j, determined in accordance with the initial conditions. One could perhaps imagine cases in which the specified initial conditions were such as to make the coefficient a_D zero. Yet, even in those cases any random shock would almost certainly bring the wicked roots into play. That is not to say, however, that the system would ever actually reach the absurd state of affairs just described. For one thing, negative capital stock is logically inconceivable. For another, negative output is economically inconceivable. Thus our model would have to be amended by the requirement that negative outputs always be replaced by zero. Now, in Equation (21), replacing a negative $*x_{fF}(t)$ by zero indicates that domestic demand for domestically produced consumers' and producers' goods must be satisfied by domestic output alone. We have seen that the negative export term $*x_{fF}(t)$ in case (5, 5) allows the domestic economy to grow at the absurd rate of 58.5 percent per unit of time, consumption and net investment of domestically produced producers' goods alone adding up to 116.9 percent of current domestic output. If $*x_{fF}(t)$ is now to equal zero, only a much lower growth rate will permit Equation (21) to be satisfied. Such amendment of the model will very substantially reduce the rate of growth of the domestic economy. But it is hardly profitable to trace events much further by verbal reasoning. Suffice it to say that when a system is heading for any of the absurd paths in time determined by any of the wicked roots, that system will run into irreversibilities and switching problems,[8] and to the extent that excess capacity is generated the system can no longer be said to be in equilibrium.

13. THE GOOD ROOTS

Whether the 36 versions of determinantal Equation (III) have wicked roots or not, each version does have a positive real root slightly above unity, varying from $+1.104$ in case (6, 1) to $+1.049$ in case (1, 6). This is the root which has the largest absolute value and at the same time gives the two elements of a column of the adjoint the same signs. A root doing this will be called a "good" root because of the absence of any absurd consequences.

[8] Leontief, *op. cit.*, pp. 68–76.

The 36 values of the good root are listed in Table 31. In the 21 cases having no wicked root, the good root listed in Table 31,

TABLE 31. Largest Roots r_d Compatible with National Outputs of Same Signs in the Two Countries

Domestic	b_{ff}		0.2	0.4	0.6	0.8	1.0	1.2
Low-saving	b_{Ff}		1.2	1.0	0.8	0.6	0.4	0.2
Economy								
Foreign High-saving Economy								
b_{FF}	b_{fF}		(1)	(2)	(3)	(4)	(5)	(6)
0.2	1.2	(1)	1.077	1.073	1.068	1.063	1.057	1.049
0.4	1.0	(2)	1.080	1.076	1.072	1.066	1.059	1.051
0.6	0.8	(3)	1.084	1.080	1.075	1.069	1.062	1.052
0.8	0.6	(4)	1.089	1.085	1.080	1.074	1.066	1.055
1.0	0.4	(5)	1.095	1.092	1.087	1.081	1.072	1.058
1.2	0.2	(6)	1.104	1.102	1.098	1.092	1.082	1.065

NOTE: All 36 roots are positive and real. The 36 elements of this table are referred to by first mentioning the row, then the column. Thus the value of element (3, 4) is 1.069.

call it r_d, will eventually cause the two economies to settle down at a *common* proportionate equilibrium rate of growth $g = r_d - 1$, this will happen irrespective of the values of the initial conditions. In the 15 cases where a wicked root exists the same thing can happen, but only if the initial conditions are such that the co-efficient a_D, corresponding to the wicked root r_D, becomes zero. Assuming that it does, one can find the 36 values of common rates of growth $g = r_d - 1$ from Table 31. They vary from 10.4 per-cent on a two-year basis in Case (6, 1) to 4.9 percent in Case (1, 6). We should emphasize that the existence of a proportionate equili-brium rate of growth which ultimately is constant in time and space is a result, not an assumption. While this difference between our model and growth models of the Harrod-Domar-Johnson type may seem quite striking, it should be pointed out that our result follows from our linearity assumption. Many readers may well feel that an even higher degree of generality is desired, and that linear difference-equation models like ours are simply not rich enough for the handling of the general case. Going back to our model, we should emphasize, too, that if the roots lower than r_d are not very much lower than r_d the latter will require a very long time indeed to swamp them, and "eventually" should be taken, therefore, *sub specie aeternitatis*.

14. THE COMMON EQUILIBRIUM RATE OF GROWTH AND THE SIZE OF THE ECONOMIES

Still assuming that if a wicked root r_D exists, the coefficient a_D corresponding to it is equal to zero, we can find the relative size of the two economies after equilibrium, at which time the common equilibrium rate $g = r_d - 1$ has been reached. In the solution of the system we found that a_d times r_d in the tth power multiplied by $P_{11}(r_d)$ gives $X_f(t)$, and multiplied by $P_{21}(r_d)$ gives $X_F(t)$. Consequently, the ratio $P_{11}(r_d)/P_{21}(r_d)$ measures the relative size of the two equilibrium gross national outputs.[9] This ratio appears in Table 32. As one might suspect, a high equilibrium common growth rate is associated with a low equilibrium ratio between the gross national product of the low-saving economy and the gross national product of the high-saving economy. In Figure 71 this relationship is shown directly. Spelled out, results may be reported as follows.

By "international" capital coefficient let us mean the ratio between imported capital stock in existence at any given moment of time on the one hand, and gross national product on the other. Then, if the international capital coefficient is about the same in the two countries, we shall find ourselves somewhere close to the northwest-southeast diagonal in Tables 31 and 32. Near this

[9] Leontief, *op. cit.*, equation (3, 11), p. 61.

TABLE 32.   Ratio $P_{11}(r_d)/P_{21}(r_d)$ between First-Row and Second-Row Element of Any Column of Adjoint of Determinant Corresponding to the Root r_d

Foreign, High-saving Economy				Domestic, Low-saving Economy b_{ff} b_{Ff}					
			b_{ff}	0.2	0.4	0.6	0.8	1.0	1.2
			b_{Ff}	1.2	1.0	0.8	0.6	0.4	0.2
b_{FF}	b_{fF}			(1)	(2)	(3)	(4)	(5)	(6)
0.2	1.2	(1)		1.14	1.38	1.76	2.39	3.65	7.51
0.4	1.0	(2)		0.96	1.17	1.48	2.08	3.13	6.46
0.6	0.8	(3)		0.78	0.95	1.22	1.67	2.59	5.43
0.8	0.6	(4)		0.59	0.73	0.94	1.30	2.04	4.35
1.0	0.4	(5)		0.41	0.50	0.65	0.91	1.47	3.28
1.2	0.2	(6)		0.21	0.26	0.34	0.50	0.86	2.11

NOTE: All 36 ratios are positive.   The 36 elements are referred to by first mentioning the row, then the column.   Case (3, 4) thus means the value 1.67.

diagonal, the common equilibrium proportionate rate of growth is around 7 percent on a two-year basis, and the equilibrium sizes of the two economies are not too different.   In fact, in Case (1, 1),

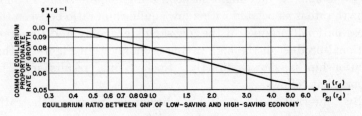

Figure 71

the ratio between the two gross national products is 1.14; in Case (6, 6) it is 2.11.

If the low-saving economy has a substantially higher international capital coefficient than has the high-saving economy, we shall find ourselves somewhere in the southwestern corner of Tables 31 and 32. Here, the common equilibrium proportionate rate of growth is generally high, culminating in Case (6, 1) with the rate 10.4 percent on a two-year basis. On the other hand, as one would suspect of such a structure of international trade, the equilibrium ratio between the gross national products of the low-saving and the high-saving economies, respectively, is now very low, e.g., 0.21 in Case (6, 1).

Finally, if the low-saving economy has a substantially lower international capital coefficient than has the high-saving economy, we find ourselves in the northeastern corner of Tables 31 and 32. Here, there are rather low common equilibrium rates of growth, e.g., 4.9 percent on a two-year basis in Case (1, 6). On the other hand, the ratio between the two gross national products is now as high as 7.5 in Case (1, 6).

These common rates of growth may be compared with the rates at which the economies would grow if isolated from one another. In Appendix II, to this chapter, such "isolation rates" are found to be 4.0 percent per two-year period in the low-saving economy and 11.8 percent per two-year period in the high-saving economy. All common equilibrium growth rates found in Table 31 lie between these two extremes.

15. THE REMAINING ROOTS

In all 36 cases examined, a double positive real root $r_j = + 1.0000$ was found. This finding necessitates a slight qualification of the rule given in Section 10. Since in our model all elements of $P(r_j)$ become zero for $r_j = + 1.0000$, see the expression for $P(r_j)$ in Section 10 above, none of the columns of $P(r_j)$ can be used in the construction of the constituent solution. As shown by Frazer, Duncan, and Collar,[10] in order to obtain the full

---

[10] R. A. Frazer, W. J. Duncan, and A. R. Collar, *Elementary Matrices and Some Applications to Dynamics and Differential Equations* (Cambridge, England: The University Press, 1938), pp. 167–172.

number of constituents corresponding to a double root (two) it may be necessary to proceed to the nonzero columns of the derivative $dP(r_j)/dr_j$. But even after that is done, the parts of the constituent solution containing the multiple root will be swamped by the larger roots r_d and r_D.

Finally let us examine the remaining roots. Almost all of them are complex, and in most cases their absolute values (moduli) are less than unity. Although the moduli of some roots are equal to or slightly in excess of unity, in no case is the absolute value as large as the absolute value of the real root r_d listed in Table 31. Consequently, roots with such moduli will eventually be swamped either by the root r_d or the root r_D.

16. CONCLUSION

For two economies with different propensities to save but with the same over-all capital coefficient, we have examined the entire field of possible combinations of international capital coefficients. In 21 of the 36 cases the equilibrium path for the two countries is smooth and clear. Eventually the proportionate equilibrium rate of growth in the two countries will be practically the same, allowing due adjustment of the sizes of the two gross national products. In the remaining 15 cases we found a highly precarious equilibrium path, which can materialize and maintain itself only under very special initial conditions indeed. Thus the skepticism about the possibility of moderate steady growth in a closed economy, already expressed by others,[11] may well be extended, but for entirely different reasons, to the international economy.

[11] T. C. Schelling, "Capital Growth and Equilibrium," *The American Economic Review*, Vol. XXXVII, No. 5 (Dec., 1947), pp. 864–876; Sidney S. Alexander, "The Accelerator as a Generator of Steady Growth," *The Quarterly Journal of Economics*, Vol. LXIII, No. 2 (May, 1949), pp. 174–197; and D. Hamberg, "Investment and Saving in a Growing Economy," *The Review of Economics and Statistics*, Vol. XXXVII, No. 2 (May, 1955), pp. 196–201.

17. APPLICATION TO EXCHANGE RATE DEVALUATION

We have seen that when a low-saving economy trades with a high-saving economy, the latter will transmit some of its growth potential to the former. Such a transfer is made possible by an export surplus in the high-saving economy and by international lending on the part of the latter. In other words, the model makes no provision whatsoever for equalization of the balance of trade between the two countries. On the contrary, had it made provision for such equalization, no international lending, no export surplus, no partial transmission of the growth potential of the high-saving economy would be possible.

Even though international lending is an essential feature of our model, limits to such lending may well exist. Should the limits be approached, devaluation of the currency of the low-saving economy might be considered. (Direct controls, interfering with our behavior equations, might of course also be considered but will be ignored here.) Devaluation may affect the international capital coefficients. Rarely are capital coefficients, national or international, fixed by physical necessity. Frequently a choice is offered between a limited number of processes (our Chapter 16). In both countries devaluation of the currency of the low-saving country will make relatively more attractive such processes which employ relatively large amounts of the producers' goods made in that country. Thus in our particular case, the domestic country will move east in Tables 31 and 32, and the foreign country will move north. Both moves have the same effects, i.e., those of reducing the common equilibrium proportionate rate of growth and of increasing the relative equilibrium size of the devaluing, low-saving economy.

Will concurrent reduction of the common growth rate and relative expansion of the size of the devaluing economy reduce the need for international lending? It is demonstrable that the answer is "No." The first step in the proof is to find a convenient expression of the ratio between the total physical imports of the two economies. First, total physical imports into the domestic, low-saving economy can be found by using Equation (2) in the form

(2) $$*x_{Ff}(t) = *S_{Ff}(t) - S_{Ff}(t-1) + *R_{Ff}(t)$$

Insert (10) and (14) and get

$$*x_{Ff}(t) = b_{Ff}[*X_f(t) - X_f(t-1)]$$
$$+ b_{Ff}[X_f(t-L) - X_f(t-L-1)]$$
$$\dots\dots\dots\dots\dots\dots\dots\dots\dots\dots\dots\dots$$
$$+ b_{Ff}[X_f(t-nL) - X_f(t-nL-1)]$$

Now assume that for a long time the gross national product $X_f(t)$ has been growing at the equilibrium common proportionate rate of growth g. Then

$$*x_{Ff}(t) =$$
$$b_{Ff}*X_f(t)\left[1 - \frac{1}{1+g}\right]\left[1 + \frac{1}{(1+g)^L} + \cdots + \frac{1}{(1+g)^{nL}} + \cdots\right]$$

For $n \to \infty$ we have

(IV) $$*x_{Ff}(t) \to b_{Ff}*X_f(t)\; \frac{1 - \dfrac{1}{1+g}}{1 - \dfrac{1}{(1+g)^L}}$$

By using Equation (4) as our point of departure, we similarly find the following expression for total physical imports into the foreign, high-saving economy

(V) $$*x_{fF}(t) \to b_{fF}*X_F(t)\; \frac{1 - \dfrac{1}{1+g}}{1 - \dfrac{1}{(1+g)^L}}$$

Taking (IV) and (V) together, we find the ratio between the total physical imports of the two economies

(VI) $$\frac{^*x_{Ff}(t)}{^*x_{fF}(t)} \to \frac{b_{Ff}{^*}X_f(t)}{b_{fF}{^*}X_F(t)}$$

The verbal equivalent is: the ratio between total physical imports tends to be equal to the ratio between the two international capital coefficients multiplied by the ratio between the two gross national products.

Using this ratio, we can proceed to answer the question of whether devaluation by the low-saving economy reduces the need for international lending by the high-saving economy. Assume, for example, that before devaluation we are concerned with Case (5, 3) in Table 32. Now assume that devaluation reduces the international capital coefficient of the devaluing country b_{Ff} from 0.8 to 0.4 while expanding that of the other country b_{fF} from 0.4 to 0.8. Surely there is no lack of response in international demand! In other words, devaluation shifts us from Case (5, 3) to case (3, 5). According to Table 32 the ratio between the equilibrium gross national products changes from 0.65 to 2.59. And according to new expression (VI) the ratio between total physical imports into the two countries is

$$\frac{^*x_{Ff}(t)}{^*x_{fF}(t)} \to \frac{0.8}{0.4}\, 0.65 = 1.30$$

before devaluation. After devaluation the ratio is

$$\frac{^*x_{Ff}(t)}{^*x_{fF}(t)} \to \frac{0.4}{0.8}\, 2.59 = 1.30$$

or the same in both cases.

In Tables 31 and 32 the two physical over-all capital coefficients are assumed to be 1.4, and the two consumption-gross national product ratios 0.80 and 0.75 respectively. As long as we do not relax these two assumptions, we can experiment further with Table 32 and shall find that our depressing result—devaluation does not change the long-run physical imports ratio—has rather general validity. The relative size of the two gross national products, which is so often used as a parameter in other models [12] but is a variable here, will stubbornly change in such a manner that the ratio between physical imports into the two countries will remain practically unchanged—in spite of drastically changed import propensities. But if the ratio between *physical* imports does not change, the ratio between *value* imports into the low-saving economy and *value* imports into the high-saving economy must rise as a consequence of devaluation, as long as both values are expressed in the same currency. Or, to put the same result in a different form, the ratio between the value *imports* of the devaluing country and the value *exports* of that country must rise as a consequence of devaluation, as long as both values are expressed in the same currency. We may then justifiably draw the following conclusion: As long as devaluation neither changes the overall physical capital coefficients nor narrows the gap between the degrees of thriftiness in the two economies, the purpose of devaluation—to reduce the need for international lending —is defeated. But of course, the lower internal rate of return in the devaluing country may force that country to save more, and the higher internal rate of return in the nondevaluing country may induce that country to save less.

APPENDIX I: INTERNATIONAL CAPITAL
COEFFICIENT COMPARISONS

The little we know about capital coefficients seems to indicate that their orders of magnitude are quite similar in different countries. [13] In addition to the sources mentioned in the footnote below, we may add

---

[12] See for example Guy H. Orcutt, "Exchange Rate Adjustment and Relative Size of the Depreciating Bloc," *The Review of Economics and Statistics,* Vol. XXXVII, No. 1 (Feb., 1955), pp. 1–11.

[13] Robert N. Grosse, "The Structure of Capital," *Studies in the Structure of the American Economy* (New York: Oxford, 1953), pp. 213–216, quoting Colin Clark, Paul H. Douglas, and others; E. H. Phelps Brown and B. Weber, "Accumulation, Productivity, and Distribution in the British Economy, 1870–1938," *The Economic Journal,* Vol. LXIII, No. 250 (June, 1953), p. 263.

an extremely rough comparison between North America and the rest of the world in respect to energy input per dollar's worth of national income. The comparison, for what it is worth, is presented in Tables 33 and 34. The degree of similarity between North America and the rest of the world in respect to this input-income ratio is striking, indeed. Lacking capital-stock data for the rest of the world, we must accept energy input as probably the best available measure of capital.

TABLE 33. Energy Supply per Dollar's Worth of National Income, 1948

	North America	Rest of World
Supply of Energy in 1948, in Billions of Tons of Coal Equivalent	1.254	1.641
National Income at Factor Cost in 1948, in Billions of U.S. Dollars	$235	$313
Supply of Energy in 1948 in Tons of Coal Equivalent per Dollar's Worth of National Income	0.0053	0.0052

SOURCE: W. S. Woytinski and E. S. Woytinski, *World Population and Production* (New York: The Twentieth Century Fund, 1953), table 395, p. 931.

TABLE 34. Horsepower Delivered per Dollar's Worth of National Income, 1948

	North America	Rest of World
Heat Generated and Motive Power Delivered in 1948 in Billions of Horsepower	1.6268	2.2132
National Income at Factor Cost in 1948, in Billions of U.S. Dollars	$235	$313
Horsepower Delivered per Dollar's Worth of National Income	0.0069	0.0070

SOURCE: Woytinski and Woytinski, *op. cit.*, p. 939.

APPENDIX II: THE RATES OF GROWTH IN THE TWO COUNTRIES WHEN ISOLATED

To find the rates of growth in the two countries when they are isolated from one another, all we need do is insert

$$b_{fF} = 0 \qquad b_{Ff} = 0$$

into Equations (I) and (II), respectively. We get the following two equations, each in only one variable

(Ia) $(1 - b_{ff} - a_{fh}a_{hf}\pi_h/\pi_f)X_f(t) + b_{ff}X_f(t - 1)$
$$- (1 - a_{fh}a_{hf}\pi_h/\pi_f)X_f(t - L) = 0$$

(IIa) $-(1 - b_{FF} - a_{FH}a_{HF}\pi_H/\pi_F)X_F(t) - b_{FF}X_F(t - 1)$
$$+ (1 - a_{FH}a_{HF}\pi_H/\pi_F)X_F(t - L) = 0$$

For

$$1 - a_{fh}a_{hf}\pi_h/\pi_f = 0.20 \qquad b_{ff} = 1.4$$

$$1 - a_{FH}a_{HF}\pi_H/\pi_F = 0.25 \qquad b_{FF} = 1.4$$

the two equations are

(Ia) $-1.20X_f(t) + 1.4X_f(t - 1) - 0.20X_f(t - L) = 0$

(IIa) $1.15X_F(t) - 1.4X_F(t - 1) + 0.25X_F(t - L) = 0$

For $L = 8$ the solution of these two single difference equations gives the following roots

(Ia)		(IIa)	
+1.040	0.000	+1.118	0.000
+1.000	0.000	+1.000	0.000
+0.419	+0.652 i	+0.433	+0.673 i
+0.419	−0.652 i	+0.433	−0.673 i
−0.209	+0.697 i	−0.216	+0.720 i
−0.209	−0.697 i	−0.216	−0.720 i
−0.646	+0.293 i	−0.668	+0.303 i
−0.646	−0.293 i	−0.668	−0.303 i

Equation (Ia) here is exactly identical to (I) of Chapter 22. Parameters and the eight roots are the same.

25

A Simple Stability Test of the Proportionate Equilibrium Rate of Growth

1. THE PROBLEM

The static determination of national output, as we saw in Chapter 3, assumes all investment to be autonomous: a constant volume of investment expenditure, irrespective of the level of national output, is added vertically to the consumption function, the result being an aggregate demand curve whose slope is the marginal propensity to consume. Since this propensity is less than one, the aggregate demand curve will run above a 45° line for outputs less than equilibrium output, but below it for outputs more than equilibrium output. We say, then, in technical parlance that the national output equilibrium is stable.

Modern dynamic models of the Harrod-Domar type have relaxed the assumption of autonomous investment. An equilibrium proportionate rate of growth is found, but the equilibrium path itself is unstable. On page 86 of *Towards A Dynamic Economics* Harrod assures us that "this kind of instability has

NOTE: Chaps. 20 and 25 are slightly expanded reproductions of the writer's "Stability and Growth," *The Economic Journal*, Vol. LXV, No. 260 (Dec., 1955).

nothing to do with the effect of lags, and strikes me as more fundamental." No dissent from this view is known of by the present writer. The purpose of this chapter is to show that the length of the time unit bears the utmost weight upon stability. The reader is reminded of the difference between the problem of the *existence* of an equilibrium path and the problem of the *stability* of that path. The former problem was examined in Chapters 20 through 24.

2. THE MODEL

Referring to the simple growth model sketched in Chapter 20, let us ask what happens should business firms suddenly start to plan for output to rise at a growth rate different from the one determined by Equation (II) in Chapter 20. Suppose, for example, that the system has been in equilibrium but that now business firms start to plan for output to rise at a growth rate *higher* than the rate determined by (II). Going back to Figure 58, we find that while $Y(t - 1)$ was equilibrium output for period $t - 1$, businessmen do not now plan for output $Y_0(t)$ but for a higher output. Figure 58 shows that for any output larger than $Y_0(t)$, the sum of consumption demand and investment demand will exceed that output. Because of the high value of the slope of the aggregate demand curve $C(t) + I(t)$ used in Figure 58, the aggregate demand curve will now run above the 45° line, indicating that inventories are depleted, and that the businessman will suspect that he did not expand his output enough. Therefore, he may well try to catch up in the subsequent period by planning for an even higher rate of growth.

Conversely, should the businessman suddenly start planning output to rise at a growth rate *lower* than the one determined by Equation (II). For outputs slightly lower than $Y_0(t)$ the sum of consumption demand and investment demand is less than that output. Again because of the high value of the slope of the aggregate demand curve used in Figure 58 the aggregate demand curve will now run below the 45° line, indicating that inventory piles up and that the businessman will suspect that he has expanded his output too much. In the subsequent period he may well try to remedy this situation by planning for an even lower rate of growth.

To summarize: Once the system deviates from equilibrium it releases forces pulling it even farther away from equilibrium. In this sense it is unstable. What makes it unstable is the high value of the slope of the aggregate demand curve $C(t) + I(t)$ used in Figure 58. The marginal propensity to consume net national output is there set equal to 0.6, while the capital coefficient is set equal to 3, causing the slope of the aggregate demand curve beyond output $Y(t - 1)$ to be equal to 3.6.

3. THE CAPITAL COEFFICIENT AND THE LENGTH OF THE TIME UNIT

At this point it becomes crucial that while the propensity to consume is a ratio between two flows, the capital coefficient is a ratio between a stock and a flow. A change in the length of the time unit used does not affect the value of the propensity to consume, for the values both of the numerator and the denominator are in direct proportion to the time length. Nor will a change in the length of the time unit change the numerator of the capital coefficient, because the numerator is a stock. The denominator will change, however, because it is a flow whose value is in direct proportion to the length of the time unit. Consequently, the value of the capital coefficient is in inverse proportion to the length of the time unit. For example, Kuznets[1] has found the ratio between the dollar value of fixed capital (structures and durable equipment) and the dollar value of *annual* net national product to be close to 3. Thus the capital coefficient on an

[1] Simon Kuznets, "Long-Term Changes in the National Income of the United States of America since 1870," *Income and Wealth of the United States*, Simon Kuznets, ed. (Cambridge, England: Bowes & Bowes, 1952), table 25, p. 127.

annual basis is 3, but on a quarterly basis it would obviously be 12, and on a decade basis 0.3.

4. RESULT

We have said that what made the equilibrium illustrated in Figure 58 unstable is the high value of the slope of the aggregate demand curve. Figure 58 was based on a capital coefficient equal to 3. If any realism is desired, this implies that the length of the time unit used is around one year. The time unit used is a business-planning period, and we assumed business firms to try to establish at the end of the current period a real capital stock

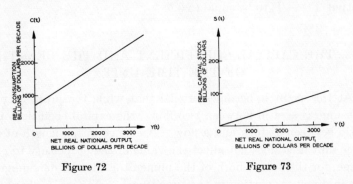

Figure 72   Figure 73

which was in direct proportion to current net real national output. So if the year is the time unit, the capital coefficient is equal to 3. But although little is known about the length of business-planning periods, we suspect that the year is much too short for this purpose. Business hardly tries to adjust its stock of structures and durable equipment to its annual rate of output, so let us try a longer time unit. For example, let us take the *decade* rather than the year as our time unit. Figures 72 through 74 show the consequences of this alteration. In the consumption function, shown in Figure 72, one now has billions of dollars per decade rather than billions of dollars per year on both axes, and consequently there is no change in the slope of the consumption function. In the capital stock-output function, shown in Figure 73, one now has billions of dollars per decade on the output axis *but still just billions of dollars on the capital-stock axis.* Consequently, on a decade basis the capital coefficient is only slightly above one-tenth of its value on an annual basis, and we are now using a capital coefficient slightly above 0.3, or more precisely equal to 0.3556,[2] as shown in Figure 73. The investment function, as developed in equation (4b) but not shown separately, has the same slope.

At this point the mathematically trained reader will have no difficulty. He will realize that in Equation (4b) the variable on the left-hand side, $I(t)$, has the dimension dollars per unit of time, but that the variable on the right-hand side, $Y(t) - Y(t - 1)$, has

---

[2] Not 0.3, because of our habit of letting a stock variable refer to the *end* of the period. On an annual basis call the capital coefficient b_1; on a decade basis call it b_{10}. Find the value of the end-of-period capital stock over the entire output of ten preceding years. Since output is growing at the annual rate g, we have:

$$b_{10} = b_1 \frac{1}{1 + (1 + g)^{-1} + (1 + g)^{-2} + \cdots + (1 + g)^{-9}}$$

If $a = 0.6$, $b_1 = 3.0$ and $y = 0.2846$; then, according to (II) $g = 0.04$ and $b_{10} = 0.3556$.

At this point the reader may become uneasy: If one keeps lengthening the time unit, may not the capital coefficient diminish to the point where the equilibrium rate of growth, defined by (II) in chap. 20, turns negative? Fortunately no such danger exists. Let b_n be the capital coefficient based upon a time unit of n-years. Then

$$b_n = b_1 \frac{1}{1 + (1 + g)^{-1} + (1 + g)^{-2} + \cdots + (1 + g)^{-(n-1)}}$$

Using the formula for the sum of the first n terms of a geometric progression, we let n approach infinity and obtain

$$b_n \to b_1 \left(1 - \frac{1}{1 + g}\right)$$

Now replacing b in (II) in chap. 20 by b_1 (formula (II) was derived on an annual basis) and inserting the value of g thus expressed, we find

$$b_n \to 1 - (a + y)$$

Or, for a time unit whose length approaches infinity, the capital coefficient will approach one minus the long-run propensity to consume. In equation (II), then, the denominator approaches zero, indicating an equilibrium rate of growth approaching infinity. This is as it should be, and there is thus no risk of growth turning into decay because of our lengthening the time unit.

the dimension dollars per unit of time *per unit of time*. Thus lengthening the time unit tenfold will increase the value of the former variable $I(t)$ to approximately tenfold while increasing the value of the second variable to approximately a hundredfold. To compensate for this variation the parameter b must be reduced to approximately one-tenth of its former value.

The nonmathematical reader may need help in the form of a numerical example. In a given year let net real national output be $100 billion and the annual capital coefficient 3. Required capital stock is $300 billion. Let the economy grow during the current year by 4 percent per annum. Next year's net real national output is then $104 billion, and required capital stock is $312 billion. Required investment will then be $12 billion per annum, and output will have increased by $4 billion per annum per annum. The ratio between the two, which is the slope of the annual investment function, is 3.

Now let us look at the same economy on a decade basis. In a given decade, let output be $1,000 billion. As explained in footnote 2, on a decade basis the capital coefficient is 0.3556, the required capital stock consequently $355.6 billion. Now something which grows at 4 percent compounded annually will grow at 48 percent per decade. Next decade's output, then, is $1480 billion, and required capital stock is $526.288 billion. Required investment is then $170.688 billion per decade. Output will have increased by $480 billion per decade per decade. The ratio between them, that is, the slope of the decade investment function, is 0.3556.

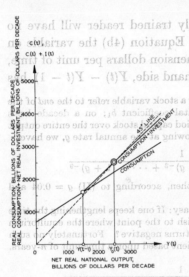

Figure 74

It is true, then, that the slope of the decade investment function is approximately one-tenth of the slope of the annual investment function. As a result, the aggregate demand curve, shown in Figure 74, now has a much lower slope over the relevant range, i.e., slightly above 0.9 or more precisely 0.9556. At outputs higher than the equilibrium output the aggregate demand curve now runs below the 45° line. And at outputs slightly lower than the equilibrium output the aggregate demand curve now runs above the 45° line. The equilibrium is therefore a stable one.

It may seem baffling that anything as seemingly nominal as the length of the time unit used in the model could have much to do with something as real as the stability of a growing economy. But the length of the time unit is not nominal, not at all. In the final analysis, the time unit is a planning period, and if the induced-investment planning period is rather short, say one year, the capital coefficient is then rather high, say 3. Should business firms for any reason plan for current output to exceed current equilibrium output by one dollar per year, they will immediately plan, carry out, and complete, *before the year is over*, three extra dollars' worth of investment in equipment and fixed plant in order to maintain the rigidly fixed capital coefficient specified. Furthermore, if the marginal propensity to consume net national output is 0.6, consumers will spend 0.6 extra dollars' worth annually on consumption. Thus every dollar's worth of deviation from annual equilibrium output will generate $3.6 worth of deviation (in the same direction) from annual equilibrium demand. As we have seen, this effect is highly destabilizing.

If, on the other hand, the induced-investment planning period is rather long, say a decade, the capital coefficient is much smaller, slightly above 0.3 The smaller capital coefficient in itself, the reader should be warned, has no effect whatsoever upon the equilibrium path. If on an annual basis $a = 0.6$, $b = 3.0$, and $y = 0.2846$, then solution (II) will render the value $g = 0.04$ per annum. Since on a decade basis, a and y are still the same, but b changes from 3.0 to 0.3556 (as explained in footnote 2), solution

(II) will render the value $g = 0.48$ per decade. This is as it should be—anything that grows smoothly at 4 per cent per annum is known to grow by 48 percent per decade. But while the shift from an annual to a decade basis does not affect the equilibrium path *per se*, it does affect the consequences of deviations from that path. If firms plan for current output to exceed current equilibrium output by one dollar per year, which is equivalent to ten dollars per decade, they will plan, carry out, and complete, *before the decade is over*, 3.556 extra dollars' worth of investment in equipment and fixed plant. Note that the same capital stock makes possible ten times as much output per decade as it does in one year! Furthermore, if the marginal propensity to consume net national output is 0.6, consumers will spend six extra dollars' worth per decade on consumption. Thus every ten dollars' worth of deviation from decade equilibrium output will generate only 9.556 dollars' worth of deviation (in the same direction) from decade equilibrium demand, clearly a stabilizing influence. Entrepreneurial growth expectations that are inconsistent with the equilibrium rate of growth, as defined by (II), may well tend to correct themselves automatically. Hence the length of the time unit should *not* be thought of as merely nominal.

5. CONCLUSION

In a growth model of the Harrod-Domar type instability can be made to shade over into stability by a simple lengthening of the time unit on which investment planning is based, a change that continuously weakens the induced character of investment. Since unstable equilibria are rather uninteresting, the notion of an equilibrium rate of growth thus assumes new importance.

26

A Technical Stability Test of the Proportionate Equilibrium Rate of Growth

1. DIGGING DEEPER

Great public interest is attached to the study of economic stability. If the proportionate equilibrium rate of growth turns out to be unstable, a ceiling and a floor must be provided as means of keeping the economy from exploding or from vanishing. If the ceiling and the floor provided by the structure of the economy itself are too far apart for comfort, public policy must provide lower ceilings or higher floors. If, on the other hand, the growth equilibrium is a stable one, the equilibrium will restore itself after disturbances. There may, of course, still be fluctuations, but they are dampened ones. Public action is called for only if the dampening seems too weak and too time-consuming.

In view of the importance of the subject we shall now apply some far more technical tools of analysis than those used in Chapter 25. Interestingly enough, the findings are only partly compatible with the results of our simple stability test in Chapter 25.

2. THE MODEL

In Chapter 22 we constructed a dynamic model consisting of 18 equations and 18 variables. From Equations (16) through (18), to the effect that any sector's expected sales must materialize, it is readily apparent that the model is an equilibrium model. The model allows no room for disappointed sales expectations or for disturbances, and provides no method of testing stability.

By a change of only one of the 18 equations, the last, the model is transformed into a model in which disequilibria become possible and disturbances may occur. Replace Equation (18) by:

$$(18) \qquad \frac{{}^{*}\sigma_{fh}(t) - \sigma_{fh}(t-1)}{\sigma_{fh}(t-1)} = \frac{\sigma_{fh}(t-1) - \sigma_{fh}(t-2)}{\sigma_{fh}(t-2)}$$

stating that firms expect the sales of consumers' goods to rise from period $t-1$ to period t by the same proportionate rate as that experienced from period $t-2$ to period $t-1$. The equation can be more briefly written

$$(18a) \qquad {}^{*}\sigma_{fh}(t) = \frac{[\sigma_{fh}(t-1)]^2}{\sigma_{fh}(t-2)}$$

The difference between the old and the new Equation (18) is a highly significant one. Formerly, with perfect foresight the businessman miraculously expected what would actually happen. Now he merely extrapolates his experienced proportionate rate of growth from the past into the future. Equations (16) and (17) are not to be changed. In other words, firms selling investment goods and households selling labor and entrepreneurship still expect exactly what is actually going to happen. The easiest way to imagine this is to think of such firms and households as working under contracts with the firms selling consumers' goods. Contracts are concluded at the beginning of each time unit. Over the time unit, firms in the producers' goods industry will sell the quantity ordered under contract, and labor and entrepreneurship will remain hired according to the contract.

3. SOLUTION

Since ex ante no longer equals ex post throughout the model, the solution becomes slightly more tedious. Its mechanics are shown in the Appendix to this chapter. The solution for gross national output is

$$\text{(I)} \quad (1 - b_{ff})X_f(t) + b_{ff}X_f(t - 1) - a_{fh}a_{hf}\frac{\pi_h[X_f(t - 1)]^2}{\pi_f X_f(t - 2)}$$
$$- X_f(t - L) + a_{fh}a_{hf}\frac{\pi_h[X_f(t - L - 1)]^2}{\pi_f X_f(t - L - 2)} = 0$$

4. STABILITY TESTING, A GENERAL PROPOSITION

Over the period from time zero to time t let some variable X_f grow at the positive proportionate rate of growth G per unit of time. Let some other variable $\overline{\overline{X}}_f$ grow at the positive proportionate rate of growth g per unit of time. A third variable Z, defined as $Z(t) = X_f(t)/\overline{\overline{X}}_f(t)$, will then change as follows:

$$\text{(19)} \qquad Z(t) = \frac{X_f(t)}{\overline{\overline{X}}_f(t)} = u^t Z(0)$$

where

$$u = \frac{1 + G}{1 + g}$$

If G exceeds g, u exceeds unity, and $Z(t) \to \infty$ for $t \to \infty$. And if g exceeds G, u is less than unity, and $Z(t) \to 0$ for $t \to \infty$. If, and only if, $G = g$, u equals unity, and also $Z(t)$ tends towards one single finite nonzero value for $t \to \infty$.

5. STABILITY TESTING, THE SPECIFIC PROCEDURE

If equilibrium is to be stable, $X_f(t)$, as defined by (I) above and based upon the new Equation (18), must eventually display the same growth pattern as $\overline{\overline{X}}_f(t)$, as defined by (V) in Chapter 22 and based upon the old Equation (18). That growth pattern is identified[1] by the equilibrium proportionate rate of growth $g = r_d - 1$. In that case, and only in that case, will $Z(t)$ as defined by Equation (19) tend toward one single finite nonzero value for $t \to \infty$. To test whether $Z(t)$ does so, set out the difference equation governing $Z(t)$, solve, and then examine its roots. The difference equation for $X_f(t)$ appears as (I) above. Divide through by $\bar{\bar{X}}_f(t)$, using definition (V) in Chapter 22, and adopt the notation

$$A = 1 - b_{ff}$$

$$B = \frac{b_{ff}}{r_d}$$

$$C = a_{fh}a_{hf}\frac{\pi_h}{\pi_f}$$

$$D = \frac{1}{r_d{}^L}$$

$$E = \frac{a_{fh}a_{hf}\dfrac{\pi_h}{\pi_f}}{r_d{}^L}$$

The difference equation in $Z(t)$ can then be written

$$\text{(II)} \quad AZ(t) + BZ(t-1) - C\frac{[Z(t-1)]^2}{Z(t-2)}$$
$$- DZ(t-L) + E\frac{[Z(t-L-1)]^2}{Z(t-L-2)} = 0$$

which is a nonlinear $L + $ 2nd-order difference equation in the variable $Z(t)$, having the parameters A, B, C, D, E, and L.

6. THE TRANSFORMATION OF THE NONLINEAR DIFFERENCE EQUATION INTO A LINEAR ONE

Little is known about the solution of nonlinear difference equations, and transformation of Equation (II) into a linear

---

[1] Cf. the closing sentences of section 16 of chap. 22.

difference equation is urgent. Such transformation will proceed as follows.[2]

For certain initial conditions we know what the time path of $Z(t)$ will be. For example, if for the last $L + 2$ time units $X_f(t) = \bar{\bar{X}}_f(t)$, then $Z(t)$ will remain equal to one. For certain other initial conditions which are close to, but differ from, the original ones we shall get not the time path $Z(t)$ but some other path $Z(t) + \zeta(t)$ where $\zeta(t)$ is small compared to $Z(t)$. Throughout Equation (II) replace $Z(t)$ by $Z(t) + \zeta(t)$ and get

$$AZ(t) + A\zeta(t) + BZ(t - 1) + B\zeta(t - 1) - DZ(t - L)$$
$$- D\zeta(t - L) - C \frac{[Z(t - 1) + \zeta(t - 1)]^2}{Z(t - 2) + \zeta(t - 2)}$$
$$+ E \frac{[Z(t - L - 1) + \zeta(t - L - 1)]^2}{Z(t - L - 2) + \zeta(t - L - 2)} = 0$$

However, whenever $\zeta(t)$ is small relative to $Z(t)$, the last two terms can be greatly simplified. Write the C-term as

$$C \frac{[Z(t - 1)]^2 \left\{ 1 + \dfrac{2\zeta(t - 1)}{Z(t - 1)} + \left[\dfrac{\zeta(t - 1)}{Z(t - 1)} \right]^2 \right\}}{Z(t - 2) \left[1 + \dfrac{\zeta(t - 2)}{Z(t - 2)} \right]}$$

Whenever $\zeta(t)$ is small relative to $Z(t)$, the last, squared, term of the numerator may be ignored. Moreover, if a number ϵ is small relative to one, dividing by $1 + \epsilon$ will yield practically the same results as will multiplying by $1 - \epsilon$. Consequently, the entire C-term can be written

$$C \frac{[Z(t - 1)]^2}{Z(t - 2)} \left[1 + \frac{2\zeta(t - 1)}{Z(t - 1)} \right] \left[1 - \frac{\zeta(t - 2)}{Z(t - 2)} \right]$$

Whenever $\zeta(t)$ is small relative to $Z(t)$, this expression is practically the same as

$$C \frac{[Z(t - 1)]^2}{Z(t - 2)} \left[1 + \frac{2\zeta(t - 1)}{Z(t - 1)} - \frac{\zeta(t - 2)}{Z(t - 2)} \right]$$

---

[2] For hints on procedure the author is grateful to Professor Abraham H. Taub.

By replacing C with E and t with $t - L$, a similar, greatly simplified expression for the E-term is obtained. As a result, we have a greatly simplified version of Equation (II) with $Z(t)$ replaced by $Z(t) + \zeta(t)$. If from this version we deduct the original version of (II) and set $Z(t) = 1$, we get the following linear difference equation in $\zeta(t)$

$$A\zeta(t) + (B - 2\,C)\zeta(t - 1) + C\zeta(t - 2) - D\zeta(t - L)$$
$$+ 2E\zeta(t - L - 1) - E\zeta(t - L - 2) = 0$$

This is the difference equation which governs the time path of the small deviation $\zeta(t)$ between the actual time path $Z(t) + \zeta(t)$ and the equilibrium time path $Z(t) = 1$. For a solution, try $\zeta(t) = z^t$, divide through by z^{t-L-2}, and get

$$\text{(III)} \qquad Az^{L+2} + (B - 2C)z^{L+1} + Cz^L - Dz^2 + 2Ez - E = 0$$

which we shall now solve numerically, utilizing different assumptions about the length of the time unit.

7. NUMERICAL SOLUTIONS

On an annual basis the empirical values of the parameters A, B, C, D, E, and L, defined in Section 5 above, are very roughly estimated in Chapter 22, Section 10. In the present chapter we shall use the same empirically plausible values, but we shall experiment with the length of the time unit. The numerical values of some of the parameters will depend upon that length.

We shall begin with L, the easiest. The value of L in terms of time units is, of course, exactly in inverse proportion to the length of the time unit. The coefficients A and B include the capital coefficient b_{ff}, which is a stock-flow ratio. The value of stock-flow ratios is known to be in approximately inverse proportion to the length of the time unit. Call the capital coefficient, if based on a one-year time unit, $b_{ff,1}$ and if based upon a two-year time unit, $b_{ff,2}$. Find the value of the end-of-year capital stock at time $t + 2$ over the entire output of the two preceding years $t + 1$

and $t + 2$, assuming that output is growing smoothly at the proportionate rate g per annum:

$$b_{ff,2} = \frac{S_{ff}(t + 2)}{X_f(t + 1) + X_f(t + 2)} = \frac{(1 + g)S_{ff}(t + 1)}{[1 + (1 + g)]X_f(t + 1)}$$
$$= \frac{b_{ff,1}}{1 + \dfrac{1}{1 + g}}$$

Thus, if the expected rate of growth is our equilibrium rate $g = 0.01985$ per annum and if $b_{ff,1}$ is 2.7728, $b_{ff,2} = 1.4000$.

The values of parameters A, $B - 2C$, and L as dependent upon the length of the time unit are shown in Table 35. If for the

TABLE 35. Numerical Values of Parameters of Equations (II) and (III) Varying with Length of Time Unit *

Length of Time Unit in Years	L	A	$B - 2C$
1/2	32	-4.5185	$+3.8645$
1	16	-1.7728	$+1.1188$
2	8	-0.4000	-0.2540
4	4	$+0.2862$	-0.9402
6	$\frac{16}{6}$	$+0.5149$	-1.1689
8	2	$+0.6291$	-1.2831
12	$\frac{16}{12}$	$+0.7432$	-1.3972
16	1	$+0.8000$	-1.4540

* The numerical values of the remaining parameters do not vary with the length of the time unit. These numerical values are: $C = 0.8$; $D = 0.7302$; $2E = 1.1684$; and $E = 0.5842$.

length of the time unit we use 1/2, 1, 2, 4, 6, 8, 12, and 16 years, we obtain eight alternative versions of Equation (III). The degrees of the eight equations will be 34, 18, 10, 6, 14/3, 4, 10/3, and 3, respectively. All eight equations were solved on the University of Illinois high-speed digital computer. As we know, the greatest root will eventually swamp all others, and the eight numerically greatest roots other than unity are shown in Table 36.

TABLE 36. Numerically Greatest Root Other Than Unity of Equation (III) as Dependent upon the Length of the Time Unit

Length of Time Unit in Years	Numerically Greatest Root Other Than Unity
1/2	0.9902
1	$-0.9916 \pm 0.1838\,i$
2	-1.7102
4	2.0344
6	1.2815
8	1.1392
12	1.0398
16	0.7302

In all eight cases, unity is a root. Figure 75 summarizes our findings.

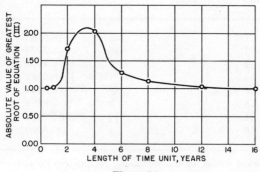

Figure 75

8. CONCLUSION

In the six cases where the length of the time unit equals 1, 2, 4, 6, 8, and 12 years, the absolute value of the greatest root of Equation (III) is in excess of unity, indicating that both $\zeta(t)$ and $[Z(t) + \zeta(t)]$ will explode. Since $Z(t) + \zeta(t)$ will *not* tend toward one single, finite nonzero value for $t \to \infty$, we see that, $X_f(t)$, as defined by Equation (I), if disturbed will *never* grow at the same proportionate rate of growth as that of $\overline{\overline{X}}_f(t)$, as defined by Equation (V) in Chapter 22, no matter how long the wait. Expectations, then, are not self-correcting, and the equilibrium is unstable.

In the two extreme cases where the length of the time unit is one-half year or 16 years, the absolute value of the greatest root of Equation (III) is unity. Here, then, $\zeta(t)$ will not explode, and $Z(t) + \zeta(t)$ will tend toward one single, finite nonzero value for $t \to \infty$, which tendency indicates that $X_f(t)$ if disturbed, eventually will grow at the same proportionate rate of growth as that of $\overline{\overline{X}}_f(t)$. Expectations are self-correcting, and the equilibrium is stable.

9. TESTING THE GOODNESS OF OUR LINEAR APPROXIMATION

In Section 6 we transformed our nonlinear difference equation (II) into a linear difference equation whose characteristic equation was Equation (III). But the linear equation is merely an approximation to the nonlinear one, and we should very much like to know how good. More precisely, what we want to know is whether or not the conclusions drawn from the solution of (III) will hold when (III) is replaced by (II). As we have already said, little is known about the solution of nonlinear difference equations. But fortunately, a recursive solution is always possible. Equation (II) is an $L + 2$nd-order difference equation in the variable $Z(t)$. Given the numerical value of $Z(t)$ for $L + 2$ successive time units, Equation (II) will provide the numerical value of $Z(t)$ for the subsequent time unit. A recursive solution, then, can be worked out by specifying $L + 2$ initial conditions and calculating the numerical value of $Z(t)$, step by step for a succession of time of any length desired. In practice, such a solution is useful only if one can keep a large number of significant figures. Consequently, a program using so-called floating-point notation was prepared for the University of Illinois high-speed digital computer.

As a guarantee of the stability test being a severe one, the initial conditions were selected in such a way as to represent a major disturbance of the system. The $L + 2$ initial conditions were simply a path ending at the value one for $t = 0$ and characterized by a proportionate rate of growth of 0.02 per half-year period. In other words, for $L + 2$ time units the economy was assumed to have been growing at twice its equilibrium proportionate rate of growth. Recursive solutions were worked out for six cases of different time units: 1/2, 1, 2, 4, 8, and 16 years. In each case, a recursive solution was attempted for a succession of 128 calendar years, irrespective of the particular time unit used. In the two cases where the time units were equal to 2 and 4 years respectively, the time path for $Z(t)$ was so violently explosive that going beyond 50 and 76 calendar years, respectively, proved useless. Findings are summarized in Table 37 and in Figures 76 through 81.

TABLE 37.   Recursive Solutions of Equation (II) Showing Time Path of $Z(t)$ for Time Units Equalling 1/2, 1, 2, 4, 8, and 16 Years

Time t in Calendar Years	$Z(t)$ for Time Unit Equalling					
	1/2	1	2	4	8	16
− 16	0.53	0.53	0.53	0.53	0.53	0.53
0	1.00	1.00	1.00	1.00	1.00	1.00
16	1.39	1.38	− 5.41	20.37	2.05	1.88
32	1.68	1.67	$−0.74 \times 10^{17}$	0.63×10^{8}	5.02	3.55
48	1.90	1.88	$−0.20 \times 10^{53}$	0.22×10^{22}	15.68	6.69
64	2.05	2.04	—	0.10×10^{43}	67.25	12.61
80	2.17	2.15	—	—	0.43×10^{3}	23.77
96	2.25	2.24	—	—	0.44×10^{4}	44.80
112	2.31	2.30	—	—	0.80×10^{5}	84.42
128	2.36	2.34	—	—	0.28×10^{7}	159.09

The general conclusion is that the linear difference equation is a fair approximation to nonlinear difference Equation (II), the variables of both equations being violently explosive for time units

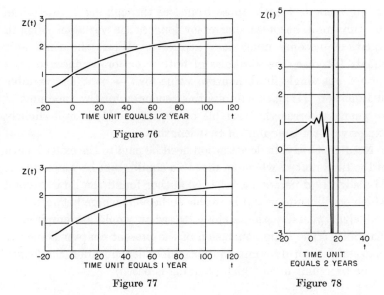

Figure 76

Figure 77

Figure 78

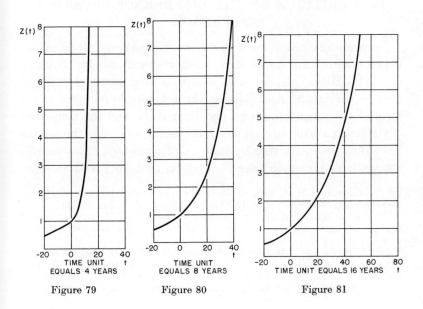

Figure 79

Figure 80

Figure 81

of intermediate length, those from two through eight years. As the time unit becomes shorter or longer, the variables of both equations become much less explosive. When the time unit equals 1/2 year, the variables of both equations appear to tend toward one single finite nonzero value for $t \to \infty$. The variable of Equation (III) also exhibits this tendency for the time unit of 16 years, whereas the variable of Equation (II) is still slightly explosive for a time unit of that length.

Needless to say, little attention need be paid to the exact length of the time unit at which an unstable equilibrium becomes stable. In a slightly different model,[3] the author found the limit beyond which equilibrium would be stable to be somewhere between four and eight years, perhaps closer to what would be empirically plausible. The main conclusion of the present chapter is merely that stability of dynamic equilibria *does* depend upon the length of the time unit upon which planning is based.

10. A CRITIQUE OF THE DIFFERENCE-EQUATION APPROACH

Dynamic analysis in terms of difference equations, pioneered by Frisch[4] and Samuelson[5] and further developed by Baumol, Goodwin, Hicks, Metzler, and others, is long on substance and operational significance: Express the behavior hypotheses in the form of difference equations, find their roots, and the properties of the time path of the economy are revealed, obviating the need to trace that time path step by step. Unfortunately, however, this approach at the same time is short on generality and validity.

[3] Hans Brems, "How Induced Is Induced Investment?" *The Review of Economics and Statistics*, Vol. XXXVII, No. 3 (Aug., 1955), pp. 267–277.

[4] Ragnar Frisch, "Propagation Problems and Impulse Problems in Dynamic Economics," *Economic Essays in Honour of Gustav Cassel* (London: Allen & Unwin, 1933), pp. 171–205.

[5] P. A. Samuelson, "Interactions Between the Multiplier Analysis and the Principle of Acceleration," *The Review of Economics and Statistics*, Vol. XXI, No. 2 (May, 1939), pp. 75–78, reprinted in *Readings in Business Cycle Theory*, Gottfried Haberler, ed. (Philadelphia: Blakiston, 1944), pp. 261–269.

For one thing, it is highly aggregative. For another, it has frequently been criticized for being "too precise" and for its failure to include money, banking, psychology, innovations, and many other things, although some critics seem perfectly content merely to enumerate verbally the missing factors. But from the statement that linear difference equations in a few variables are inadequate for a full analysis, it does not follow that one should confine himself to verbal analysis. Richard Goodwin[6] has aptly defended his use of linear relationships by saying: "Otherwise in most cases a mathematical, and a fortiori a verbal, analysis of this type of problem is impossible."

In his later writings, however, Goodwin dropped the linearity assumption. The mathematical difficulties involved in nonlinear systems may be overcome either by constructing linear approximations as we have attempted, or by relying upon recursive solutions, entirely practicable when digital computers are used. Or, finally, the difficulties may be overcome by simply observing and recording the behavior of physical systems that are analogues of the economic systems. Strotz, McAnulty, and Naines[7] have presented an electro-analog solution of Goodwin's nonlinear system, and in his *Mechanism of Economic Systems*,[8] Tustin makes extensive use of such analogues. The manner in which various economic quantities, such as income and investment, influence one another is said to be precisely the kind of relationship that engineers have investigated in their construction of control systems, such as automatic pilots and temperature regulators. Thus Tustin was able to make use of the powerful concepts of control system engineering in application to problems of aggregative dynamics.

[6] Richard M. Goodwin, "Secular and Cyclical Aspects of the Multiplier and the Accelerator," *Income, Employment, and Public Policy* (New York: Norton, 1948), footnote on pp. 112–113.

[7] R. H. Strotz, J. C. McAnulty, and J. B. Naines, Jr., "Goodwin's Nonlinear Theory of the Business Cycle: An Electro-analog Solution," *Econometrica*, Vol. 21, No. 3 (July, 1953), pp. 390–411.

[8] Arnold Tustin, *The Mechanism of Economic Systems* (Cambridge, Mass.: Harvard University Press, 1953).

APPENDIX: THE MECHANICS OF FINDING
SOLUTION (I)

Write (18) as

(18a)
$$*\sigma_{fh}(t) = \frac{[\sigma_{fh}(t-1)]^2}{\sigma_{fh}(t-2)}$$

On the right-hand side of (18a), insert (15), (10), (6), (17), (14), (9), (5), and (12) in that order and get

(18b)
$$*\sigma_{fh}(t) = a_{fh}a_{hf}\frac{\pi_h}{\pi_f}\frac{[X_f(t-1)]^2}{X_f(t-2)}$$

Next, insert (8) and (11) into (2), replace t by $t-1$, and compare the outcome with (1); it is demonstrable that $S_{ff}(t-1) = *S_{ff}(t-1)$. Use this result, (3), (4), and (12) upon (1) and get

$$x_{ff}(t) = b_{ff}[X_f(t) - X_f(t-1)] + x_{ff}(t-L)$$

In order to express the last term of the preceding equation by $X_f(t)$ we shall use (8), (13), (16), (7), and (12) in that order and get

$$x_{ff}(t-L) = X_f(t-L) - *\sigma_{fh}(t-L)$$

In (18b) replace t by $(t-L)$, insert here, and insert the outcome into the equation for $x_{ff}(t)$ above. But according to (8), (13), and (16), $x_{ff}(t) = *\sigma_{ff}(t)$. Insert the result together with (18b) into (7) and get Equation (I).

CONCLUSIONS

While Parts I–III were entirely static, Part IV is dynamic. Needless to say, this particular order of presentation does not imply the superiority of Part IV over the preceding parts. Part IV is simply devoted to an entirely different kind of problem, that of long-run growth. The conclusions derived in Parts I through III are in no way invalidated when applied to short-run policy. But which conclusions can be drawn from Part IV? The first and most important one is that the short-run impact of saving is the reverse of the long-run impact: In an underemployed economy the capitalist-saver, while increasing his propensity to save, will reduce the momentary level of output but will expand the long-run growth potential of his economy. The simple models of the early chapters of Part IV as well as the later more complicated ones agree on this conclusion.

The Harrod-Domar model determined one over-all proportionate rate of growth. As shown in Chapter 21, it is not difficult to set out a model characterized by different, but constant, rates of growth of output, labor force, hours, and productivity. Such a model permits the drawing of a number of important policy conclusions. In underdeveloped and mature economies alike, as high as possible a growth rate of output per man-hour is deemed desirable. The model shows that this goal is approached by a reduction of the propensity to consume, a reduction of the capital coefficient, a slowing-down of population growth, increasing demand for leisure, a reduction of the number of idle machine-hours, and finally an increase in the business propensity to withhold earnings.

The Harrod-Domar model also assumes that the proportionate rate of growth is constant in time. Testing this assumption by replacing the net by the gross approach to national output, we found in Chapter 22 the assumption to be a moderately satisfactory one.   Essentially, our old policy conclusions can still be drawn: that the proportionate rate of growth will rise if the community gross propensity to save rises, and if the capital coefficient falls.   A new conclusion was that the same would happen if the useful life of producers' goods rises.

But even further refinement was desirable.   In illuminating the effect of various types of technological progress, the model was further disaggregated, and business earnings and their distribution as dividends were explicitly related to such progress.   In accordance with empirically plausible assumptions it was shown that the four types of technological progress frequently but not always accelerate growth.

A disaggregation in a different direction was undertaken in Chapter 24, where the assumption of a closed economy was abandoned.   Although the interaction of two economies, each with its own growth potential, was not always smooth and harmonious, a majority of cases remained in which the two economies would eventually wind up with the same proportionate rate of growth, but not until after due adjustment of their relative sizes had taken place.   The introduction of relative size as a variable thus proved highly useful.   The results were finally used to show that devaluation might in the long run fail to reduce the need for international lending.

The last two chapters of Part IV were devoted to a test of the stability of the equilibrium growth path.   The study was undertaken at an elementary and then at an advanced level.   Both gave the result that stability, among other things, is related to the length of the investment-planning period adopted by business. While the two tests did not quite agree on the one particular length most favorable to stability, they did agree that medium lengths of between one and ten years are unfavorable and that very long lengths are favorable.   But while the elementary test would indicate extremely short lengths, those less than one year, to be unfavorable, the advanced test would indicate them to be favorable.

Epilogue

The economic theory of our time seems to be moving swiftly in the directions both of more substance and of more operational significance (in the senses used in Chapter 1). In statics, major advances like the theory of games, linear programming, and Leontief input-output models exemplify this trend. In dynamics, the trend is visible in the Harrod-Domar growth models, the linear and nonlinear difference equations used by Frisch, Goodwin, Hicks, Metzler, Samuelson, and others, and the majestic dynamic Leontief model. The specificity of the premises of such models has frequently required extensive use of mathematics for extraction of conclusions. In some instances substance and operational significance have been bought by the sacrifice of generality and validity, and critics can be depended upon to call attention to this sacrifice. Such criticism may give rise to the construction of new models whose richness of substance will not be gained at the expense of quite as much generality and validity. As a result of such continuing interaction between construction and demolition, further mathematization of economic theory is to be anticipated.

INDEX

Abbott, Lawrence, 186 n.
Abramovitz, Moses, 249
Absorption approach, 108
Accelerator, 14, 289–314
　　See also Capital coefficient
Active money, 38
Active processes, 170
Activity, 164 n.
Adelman, M. A., 89 n.
Adjoint, 297
Advertising, 85–90, 185–201
Aggregation, 11–14
Åkerman, Gustaf, 213 n.
Alchian, Armen A., 216 n.
Alexander, Sidney S., 308 n.
Allen, R. G. D., 4 n., 130 n., 136 n., 216 n.
Andrews, P. W. S., 37 n.
Australia, 92, 120, 268 n.
Automobile industry, obsolescence in, 87, 287–288
Automobile Manufacturers Association, 88 n.
Autonomous consumption, 16, 21, 36, 59, 95, 127–128, 139, 143, 234
Autonomous investment, 19, 20

Balance of trade, 30
Balanced-budget multiplier, 72–75
Balanced foreign trade, 91–123
Balanced foreign-trade multiplier, 91–106
Balance-of-trade multipliers, 30
Banks, liquidity preference of, 39–40
Barfod, Börge, 186 n.
Basic solutions, 171
Baumol, William J., 14 n., 35 n., 74 n., 75 n., 233 n., 261 n., 263 n., 296 n., 297 n., 334
Bhatt, V. V., 212 n.
Blyth, Conrad H., 213 n.

Böhm-Bawerk, Eugen von, 7, 12 n., 202–211, 224–225
Boundaries, *see* Price boundaries
Bowen, William G., 74 n.
Brems, Hans, 90 n., 186 n., 334 n.
Britain, *see* United Kingdom
Brown, A. J., 39 n., 118 n.
Bureau of Labor Statistics, 130
Bushaw, D. W., 21, 130 n., 296 n.
Business net saving, 244, 250

Canada, 5, 268 n.
Capital, accumulation, 210
　　coefficient, 3, 231, 234, 248, 256, 259, 260, 270, 275, 293, 309, 312–313, 317–318, 328–329
　　concept, 204–205
　　intensity, 212, 224–226, 242
　　stock, 208, 224, 234, 241–242, 256, 259–260, 275, 293
Cassel, Gustav, 50 n., 232 n.
Chamberlin, Edward H., 83–85, 186 n.
Chandler, Lester V., 35 n.
Chang, Tse Chun, 118 n.
Charnes, A., 166 n., 179 n.
Chenery, Hollis B., 187 n., 218, 219
Chipman, John S., 178 n.
Circulating capital, 202–211
Clark, Colin, 312 n.
Closed Leontief model, 138–147
Clower, R. W., 21, 130 n., 296 n.
Collar, A. R., 307
Common equilibrium rate of growth, 304–305
Common Market, 108
Communication, 6–7
Computer, *see* Electronic high-speed digital computer
Concave demand curve, 195
Constancy of proportionate rate of growth, 254–272